bowraville

Dan Box won two Walkley Awards for his reporting on the murders of Colleen Walker-Craig, Evelyn Greenup and Clinton Speedy-Duroux, published in *The Australian*. He has also worked for London's *The Sunday Times* and the BBC.

DAN BOX

bowraville

VIKING
an imprint of
PENGUIN BOOKS

VIKING

UK | USA | Canada | Ireland | Australia
India | New Zealand | South Africa | China

Viking is part of the Penguin Random House group of companies
whose addresses can be found at global.penguinrandomhouse.com.

First published by Viking, an imprint of Penguin Random House Australia Pty Ltd, 2019

Cover photograph by Chris Graham
Cover design by Alex Ross © Penguin Random House Australia Pty Ltd
Typeset in 12.15/18pt Adobe Garamond Pro by Midland Typesetters, Australia
Printed and bound in Australia by Griffin Press, part of Ovato, an accredited ISO AS/NZS 14001
Environmental Management Systems printer.

 A catalogue record for this
book is available from the
National Library of Australia

ISBN 978 0 14378 439 5

penguin.com.au

A major theme in this story is that of the Maangun 'the Law' by which anyone responsible for another's death accepts that there must be pay-back.

Gumbaynggirr Yuludarla Jandaygam

The conviction of the guilty is a public interest, as is the acquittal of the innocent.

Attorney General (NSW) v Hide
Written submissions filed by the Applicant

He asked me if I did it and I said 'No.' That's it.

James Hide
Interviewed by NSW Police, 8 April 1991

Sunday, 16 September 1990

It was only three days after Colleen had gone missing that anybody told her mother, Muriel Craig, and the news made no sense to her. No sense to her at all. They told her Colleen had been at a party. On the Mission in Bowraville. The party was at Fred's place; opposite the Tree of Knowledge. The house at number 4, on Cemetery Road.

Muriel had driven down that morning from her home in Sawtell, less than an hour from Bowraville, just further up the coast. When she went to the Bowraville police station, she couldn't get an answer to her knocking. Maybe it was shut up for the Sunday. She tried again on Monday, climbing High Street to the hilltop, walking through the gate in the white picket fence outside the neat, Federation building and this time, finding the door open, walking in, out of the sunlight, and ringing the bell on the counter inside. The policeman in his blue uniform looked up and saw her standing there, but took his time to answer. Muriel told him that Colleen was missing. Her daughter was sixteen, she said.

'How long has she been missing for?' the policeman asked her.

'Well, they said she was missing the Thursday night and it's Monday.'

Muriel showed the man a photograph: Colleen looking confident and beautiful, with red lips just about to smile.

'This is your daughter?' he asked her, doubtful. 'She doesn't look Aboriginal.' Colleen had pale brown skin – their family had some white blood in it. The policeman didn't take a statement. He filled out some paperwork. Maybe he told her Colleen had gone walkabout – Muriel isn't certain. It's been so long since it happened and it's so hard to remember, what with the fear and the emotion.

Muriel said nothing. She couldn't backchat the police.

It seemed they were not going to help her. Instead, Muriel went home, gathered up her remaining, younger children and moved the family to Bowraville, a small town of something like a thousand people that nestled in a loop of the green Nambucca River on the mid-north coast of New South Wales. There she spent her days driving up and down the Mission, which was just the eight brown-brick houses built along one side of the long stretch of Cemetery Road, pleading or demanding that people tell her if they had seen her daughter. But people only told her fragments. Some said that they'd seen Colleen drinking at the party. Some said they'd seen her outside, where the music and the people had spilled out that night across the road. But the times and names and details were all different. Muriel had to fit these broken pieces back together into a whole.

Michelle Flanders, who got to the party around 8.30 p.m. after finishing her work at the play centre on the Mission, said she found her boyfriend drinking and singing with about eight other boys when she arrived. The drinking had started early but he got up when he saw her and the two of them walked outside number 4, through the wire gate and across the pitted bitumen to where Colleen was sitting underneath the spreading white mahogany they called the Tree of Knowledge. She was one of those gathered round the fire with Kelly Jarrett, who was celebrating her eighteenth birthday. James Hide was there with them and some others who Michelle could not remember. The boys were smoking yarndi, or marijuana, while the girls were drinking Passion Pop. When the couple arrived, James handed them a stubbie but Michelle's boyfriend spat it out and told him, 'That's not beer.'

It smelled like bourbon, Michelle thought.

For Muriel, the story got more confusing. The party was at the home of Fred Buchanan, who was Colleen's cousin. Fred later remembered that he'd been drinking all day in the house, sitting in his bedroom with the other blokes before crashing out at about 8 p.m. Colleen had come late to the party and hadn't stayed there. She was wearing a white jumper with a blue-and-red band and light blue jeans cut short to the knee, he remembered.

Fred said Colleen had walked into the bedroom, holding a bottle of Passion Pop and talking about catching the train to Goodooga in the morning. Goodooga was out west, more than a day's journey from Bowraville via Sydney. After the party, he heard that a white Holden Commodore had come along outside and someone from inside had called out, 'Uncle George, where are you going?' It sounded like it had been Colleen talking, someone told him, though Fred didn't see or hear it for himself. He blacked out and woke up something like twelve hours later, long after the early morning train for Goodooga had gone.

Martin George Greenup was drinking in the lounge room at the party with James Hide, who was the only white man among the crowd of blackfellas, and remembered that he overheard James saying, 'Come on babe, Colleen, I want to see you tonight.' Colleen got upset, walked outside the house, and sat on the front step. She was a pretty girl, with dark, curling hair and an easy smile. She looked like her mother, Muriel.

Sometime around two or three in the morning, after the other boys had finished drinking and crashed out, Martin said that he had left the party and seen a white Commodore parked outside up the road, facing towards the cemetery. Colleen, who was in the front seat, waved and sung out, 'See ya later, Uncle Martin.'

'See ya later, Col,' he told her.

Or maybe Colleen was sitting in the back seat and yelled out 'How you going, Uncle George?' It was hard to remember. Anyway, as he was walking away from the party, the Commodore drove past him, heading into Bowraville.

Muriel kept searching for her daughter, trying to make sense of all these different versions, but what people were saying wasn't straightforward or it changed with each telling or what one person said was contradicted by another. One of Colleen's cousins said he'd seen her two days after the party, talking about the footy knock-out tournament she was due to go to. Kelly Jarrett, whose birthday party it had been that night, told Muriel that she last saw Colleen outside at the party. The two of them had gone over to Fred's house and stayed there drinking. At about 11.30 p.m. Colleen had come over to where Kelly was standing by the fire. But after that, she hadn't seen her.

As the weather got hotter ahead of the coming summer, Muriel found that her suspicions worsened. She was a proud lady. Defiant, you might call her. She'd grown up on the Mission and many of the people living there were family. But it seemed they could not, or they would not, tell her what happened to her daughter. Their versions were all different. They couldn't all be true.

The last time that her mother saw her, Colleen had given her a kiss and said, 'Mum, I'll see you Sunday.' That was on the Monday, 10 September. Muriel had not worried about letting her daughter travel down to Bowraville. Colleen would do what she wanted. A few months earlier, in March, she'd got sick of school and left it behind her. Yes, Colleen drank a bit and smoked a little yarndi, but she'd been to Bowraville before, staying there with family, and she'd also spent time living in Macksville, the next town down the river. But each time she went away, when Colleen asked her, Muriel had picked her up and they'd gone home together to Sawtell.

After school, or at the weekends, Muriel's other children went out with her around Bowraville, looking for their sister. They didn't fully understand her absence. The youngest, Lucas, who was only eight or thereabouts, watched his mum running around and saw that she was panicking and hurt. But they were only children. Lucas felt guilty there was nothing they could do.

The days turned into weeks and Muriel's suspicion expanded. If no one was telling her what really happened to her daughter, maybe they were hiding what they knew. She started to look at people differently, asking herself if they were acting smart. She needed to find a common thread, something she could follow, which ran through all the various accounts. Something that would lead her to her daughter. Like the white Commodore, perhaps, which people told her Colleen had been sitting in that night.

Jason Buchanan had been at the party and said he saw the car parked up outside the house at about 11 or 11.30 p.m. Beyond it, the fire was burning across the road by the Tree of Knowledge, where he recalled James and another fellow had two crates of VB. Jason went to have a drink and Colleen joined them. Jason said he heard a woman laughing in the Commodore and recognised the voice as Maxine Jarrett's. He last saw Colleen at about 12 a.m.

Maxine Jarrett said she'd been drinking at a nightclub in Nambucca Heads, about 20 kilometres from Bowraville until sometime after 1 a.m., when she met a bloke who said he had a car and offered to drive her home. When they arrived at Cemetery Road, she didn't see anybody underneath the Tree of Knowledge. They were the only people in the Commodore, she said, just her and the driver.

Now all Muriel had was more suspicion and confusion. She just wanted to find the last person who had seen her daughter.

Patricia Stadhams said that she had seen her. Patricia had been walking along the Mission shortly after 12 a.m. on the night of the party. She had seen Colleen outside the house next door to the party. Kelly Jarrett had been across the road, underneath the old mahogany and sung out, 'Where you going?'

'I'm just going round here,' Colleen answered, but Patricia did not see where Colleen went.

It was dark out there, without streetlights. Patricia said that she passed James on the footpath. She saw a white Commodore drive past her and stop a little further up the road.

Later, when the police interviewed her, Patricia said that Colleen wasn't on the footpath, but heading down a side street beside one of the other houses on the Mission, the next-door one to where the party was that night. That was the same way James was walking, said Patricia.

Years later, Patricia's story changed again.

Interviewed by detectives seven years after Colleen's disappearance, Patricia remembered seeing another car, a red Chrysler Galant belonging to James's mother, parked in the driveway at the back of the Mission. She'd stopped and watched Colleen walking down the street beside the house towards where the car was parked, and watched James go through the gate and down the other side of the same building.

'He looked suspicious so I stood there and watched him,' Patricia told an inquest in 2004, fourteen years after the teenager went missing. She watched both James and Colleen walk away from her, towards where the car was waiting. The next day, both Colleen and the red Galant were gone.

Tuesday, 16 September 2014

Detective Chief Inspector Gary Jubelin asks to meet me on a hot spring morning at a cafe near the headquarters of the New South Wales police force in Parramatta, western Sydney, where the sunlight casts a sharp divide along the footpath. Taking off his sunglasses and folding them on the cafe table, Gary says he wants to talk about three murders. The victims were all children: sixteen-year-old Colleen Walker-Craig; four-year-old Evelyn Greenup and Clinton Speedy-Duroux, who was also sixteen. No one has been jailed as a result.

I'm a crime reporter with *The Australian* newspaper but this is the first time a detective has come to me with a story. It's usually me asking them to tell me what they know.

Doing this job, I know a little about murder. I remember the first time I sat in court and watched someone be convicted, and thinking how ordinary he looked, this person who had taken another's life. Most recently, I've been covering a lot of child sex cases, meeting with the victims and sitting in court to watch the men – it's mostly men – who hurt them try to plead or lie or bully their way out. It's taught me about power and violence and cruelty and contempt. But also about courage and determination, at least on the part of the victims and their families. Gary says that both these things are in this story too.

As a newspaper reporter, I also know a little about true crime stories. I know that a true crime story often cannot be believed, at least at the beginning. Gary tells me that each of the three murdered children was Aboriginal. All three disappeared over five months, during the spring and hot summer between September 1990 and February 1991. All three went missing from Bowraville, which sits in the Nambucca Valley where subtropical farming country is sliced apart by rivers running down from the Great Dividing Range towards the southern Pacific Ocean. The bodies of Evelyn and Clinton were found dumped beside a dirt road running through the dark gum forest above Bowraville, says Gary. Colleen's body has not been recovered, although her clothes were later found in a river near the forest, weighted down with stones.

Bowraville is a six-hour drive north from where we're sitting, Gary says, ordering a green tea from the cafe waiter. He's been wrestling with these murders for almost twenty years now and has made the journey from Sydney to where they took place over and over during that time. Mostly, once you leave the city, the road snakes through gum forests or fields of cattle and horses, with relatively little traffic, which means you spend the time alone behind the steering wheel thinking. He tells me his thoughts.

Gary believes he knows who killed the children. He won't tell me his suspect's name, saying only that 'he's smart. He hasn't got a formal education but I think he's got a rat cunning.' His suspect is a white man, Gary says, who grew up in Bowraville and worked in the town's hide factory, shifting the bloody skins around for tanning. Gary says that Colleen, the first of the three children to go missing, was last seen walking down one side of a house on the Bowraville mission, while his suspect was seen walking down the other side.

The tea arrives in a neat china teapot and he pauses to pour it. Looking up, Gary says his suspect knew all three of the murdered children and that different witnesses saw him at the parties where each of the victims went missing. Only, his suspect has already been found not guilty of the murders. Twice.

A true crime story is always more complicated than fiction. As a reporter, I've found that real life defies your attempts to make a story from it. It's ugly, sometimes too ugly to put in the paper. You cannot always trust the people you encounter. Sometimes you have to choose between two competing versions of the truth. If, like me, it is your job to tell it, then a true crime story is always more complex than you would like.

I study Gary while drinking my coffee. He's tall and tough and broad-shouldered, wearing a well-fitted black suit with a white shirt and a plain black tie. His skull is shaved, his cheeks are hollow and his nose looks like it's been broken. While this is the first time I've met him, I know a little of his reputation. When another detective heard who I was meeting, he told me to be wary. 'If it was you that had been murdered, you'd want Gary standing over your body, leading the investigation,' that detective told me. 'But he isn't perfect. He pushes people hard. He's single-minded. He's a zealot.'

After an hour or so of talking at the cafe, Gary invites me into the police force building and we take the lift together up to level eight, which houses the offices of the Homicide Squad. Through the glass door, we walk past a wall hung with yellowing newspaper front pages – 'Killer within', 'Murder hunt' and 'Guilty' – and he leaves me sitting alone in a small, windowless room, then comes back carrying two battered cardboard boxes, both beaten up from where the files inside have been pulled out and shoved back in many times before.

Gary picks out some old transcripts of court hearings into the children's murders and of his own evidence when called as a witness to a parliamentary inquiry, which was held a few months before. Does he have permission to bring me in here and show me these documents? I wonder whether he chose not to seek permission, knowing that it might be refused. I wonder, also, what he expects me to do with the story now. I guess that Gary wants to use me, to have me write something in *The Australian*. That might mean that his bosses pay more attention, or dedicate more money, to the the case. I think this while scanning through the transcript of Gary's evidence to the parliamentary inquiry. Then one line makes me stop and stare.

'The families have been let down by the justice system,' Gary told the inquiry. 'It's very nice for society to say that all victims are treated equally. Unfortunately in this situation I do not think that is entirely correct.' I look up from the transcript and see Gary watching. He knows what I am reading. 'I am a homicide detective,' the transcript continues. 'I'm not a do-gooder or a bleeding heart. However, race and to a lesser degree socio-economic factors have impacted on the manner in which these matters have been investigated . . . The families know the reason . . . They said "It's because we're Aboriginal."' I look up at Gary. He sits in silence, looking back.

A spill of other documents is now covering the table. Continuing the transcript, I learn Gary believes the police already have the evidence to convict someone over the children's murders, but they are being prevented from doing so. He blames the courts; he blames the lawyers – 'there have been mistakes'; he blames the state government itself – 'people do not care'.

I don't know whether to believe him but then, I think, this is a true story and they are very rarely certain. But then, I think, this is the unsolved murder of three children. That demands attention. Promising Gary nothing, I gather up the photocopied transcripts. The glass door swings closed behind me as I head towards the lift.

At the offices of *The Australian* an older reporter asks me what I'm working on.

'The Bowraville murders,' I say, looking up from the documents that Gary gave me.

'Oh, the Beaumont murders,' he replies, leaning back in his chair and nodding. 'I know all about those.' Those victims were three white children, two sisters and a brother, who disappeared from Glenelg Beach, near Adelaide, in January 1966. The case had been replayed over and over in the years that followed on television and in newspaper reports.

'No,' I tell him. 'The Bowraville murders.'

'Never heard of them,' he says.

I feel a flare of resentment.

I realise that now I am committed. Because three black children were murdered a few hours away from the office in which we are sitting, and he should hear about them too.

*

Later, I learn more about the children. Colleen had four sisters and two brothers. The last time her younger sister, Paula, saw her, they were lying up in the bedroom together at home watching television, with Colleen telling scary stories, trying to make her sister laugh. She was generous and outgoing and popular. Before her disappearance, Colleen taught her brother Lucas how to swim, down at the Sawtell coast where Bonville Creek meets the Pacific Ocean. He made it to the state-level championships in school.

Evelyn was shy and quiet. A photograph taken the week before she went missing shows her sitting in a blue-and-red checked dress, a red ribbon tumbling from the neck down her chest. The eldest of her mother's children, Evelyn always had her three-year-old brother Aaron with her. Her mother, Rebecca, said they were like two peas in a pod, the two of them, you couldn't part them. Clingy, people said of her, not the sort to leave the shelter of her family and wander off alone.

Clinton was tall, strong and good-looking. The kind of boy who would be good at anything. He played basketball and footy, and when his team made the grand final, he scored two tries and won them the game. Clinton's family called him Bubby. He loved dancing and had Michael Jackson posters plastered across his bedroom wall. Like Michael Jackson, Bubby cared about his appearance. So much so that he never left the house without his favourite pair of shoes.

That fact was important, I would learn.

Tuesday, 16 February 2016

Since meeting Gary, I've spoken to the children's families by telephone, but this visit is the first time I've managed to convince my editors to let me visit where the children disappeared. Travelling with a producer from *The Australian*, Eric George, I'd planned to be in Sawtell a week earlier to meet with Colleen's mother, Muriel Craig. Only Muriel arranged to meet with a psychic, to talk to her daughter, so she said we'd have to wait until today.

From outside, the home where Colleen spent most of her childhood seems ordinary. A brick building with hanging baskets out the front and a neat patch of lawn. An ornamental wishing well stands in one corner of the garden, surrounded by statues of a duck, a swan and a garden gnome, all huddling together as if seeking shelter from the sunlight in the shade of the fence. It's just like countless homes on countless quiet roads across the country, except that this one contains a grieving mother, and that it is from this house in Sawtell that Colleen left to travel south to Bowraville, from where she disappeared.

Inside, the television casts a pale light on the dark, heavy furniture. The ceiling fan is thudding. A big, wary woman with a shock of black hair, Muriel sits with her hands resting on her stomach and says the psychic told her where to look for Colleen's body, and also told her several other people are hiding what they know about her daughter's death.

Muriel and I are each a little cautious of the other. She'd called me once, late in the evening, after I'd written a small article in the newspaper about the children's disappearance. Expecting her to thank me, I had instead been thrown backwards by her fury. The families of Evelyn and Clinton had been quoted, she'd said, but there was nothing from any member of her family. I said that I called her and left a message but heard nothing back. It wasn't good enough, she spat at me. I should have waited. I'd stammered an apology. It was a lesson in grief.

Muriel suggests we go out into her back garden, where lorikeets are screeching in the tree branches above the fence. I pull my chair close to hers, but not too close, and try not to stare directly at her as I ask my questions, not wanting to turn this into another confrontation. After what happened when she called me, I try to start again.

Muriel says that Colleen was her second baby, back when they were living in Bowraville, and she grew up to become her mother's helper. They used to clean the little Mission house together. 'Mum, I'll do it, leave it,' Colleen said. Talking about her daughter, Muriel looks up and to one side, smiling. When Colleen was little, the family moved from Bowraville to Sydney, then up the coast again to Coffs Harbour before settling in Sawtell, in the brick house outside which Muriel and I are sitting. Colleen was seven then.

Colleen slept here on the night before she left for Kelly
Jarrett's eighteenth birthday party in Bowraville. On the Monday,
Colleen helped her mother clean the house in the morning,
then gave her a kiss and said she'd see her that weekend at the
footy knockout tournament in Macksville, the next town down
the river from Bowraville itself. Remembering that moment,
Muriel looks down, stops smiling and shakes her head.

'Don't forget to pick me up now,' her daughter told her. Colleen
then left the house in a car driven by the partner of one of Muriel's
cousins. He offered to drive her down to Bowraville, alone, and she
trusted people. Muriel says her daughter was smiling as she got into
the car.

This was Colleen's country. From Sawtell the road heads south
over the Bellinger and Kalang rivers, looping through fields of
bananas with wide green leaves, which give way in time to eucalyptus forest, past isolated gardens where the trees burst with purple
flowers. Outside, the only sounds were birds and insects. Wooded
mountains formed the horizon against a bright blue sky.

There is a story about the making of this country. A young
Aboriginal man, a goori, saw a handsome stranger coming, a
stranger who was shining like the sun. The young man and the
other gooris followed and the stranger led them east towards
the ocean. But every time they got up close behind him, the
stranger made a river and cut himself a canoe to paddle across.
Some of the young men followed and, as they crossed each river,
the stranger gave them names and made them talk in different
languages. Eventually, as he led the gooris further, more of the
land and people were divided by these rivers and became the
Bandjalung, the Yaygirr and Dhanggati. Each spoke a different
language from the others. The Gumbaynggirr went the furthest,

following the stranger all the way to where the Nambucca River meets the ocean, but they couldn't catch him. That was there they finished up, the last place they followed him. The stranger went away then, leaving the people divided by the rivers and speaking different tongues. This land between Sawtell and Bowraville is Gumbaynggirr country here.

After driving out of Sawtell for somewhere around half an hour, the road turns west, inland, and here, the car in which she was travelling made its way through a patchwork of gum forest divided by lush fields and bare hilltops with scattered houses. In the 1800s, white settlers arrived in the Nambucca Valley, looking for the tall cedar trees found in its upper reaches, 30 metres to the first limb and several metres in girth. These trees were felled, ripped apart with pitsaws, then hewn into timber, dragged out by bullock-teams and carried down the river to the coast and on to Sydney for a profit. In a few decades, the valley had been stripped of cedar. Bowraville itself grew out of a cedar-getters camp.

Cattle farmers followed, clearing more land along the river-banks. These settlers left their names – the Buchanans and the Jarretts – and they also put up fences, meaning the Gumbaynggirr had to move, or were moved, to government reserves and the church missions. In 1883 the government declared an Aboriginal reserve would be established on Stuart Island, at the mouth of the Nambucca River, where the gooris chased the handsome stranger. Black people from the surrounding area were taken from their lands and forced to move there. In 1952 the Lands Department declared the island a recreational reserve and it was turned into a golf course. The people living on it had to move again.

Colleen's family settled upriver from Stuart Island, on the Mission in Bowraville, where her great-grandmother worked as

a cleaner for a white man in town. Over the years, more people
came to the Nambucca Valley, and the cattle were fed into the abat-
toirs to feed them. It seemed to the Gumbaynggirr as if the rivers
were the only thing that did not belong to the white man.

Near Bowraville, the road ran deeper through the forest, closer
to the Nambucca River, where the light reflected from the water
through the trees. Suddenly, they swooped out from under the tree
branches into daylight, down a sharp hill and around the perimeter
of the local racecourse, then on and over an old bridge, where the
worn-out planks shuddered under the car wheels with a rhythm
like a train riding on the tracks.

Beneath the bridge brown children played in the warm river
water. Beyond it, imported pines stood in the fine gardens of modest
timber houses. The road dipped in front of the pretty pastel-painted
church and rose between the school and the first of the storefronts.
On one side was the butchers and Bowraville Motors. On the other
the tiny red-brick courthouse and the neat police station.

The night after her daughter Colleen had driven down to
Bowraville, or maybe it was the next one, Muriel says she dreamed
about her daughter. Colleen was running between the trees on the
wide, flat land opposite the Mission and singing out for help. There
wasn't just one person chasing, there was a group of people. Muriel
could see their legs as they ran after. There might have been about
four or five. The dream didn't show her who these people were, she
just saw them chasing.

'Then I seen a figure, a person digging with a shovel,' Muriel says
as we sit in her garden. When the dream showed her the hands of that
person, they were white

*

On the Sunday after she waved her daughter off to travel to Bowraville, 16 September 1990, Muriel Craig drove down to the Macksville knockout tournament to meet Colleen with a car full of kids. Arriving at about 10 a.m., she parked the green station wagon on the grass close up to the action, where she judged that her daughter would find them. There were a lot of people at the footy oval, a few hundred, maybe more, so Muriel sat her kids on top of the car where they could be seen, and could see out over the crowd, to wait. She knew Colleen would be looking for her there.

Another woman from the Mission, Marjorie Jarrett, approached her. Marjorie lived at number 3 with Thomas Duroux, next door to the party, and Colleen was supposed to be staying with them there, but Marjorie was angry. Colleen had taken off, she said.

'Went somewhere on Thursday,' Marjorie was saying. Thursday had been the night of the party. 'She never came. I never seen her, I never seen her since.'

'If she wasn't there Friday then why didn't you ring me and tell me?' Muriel responded. This was Sunday. Three days since the party. 'You should have called me if she was missing all that time.'

Marjorie said something about Colleen catching a train to Goodooga in the early hours of Friday morning, but that made little sense to Muriel. Goodooga was a long way out west and getting there meant travelling to Sydney by train, then a stopover, a train to Dubbo, a coach from Dubbo to Lightning Ridge, then on to Goodooga by car. If Colleen was heading out that way, she would have called her mother. And, anyway, she wouldn't have gone there without saying, as she was supposed to be here at the knockout.

'I think then I already knew that she was gone,' Muriel tells me.

One of the kids was sent running into the crowd to find Muriel's sister. Along with the cousin who'd been staying with Muriel, they all piled into cars and headed straight to Bowraville, passing through the deep shadows of the forest outside town. Muriel, worried, asked if her cousin's partner, who had driven off with Colleen the last time she'd seen her, could have harmed the teenager.

'I don't know. It's possible,' her cousin replied.

The road to Bowraville from Macksville follows the green Nambucca River, entering the town from the south, closer to the Mission. Colleen, driving from Sawtell, would have come in from the north and driven down High Street, past all the white people's houses, to get to Cemetery Road. When Muriel arrived, the Mission was silent, its residents having mostly left to go to the footy tournament. Of the few people they found among the deserted houses, none had seen Colleen since the party. Muriel went to the two-man Bowraville police station, but it was closed for the weekend.

Muriel spoke to Kelly Jarrett, and to others who'd been at the party. She spoke to Martin Greenup, who said he saw Colleen out the front of the houses speaking to someone in a white Commodore. Someone on the Mission told her James Hide was also at the party, so she went to find him, driving over to his mum's place – you turn right off the Mission, then left, then right again, it's easy – and found the caravan he lived in. She knocked and James came to the door. He was big enough to fill it, and much taller than Muriel. He said the last time he'd seen Colleen she was sleeping on the couch at Freddo's, meaning Fred Buchanan's at number 4, the house of the party. James was smiling as he spoke.

I notice Muriel is staring past me, at the blank windows of her house.

'Sometimes I think I'm going silly,' she says. 'I sit here and she talks to me, all of a sudden. I can hear her in my mind.' Muriel says that Colleen tries to reassure her mother. They lie in bed together sometimes, and Colleen puts her arm around her, but then there are also times when Colleen gets angry, and things fly sideways off the table. When that happens, Muriel says she reaches out, trying to hear what her daughter wants to tell her. One time, Colleen told her mother to put the names of some people in Bowraville on Facebook, saying that they knew what happened to her. Muriel didn't do it and, the next morning, sitting on her lounge, she heard her daughter's voice: 'Mum, you didn't do what I told you to do. You didn't put the names in.' Frightened, Muriel got on the computer and posted the names online. The police made her take them down eventually, not wanting to inflame the tensions and suspicions now running through the Mission, but not before other people saw what she had written online.

'I know I shouldn't say this, but I hate the place,' says Muriel. 'I grew up there, I had a lovely childhood. But since all this happened, Bowraville is not the same,' she pauses. 'There is a lot of hate.' She looks straight at me. 'There's a lot of people in Bowraville I do hate, believe me.'

Eric and I look at each other in silence, and prepare to leave.

Wednesday, 17 February 2016

'So, this is the Mission here,' says Michelle Jarrett, pointing through the windscreen at the row of single-storey brick houses strung along one side of the unmarked, pitted strip of bitumen that is Cemetery Road. She wants to show us where her niece, four-year-old Evelyn, went missing, the second of the children to disappear in Bowraville.

Behind us is the town itself, which we left just a few minutes earlier, following Michelle's directions, driving down High Street and turning right at the white timber house with empty, lifeless windows, past the wrecked car, the shattered glass of which is spilt across the road, then left, as if crossing a divide, and downhill towards the spreading white mahogany where she told us to stop the car.

Here, there is silence for the moment. The row of houses beside an empty footpath, a few beat-up cars parked one behind the other and, across the road, a park and beyond it, a golf course.

Surrounding everything is bush, alive with the stabbing noise of insects. Looking up, I see the hills towering over Bowraville, covered with their dark shrouds of eucalypt forest. Down here, each of the Mission homes has a little, dry and faded, scrap of lawn.

The Mission homes are mostly neat, the muted colours of their brick walls and gum-green metal fencing matching those of the bush around them. A police van is parked outside one of the houses, where the footpath is scattered with brightly coloured toys. Nothing, except for us, is moving. The road itself has been renamed since the children's disappearance, Michelle tells me. Cemetery Road is now Gumbaynggirr Road.

Michelle herself is big and bold and angry and I like her. Her voice rasps, her skin is a rich brown and her greying hair is pulled up into a tight bun above her face. She wears a bright pink footy shirt printed with butterflies and a photograph of Evelyn.

She says to start the car again and turn left at the old tree, the big mahogany.

'They call it the Tree of Knowledge,' she says. I ask her why. She shrugs and points to the house opposite. That's where Colleen was staying. There are car tyres stacked up alongside the fence, a street sign that belongs to someplace else propped up beside the door and the heavy curtains, half of which are closed. Keep on driving, Michelle says. Two doors up, at number 6, that's where Evelyn was taken. A smaller house. Two windows and a covered veranda hung with mesh to provide some shelter from the sun.

Evelyn was asleep in the room closest to us on the night that she went missing, says Michelle. The window there, the one with the striped curtains. Michelle's sister, Evelyn's mother, went to bed in there with the four-year-old and her two little brothers, aged just three and one.

'Back then it didn't have a fence around it,' Michelle says, so anyone could walk in. When Evelyn's mother woke up, her daughter was gone.

We get out of the car and the realisation of just how close the houses are together twists inside my stomach. A stereo blares inside a third building, on the front wall of which someone has painted a man-size picture of the South Sydney bunny and the Parramatta eel. Evelyn's father, Billy Greenup, lives there now, says Michelle quietly. Two doors down from where his daughter disappeared.

Evelyn went missing three weeks after Colleen, on Thursday, 4 October 1990, following another party. It was another Thursday – payday, says Michelle, meaning welfare money. Payday meant a party, with some choosing to spend their money on grog and yarndi in a two- or three- or four-day rush. Dozens of people would crowd into one house, or on the road outside it. The party would jump from house to house like wildfire. The money, the food, the grog, keeping an eye on the children, everything was shared out between them.

'If you get paid, then you shout,' Michelle tells me. 'That person got to shout when they get paid. That's how it works.'

Three weeks after Colleen's disappearance, Evelyn's mum, Rebecca Stadhams, and her grandmother, Patricia Stadhams – who said she saw Colleen and James Hide walking down the side of the house at number 3 on the night the teenager disappeared – were at the party, drinking. They argued, badly, over whether Rebecca should take the children home and James stepped in to sort it. Rebecca and the children stayed.

The next day, Michelle got home from work about six thirty or seven in the evening and was lying in her room when Rebecca came to the door.

'Look, Evelyn is missing.'

'What do you mean she's missing?' Michelle asked her sister. Rebecca said she hadn't seen her daughter since the night before.

'Have you called the police?' asked Michelle.

No. Rebecca hadn't. Michelle got up, found a photograph she'd taken of her niece a week before, the one where she had the blue-and-red checked dress on, and went with her sister to the police station.

'I just want to report my niece missing, she's only four years old,' Michelle told the policeman.

He looked down at the photograph.

'What do you want me to do about it?' Michelle says he asked her.

'Help us. She's gone missing, we can't find her.'

'Well, I'm just about to knock off,' she says the policeman told her. By this time, it was around eight in the evening. Michelle drove to a cousin's house and told them that Evelyn was missing. They started looking for her themselves around the Mission. While they were out, Michelle saw a police car driving around, doing a patrol.

'What about the day after that, and the day after that?' I ask Michelle.

'Nothing, no police, nothing.' Sometimes, she or Rebecca would go up to the police station and tell them again, 'We can't find Evelyn.' One night, says Michelle, the officer behind the desk told them Evelyn had gone walkabout, as if that might explain why she disappeared. But that made no sense. Not Evelyn. She wouldn't wander off alone and leave her family. Evelyn was clingy. And kids like that don't go walkabout. She was only four years old.

Newspaper reports from the time of Evelyn's disappearance give a different account of what happened.

'We've dragged the river once,' one policeman told a local paper. Another reported how 'police and fifty locals' searched two hundred houses in Bowraville, looking for Evelyn in the days after she was reported missing. They searched the waterhole beneath Lanes Bridge, where the local children played together and over which Colleen had driven into town. Four homicide detectives from the regional crime squad in Newcastle were sent up for a week to help.

A photograph beside one of these early newspaper articles about her daughter's disappearance shows Rebecca, hollow-cheeked and wide-eyed, with her lips hidden behind thin fingers. 'Still hoping', the caption reads.

This was the second child to disappear from Bowraville, but the police did not believe they were connected. Instead, both were treated as classic missing persons cases; the police were focused on finding them, not trying to establish where they'd been and who else had been there at the time. Police records show that they followed rumours: Evelyn was seen on the Mission, in town or playing at the waterhole. Children were interviewed about this without their parents present. When Michelle first went to report Evelyn missing, she'd repeated what she had been told by someone else – that Evelyn was seen among a group of other kids in town the day following the party. The idea was planted. The conviction that Evelyn was last seen alive the following morning is repeated again and again in those early police reports.

In public and in private, the police denied any connection between the disappearances of Colleen and Evelyn. Witnesses, they said, had also seen Colleen alive after her mother said that she went missing. One witness put her on a bus travelling in Queensland. A police sergeant told one newspaper she might have moved to Sydney. A detective was quoted saying they were looking at whether Evelyn was taken by a childless couple and could be living 'safe and well'.

Standing outside the houses from which Michelle says the two children went missing, I think how three weeks and about 100 metres separated these disappearances. It's hard to believe the police did not accept that they might be connected, too.

Evelyn's mother, Rebecca Stadhams, twists her hands together. She's forty-nine and has nine children, the youngest now the same age Evelyn was at the time she disappeared. Rebecca says that she left Bowraville after it happened, and kept drinking. She's come back to mark what would have been her daughter's thirtieth and her sister, Michelle Jarrett, has arranged for us to meet in her house on the edge of town.

It's difficult, Rebecca says. Earlier, she met up with Evelyn's father, Billy Greenup, telling him, 'Before we get too drunk we have to get out to the cemetery and wish her a happy birthday.' But their daughter has missed so much, and all that they can do is kiss her grave.

On the night of the party when Evelyn went missing, Rebecca says that she was walking to the Mission with her children when they ran into James Hide. A big bloke, whose skin was often stained and dirty from work at the tannery, he asked what they were up to. 'Oh, we's nothing, going home,' she told him. They agreed to get some grog together. James had money and a car.

They went to the party, where everyone was drinking. It was only a few hours later that James had to step in to calm the fight between Rebecca and her mother, Patricia, over taking her kids home. The next morning, Rebecca says, she remembers waking up inside the bedroom and seeing her two boys sitting together on the mattress. She asked them, 'What is you two doing?' They turned to look at her. Evelyn wasn't in the room.

Rebecca went outside, looking for her daughter. One of Evelyn's pink shoes was lying beside the house.

Like Michelle and Colleen's mother, Muriel Craig, before her, Rebecca says she is happy to be interviewed, though it's obvious that talking hurts her. Her mother, Evelyn's grandmother, Patricia Stadhams, is also in the kitchen. Her face is wet with tears.

Patricia says she stayed awake on the night of the party until around three o'clock, after almost everyone else had crashed out where they stood or gone to bed. James was awake also, she says. He was mainly into whiskey. You never knew how drunk he was, because he didn't look it, but there was heaps of drink that night. Sometime during the dark of the early morning, Patricia says that she heard Evelyn crying. When Patricia woke up around about seven, she started to clean up the house. James was not there then.

I drive back to the Mission. Outside the house marked with the graffiti of the Souths bunny, I speak to a woman called Fiona Duckett, who says she was also at the party and had slept there that night. Sometime in the early hours, Fiona woke up to feed her baby.

'I seen James Hide walk out of the room next to me,' she says. That was the room in which Rebecca was sleeping with her children. James was wearing thongs and light blue stubbies, Fiona says.

'I followed him down the hallway, by the time I got to that front door, and the light was on, the door was open, I couldn't see that man.'

Over the decades, other reporters had covered the children's killings. I'd searched through the archives and read several of these old articles before leaving Sydney to visit Bowraville, trying to learn whatever they could teach me before meeting the children's families for myself. Some of the earliest reports talked about rumours of devil worshippers, heroin dealers and a branch of the Ku Klux Klan active in the Nambucca Valley. In 1996, the *Daily Telegraph* reported that police were searching for Colleen's remains on a sacred Aboriginal site, inspired by a child's dream.

In 2010, *The Monthly* described how when Evelyn's mother, Rebecca, woke up on the morning after the second party on the Mission, she found that her pants had been pulled down during the night. The year after that article was published, the ABC's *Four Corners* reported that James Hide, who had been at the party, had his eye on Rebecca.

And yet it seemed as if these reports had been met by a great silence. Reading through my photocopied versions, nothing in them helped explain why there had been so little public reaction or any kind of progress since. No one had been jailed for these three children's murders.

Instead, it felt like this serial killing had been allowed to slip into some kind of public forgetting; either that or the police, the courts and the state government had come to accept that three children could go missing and that whoever killed them could be walking free today.

The first time I spoke to someone from the children's families by telephone, I said that I was sorry. Sorry that I'd lived and worked as a crime reporter, and maybe even heard the name of Bowraville before somewhere, or read it, yet paid so little attention to what had happened there before now.

'Thank you,' said Leonie Duroux, whose late partner had been Clinton's brother. I asked if I could speak to other family members, and wrote a few small articles for *The Australian*, but these were also met with silence. No other reporters followed up the story. One, working for a rival newspaper, even questioned why I bothered; the story was cold and old, he told me. It wasn't going anywhere.

It was Michelle who made me decide to try something different. Two months earlier, in December 2015, she'd been one of a few dozen of the children's family members who gathered to hear the decision of a government review into the laws surrounding murder prosecutions. I wanted to cover the result for the newspaper, trying to explain how the children's families had campaigned for reform, believing it might allow the courts finally to jail their loved ones' killer and how they feared that without this change – a quarter-century after the children went missing – there would be no further legal action in relation to the deaths in Bowraville.

Only, when the announcement came, the government said it would not change the law. A photographer working for the paper filmed the families' reaction. Among the crowd, Michelle stood out, shouting, 'Twenty-five years, another year! Another day! Another minute! Another second! There's another day our kids go without justice. Everybody else in this Australia gets justice, but not our kids.'

Weeping, Michelle raised her hands to cover her eyes. Others among the children's families were also crying.

'Not our kids.' Michelle choked on the words as she tried to stop the flow of tears. I watched the footage over and over, then showed it to my colleagues. I watched their shocked reaction to what they were seeing.

'This is awful,' another reporter told me. 'Why won't somebody do something about it?' It was as if Michelle's voice had overcome the silence surrounding what had happened to the children. It wasn't just a cold case; it was a real woman who had lost her niece and who was hurting.

This is how to tell this story, I thought. Not in my words printed on the pages of the newspaper, but through the living voices of the families. The idea, then, had been to make a podcast – an audio documentary series published online by the newspaper. Eric George, the producer from *The Australian*, would record my conversations with the people who were directly caught up in the children's disappearances as they told their stories: the relatives, the police, the lawyers, witnesses, maybe even the police suspect, if he would agree to speak.

A podcast might be a different way to tell this true crime story. At least, people might listen. That idea had brought me here, to the Mission in Bowraville a few months later, in February, where I am now standing looking at the houses from which Colleen and Evelyn went missing. The short stretch of road between them seems to sway in the heat, as if I have a fever. I feel bare and unprotected. Neither the newspaper nor I have done anything like this before.

Thursday, 18 February 2016

Somehow, Thomas Duroux endured this. His sixteen-year-old son, Clinton Speedy-Duroux, was the third to go missing in Bowraville, and it was at Thomas's house on the Mission that Colleen was staying when she became the first to disappear. Evelyn, he tells me, used to turn up at with her brother Aaron at his house in the mornings to have breakfast. Until, of course, she didn't. Thomas's voice is soft and distant. I have to lean in close towards him with the microphone to catch the words.

Thomas and I are sitting outside his front garden in the cool of the early morning, underneath the Tree of Knowledge. He's wearing a footy jersey covered in silhouettes of fishes with staring white eyeballs. His own eyes are surrounded by dark shadows. The two of us sit side by side, our knees almost touching, staring forward. Eric George, the podcast producer, crouches beside us, ready to record. Before we came to Bowraville, detective Gary Jubelin told me that conversations follow different rules among Aboriginal communities such as that on the Mission. Eye contact can be seen as confrontational, as can asking direct questions. Long silences, such as those during which Thomas and I both stare at the parched grass in front of us, might be a politeness showing that a question is being taken seriously and consideration given as to what to say.

As the interviewer – as an interloper – Gary says I also cannot expect just to turn up, ask my questions, and then leave. This is the opposite of what my first boss as a reporter told me. He said journalism was simple: you read the newspapers, pick up the phone and write it down. Gary says that on the Mission, you need to show people respect by spending time with them. Sometimes the best way to elicit information is to share what you know first.

I make a clumsy effort to follow these instructions. Thomas talks about the pride he has in all his children. He remembers Clinton following behind him when he went down the river, fishing, or playing with his brothers out the back. Football, baseball, cricket, whatever Clinton wanted he would mainly do it. Thomas pauses.

'Terrible, blamed myself,' he tells me.

'You blamed yourself?'

'I still do,' he answers. 'Still blame myself for letting him come down.'

Thomas separated from Clinton's mother, June Speedy, but the family were close and his son still came to visit him in Bowraville. Just before Christmas 1990, three months after Colleen's disappearance and two months after Evelyn went missing, Thomas drove north to Tenterfield, up near the Queensland border, where Clinton was living. He was packing up and ready to head back south again for home when Clinton jumped into the car.

'Had his swag and everything already in there and you couldn't say no to him,' says Thomas, staring forward. How would you say no to a sixteen-year-old boy? 'It's now maybe I wish I would have,' says Thomas.

He drove Clinton down.

The two of them were home together on the Mission on the morning of 31 January 1991, less than four months after Evelyn went missing. It was a Thursday – payday. Thomas remembers Clinton leaving for a party wearing a pair of shorts, a t-shirt and his trainers. The next morning he found the trainers sitting on the veranda outside his front door.

The fear. You could almost touch it. Thomas was told Clinton's girlfriend, Kelly Jarrett, had brought the shoes home that morning.

'That's when I started to get worried and I started to walk around looking, asking people had they seen him,' says Thomas. Clinton wouldn't have gone anywhere without his shoes. Thomas explains that Clinton was particular about them. He'd been that way since he was a young bloke. Other boys liked to go barefooted but not Clinton. He'd put his shoes on when he woke up in the morning, no matter what the weather, and about the only time he didn't have them on him was in the shower or bed.

Thomas went up to where the party was the night before, in one of the flats just around the corner from the Mission, and found Kelly.

'Where's Bubby?' he asked her.

'I thought he was at home.'

Kelly said she'd been with Clinton at the party. She'd arrived around midday, carrying a bottle of Bundaberg and some coke to mix it. Clinton himself was drinking a stubby when she got there and looked already halfway gone. Normally, Clinton didn't drink much, but he did drink that day, said Kelly. They finished the rum.

James Hide had been there, Kelly told him, drinking in the kitchen. At about 10 p.m. and again around midnight, James went up to the Ex-Services Club in Bowraville on High Street to buy more grog and he came back with a bottle of Jim Beam each time. Sometime after midnight, Kelly and Clinton and James were all outside talking. The three of them walked off together, around the corner to the property on Cohalan Street where James was living in a caravan in his mum's garden. Clinton had stopped drinking but the others shared the bourbon. Inside the caravan they watched music videos and finished off the bottle, then James offered to let his guests sleep on the double bed, while he crashed at the far end of the room.

When Kelly woke up the next day, Clinton wasn't with her. She said her shorts and pants had been removed and were lying on a table in the caravan. She remembered James, who must have left the caravan while she was sleeping, coming back early in the morning and waking her up, saying, 'See you later, Kelly. We will go for a charge.' She remembered James laughing. Clinton must have gone somewhere, she reckoned. When Kelly got out of bed, she found Clinton's shoes, so she took them over to his father's.

Thomas tells me that, after speaking to Kelly, he walked through Bowraville, down to the river, searching. At the Ex-Services Club, he checked the bar, poker machines and tables. No one had seen Clinton. He walked to James's caravan. They knew each other well enough. Would drink together sometimes.

'I got on with him quite good actually,' says Thomas. The caravan was open, so Thomas knocked, but got no answer. He put his head through the doorway and saw James asleep on the double bed, with no cover on him and wearing only a pair of shorts.

'James,' called Thomas. James was sprawled out. A big bloke, bigger than most of the others on the Mission. 'James,' he called again.

He got no response.

Thomas went to the police, who said it was too soon to report his son missing. He had to wait twenty-four hours before he could report it. Thomas went back the next day and tried to tell them about Clinton being in James's caravan. He tried to tell them that James was one of the few blokes big enough to do his son harm.

'I don't know, they just didn't want to believe something like that,' says Thomas, staring at the grass. I think about how other detectives have told me that those first few hours, or days, after a killing are critical to a police investigation. In that time, bloody clothes are being burned or cleaned, weapons thrown into the river, an alibi invented. Witnesses are starting to trade fact and rumour between them, discolouring their memories. That must especially take place in a small town like Bowraville, I think, where everybody knows each other and everybody talks. Once again, the police treated Clinton as a missing persons case. Again, they publicly rejected the idea of a connection between the disappearances of the children.

'They said he'd gone walkabout,' says Thomas.

That evening, Eric and I stand at the far end of the Mission, looking back along the line of houses. The only sound is someone, somewhere, shouting. Among the trees behind the houses, at least a dozen burnt-out cars sit radiating the heat they soaked up in the hours of sunlight. Looking at the pitted road and homes with sheets hanging crookedly across windows in place of curtains, Eric says, 'I've never been anywhere like this before.'

A girl of about four or five rides up on a pink bicycle. She stops, leans her head to one side and stares at us in silence, then asks, 'What you doing?'

What to tell her? She doesn't need to know that we are here because three children staying on this street went missing. I think of my own daughters. I wouldn't tell them about a killing, or that a killer was still out there, somewhere. Uncertain how to explain our presence, I say nothing. Eventually, the girl gets bored of waiting, grins and turns her bike around. As she pedals away towards the houses where Colleen, Evelyn and Clinton were staying before they went missing, we listen to her singing.

Later that night, in a pub at Macksville, the next town along the Nambucca River, I arrange to meet a doctor who ran a small clinic on the Mission in the years after the children disappeared. He says he remembers treating children there, those aged between three and six, whose rates of skin and ear infections far outstripped those in the local white community. Kids coming in with pus dripping out of their ears. Eventually, the doctor says, their immune systems matured and he would not see the children for years. Then, during high school, they'd return to his clinic, often for something to do with alcohol misuse or drugs or solvents, or because of pregnancy.

In those few years away, he said, the kids changed. Something was lost. They'd become fatalistic. Ahead of them in adulthood lay killers: heart disease and diabetes, both much higher among the black population than the white. Blokes dying in their thirties, which was unheard of in Bowraville outside of the Mission. It's just with poverty, the doctor says, that you get these diseases. The children growing up in Bowraville were vulnerable because their whole community was vulnerable.

'Basically,' the doctor tells me, 'life's running you over like a truck.'

*

The next morning, I sit down again with Thomas underneath the white mahogany. His granddaughter is buried in the cemetery here, he says. She died of cot death. Another of his children, Clinton's younger brother, died the same way. After Clinton disappeared, another of his brothers, Marbuck, was diagnosed with motor neurone disease. Of Thomas's six boys, just three are left alive.

After the doctors told him that the disease would be fatal, Marbuck always said he wanted to live long enough to see justice for Clinton. At least, unlike his brother, Marbuck had a chance to fall in love and have children. His partner, a white woman called Leonie, took his surname, Duroux. Early in their relationship, when he was drunk, he told her about Clinton. Later, while Leonie was pregnant, she and Marbuck moved from Tenterfield to Bowraville itself.

One day the two of them pulled up outside the takeaway behind a red Galant, belonging to James Hide's mother, Marlene. Marbuck gunned the engine. He released the brake and their car ran into the red one, shunting it forward. After their son was born, Marbuck was jailed for breaking the Galant's window. Leonie watched him being escorted from the courtroom then walked out, slamming the door and shouting, 'What about his fucking brother?'

Inside the building, Marbuck was wailing 'What about my brother?' too.

A mob of shrieking magpies – the correct term for a group of these birds is 'a murder' – is sitting in the tree above us, launching themselves in short flights from the branches to the metal roof of a memorial to the three children which now stands in the parkland outside Thomas's house. He looks up at them and talks about how the families only want to get some justice; how they have put their hopes in the police, the courts and the politicians, only to be kicked in the guts each time. No one has ever been convicted, he says. Nobody listens to them. They tried to get the New South Wales attorney general, who's responsible for all the state's courts and tribunals and who appoints all the judges and magistrates, to come up to Bowraville and see where the children went missing, but he wouldn't.

'How does that make you feel?' I ask.

'Angry.' He pauses. 'Because you can't do nothing, you've just got to wait for the government. If they say yes, well it's okay but more often than not we're getting knocked back.'

'Does it make you feel powerless?' I ask him.

'Yeah, it does. Yeah, it's just sitting back, waiting, getting no answers, nothing being done.'

We sit in silence.

'If it was some other kids, different town, different circumstances, yeah, probably this would have been over and done with,' Thomas says. I think he means that if it were white kids who vanished then the result would have been different. The magpies are still screeching above us in the branches. Having not been able to get an explanation when I asked Michelle Jarrett, Evelyn's aunty, why people call this the Tree of Knowledge, I try again with Thomas but he just shrugs and says that no one knows the answer. It's just a place where the old people on the Mission would meet, he says, and maybe have a sip, and talk in the Gumbaynggirr language. Privately, I question whether there is more to this that I am not being told.

We stand and walk together to the memorial to the three murdered children. 'What would you do if you could?' I ask him.

'If it was up to me it would be over and done with by now, but I'd end up in jail.'

'What would you do?'

He laughs. 'Do I have to answer?' Thomas looks down at the twigs and displaced gravel scattered across the stone floor.

'I'll come out here with a broom, tidy it up,' he says.

Friday, 19 February 2016

Twenty-five years before my visit to Bowraville, in the weeks after the three children went missing, another reporter for *The Australian* visited the town. He wrote a long and troubling account of what he found there: a town divided between its white and black populations, each looking at the other with suspicion.

One night in a pub in Bowraville, the reporter describes meeting a 'fat white man' who announces that he'll be happy to share his knowledge of what happened to the children, but only if the reporter doesn't use his name:

> *Speedy, he says, was murdered by dope growers who spotted him looking for crops. Colleen Walker travelled by train from Macksville to Sydney, and is now living in Redfern. Evelyn Greenup, about to be taken from her mother by welfare authorities (a persistent rumour), was sent into hiding with relatives in Queensland.*

How does the Fat Man know all this?

Because, he says, he has a mate in the Federal police.

'Know what I'd like to do with all these Abos? I'd like to take a great big bus and take them all out and dump them in the Simpson Desert.'

Right, we say. Thanks for your time.

'Hey,' he says, a little later. 'What'd they do with the Abos in Tasmania?'

. . .

'They wiped them out,' I tell him.

He winks: 'That's the way to go. Useless, the lot of them.'

Standing outside the same pub, looking down the empty High Street, it seems as if the town has not moved forward since that first reporter's visit, or at least not on the surface. The courthouse is silent now, as is the little police station. The pharmacist is shuttered. Several of the other more imposing buildings sit silently, with empty, wooden verandas and closed curtains. The only movement is on the far crest of the hill on which I am standing, beyond the tiny cinema, the empty corner store and the war memorial standing alone in the middle of the road, where three men in yellow high-vis trousers and with sun-darkened skin are drinking, bare-chested on the footpath.

Behind me, in the shattered window of the darkened service station, hangs a handmade sign. It reads, 'Welcome to Bowradise'.

Walking down, past the corner store, I notice a black-and-white photograph, blown up and bolted to the wall overlooking the crossroads that forms the centre of the town. It shows a team of oxen standing ready to pull the cedar logs as wide as their bodies. With them are a man and a boy, their faces indistinct, the shoulders of the man slumped forwards. Behind them, on top of a stack of freshly cut lumber stands another figure, in shirt and tie, his hands on his hips, exultant. Does this photograph show one of the settler's camps, from which Bowraville was founded? There is no explanation, just the picture of the men and the fallen timber, where a clearing has been carved in the dark forest.

I decide to break the silence and start knocking on people's doors.

The first couple to answer say that they'll talk, and will be recorded for the podcast, but want to remain anonymous. They say it's for their own protection, as every time the disappearance of the children gets mentioned in the news, it stirs up something ugly. They talk about blackfellas coming up from the Mission, walking down the streets between the rows of white people's houses and pelting the walls and roofs with stones.

Bowraville has changed little since the children were taken, the man tells me. According to the census, the town's white population has grown slightly over the decades since, to around 1100, while the black population has remained fairly steady, at about 160 – still about five times higher, as a proportion, than the country as a whole.

'There's still a lot of hatred here,' the man says, smiling. 'Why the blacks hate us is because of the Bowraville murders.' As we talk, children run in and out of the house behind them. Lighting a cigarette, his partner tells us how she was driving home last night, or maybe the night before, when two Aboriginal kids on bicycles called out.

'Fuck you, you white cunt,' they shouted.

'What did you say?' she demanded, not taking shit from any ten-year-old or thirteen-year-old.

'Fuck you, you white bitch.'

'What for?'

'This is my land. What are you driving on my land for?' one child called out.

'You own shit. You own that bike that you're riding on,' she told him.

'I want to stab you, whitefella.'

'Why be like that?' she asks me. 'Why?'

Nothing has changed since the murders, she says, stubbing out her cigarette on the steps up to her front door. Bowraville is small, she tells me. These people are your neighbours. You leave, you come back. Same people are going to be there.

Eric George, the podcast producer, and I are staying at the Coach House Inn on the High Street in Bowraville. The hotel has a peeling grandeur, with empty corridors and rusting wrought-iron chairs stood on the balcony outside. At the time the three children went missing, around 1990, so well within my lifetime, Aboriginal people were not served at the bar in here, but drank instead in the stables out the back, where our car is parked.

Returning here each evening after days spent speaking to the children's families, I feel myself being pulled, helplessly, beneath the surface of the town.

Nearby is Bowraville's old hospital, a single-storey wooden building where black women were once not allowed to have their babies. Colleen's mother, Muriel Craig, told us how her mother had to walk to Bellingen, a long day on a dirt road climbing steeply through the forest, to get to a hospital where she would be accepted. Having given birth, she then walked home carrying the newborn child.

Muriel also told us about growing up in Bowraville in the 1950s and 1960s. Her family lived in one of the eight Mission houses. The Mission used to be on the other side of the Cemetery Road, Muriel said, but it got moved, before the murders happened, closer to the town's garbage tip, piggery and graveyard. The town's golf course stands on the old site today.

As a child, Muriel's home had three bedrooms and a kitchen. A shilling in the machine bought you an hour's worth of electricity. The children – her mum had fourteen kids in total – went to school and church in Bowraville, where there they taught them to believe in God and not to speak the Gumbaynggirr language. Her father worked on the banana plantations outside the town. It was hard work, but worth it, and they were the first family on the Mission to get a TV. The other kids would crowd into their house to watch the *Six Million Dollar Man* then tumble out and set off for the nearby orchards to get mandarins and oranges, or steal corn from people's paddocks, which they'd roast inside the husk on a fire outside, because it tastes good like that. Good times, they were, said Muriel. A happy childhood.

Once, in town, one of Muriel's white friends said they should go and get an ice cream milkshake.

'Come in with me,' she'd pleaded.

'I'm not allowed to,' Muriel replied. Blackfellas weren't allowed into many of the shops. When she was ten, in 1965, Muriel remembers a big bus arriving in Bowraville and these fellas, white and black, up from Sydney University, protesting at the racism in country New South Wales. They called it the Freedom Ride, after similar rides by civil rights activists in the segregated American Deep South. After leaving Sydney, the bus had already been to more than a dozen towns and cities across New South Wales and over

the border into Queensland, but one of the riders, the historian
Ann Curthoys, wrote in her diary that Bowraville was 'absolutely
shocking – by far the worst we'd encountered'. It had a brooding
kind of menace, the riders found.

Journalists from the newspapers in Sydney also followed their
protest and the manager of the Bowraville milk bar told the *Daily
Telegraph*: 'The aborigines never get milk shakes here. If I served a
milk shake to one of them I would lose the trade of 20 white people.' The riders decided to challenge that, and took some of the
Aboriginal kids with them into the milk bar and made sure they
were served. Muriel was one of those children. It was the first time
she'd had an ice-cream milkshake. It tasted good, she told me.

Less than a decade later, Muriel became a mother, giving birth
to Colleen, her second child, in 1974. Shortly after Colleen's birth,
a local paper published the *Bowraville Centenary*, a short book
marking one hundred years since the town was established. Its
forty-six pages listed every local headmaster, bank manager and
postmaster to work in the town during the past century; it gave
a history of the dairy company, the police station and the CBC
Bank, which opened for business in 1885; but it made no mention
of the Mission. Nor did it name a single Aboriginal person living in
Bowraville over the years.

Listening to Muriel tell the story of her childhood and Colleen's
birth, I'd felt again that sense of being adrift in the water and strug-
gling to swim against the tide. It was as if this history was like a river
eddy, circling back and back upon itself, with everything the water
carried trapped, unable to move forward. I thought again about
the old Gumbaynggirr story about how this country was made
by the formation of the rivers, which separated the people into
different tribes. When Eric and I return to the darkened Coach

House Inn this evening, we learn there is no phone reception, so instead we are told to walk down the empty road, between the pools of dim light which spills through the windows of the deserted pub to find a payphone. I try to call my wife, but cannot get an answer. Instead, back at the Coach House Inn, I lie awake in the dark of my bedroom and listen to the cockroaches. It feels as if the waters are closing over my head.

During the weeks and months after the children went missing, the Mission swam with rumours: the white man, James Hide, was at each of the parties where the children had been; James, who'd been in a relationship with Colleen's aunty, Alison Walker – he even had a kid with her – liked black girls, people were saying; before the children went missing, someone had seen James chasing an Aboriginal girl across the golf course opposite the Mission, only he didn't catch her; James once got into an argument with someone on the Mission and smashed down their door with a golf club; James had let himself into people's houses after they were sleeping and stood there, watching them in bed.

But it felt like the rumours were not being answered, or were not being heard. The police, who people said should be doing something, were used to treating the Aboriginal population as suspects, or prisoners, not victims. They weren't used to listening to them. When they visited the Mission, it was usually to break up something or drag someone off.

The blackfellas, too, weren't used to trusting the police long enough to tell them something. One time, a new and young detective went there to arrest a teenager, only the boy took a swing at him, so the policeman hit him with his baton and the two of them ended up grappling on the ground. Soon they were surrounded. One girl grabbed a length of wood and the teenage boy was shouting, 'Hit him, hit him', meaning the policeman. Another time, the wife of the local police sergeant was walking down High Street when some of the blackfellas started barking, calling her a dog for marrying a cop. The local constable, out buying a newspaper, was physically attacked.

Someone, either on the Mission or in Bowraville, knew what had happened to the children. And while it seemed that those still living on the Mission had a suspect – James – those white people living in town thought that he was innocent. Such was the mistrust between them that every so often, usually after she'd been drinking, Evelyn's mum, Rebecca Stadhams, would go into town and smash things. One time, around 2 a.m., she went up and down High Street, breaking windows. She didn't care which window, any window. Rebecca got arrested and sentenced to three weeks in Grafton Correctional Centre. Much of the time she spent curled up on the cell floor, refusing to talk.

Eric and I visit the property on Cohalan Street where James lived with his mother, Marlene, at the time of the children's disappearances. The yellow Viscount caravan he slept in is now gone. In its place, I count seven wrecked cars lying around the house itself amid a sea of abandoned motor parts, tools and domestic wreckage. A stack of polystyrene crates, each filed with crushed Coke cans, are piled outside the door. Marlene still lives there. We knock on the door.

Her partner, Noel Short, answers. A big man – too big it seems for the single-storey building to contain him – he leans half out of the screen door to talk.

'I saw youse earlier,' he says, his eyes moving between us from behind long grey hair that falls like iron bars in front of his face. 'You were over there,' he says, nodding at one of the houses opposite. He's right. We spoke to his neighbours, who'd warned us he might chase us off his property. I eye the sledgehammer lying beside the door.

I say that we are working on a report about the disappearance of the children. 'One thing that doesn't ever get told in all of this is James's side of the story,' I tell him.

'No,' he says. 'We won't talk 'cause it's what we were told not to.'

'By whom?' I ask.

'Solicitors, the barrister.'

'When was that?'

'When first, like, it happened,' he says.

'You've never spoken since then?'

'No, never spoken about it, no.' A couple of goats that live fenced inside the property walk up and are bleating at us.

'It still hasn't finished, has it?' Noel says. 'There's still her in Newcastle. You could put that in your report.'

'Which her was that?' I ask him, confused.

'The Walker one.' Colleen. 'A mate of mine saw her in Newcastle. She's still a-fucking-live in my books.'

'They found her clothes in the river,' I tell him.

'Yeah, well, but nothing else, did they?'

'No.' I feel a rising anger.

'And someone could throw her clothes in the river, now that's all I'm gonna say, thank you.' Noel turns his back on us and we pick our way back past the crates of empty Coke cans and other piles of rubbish to the footpath. I think about sitting with Colleen's mother, and the trauma she carries, caused by her daughter's death.

Later, we visit James's uncle, Brent Fletcher, who lives behind the main street of Bowraville. A friendly bloke who meets us at the gate when we approach, Brent worked with James at the tannery. Helped James get a job there, in fact.

'What was he like as a bloke then, growing up?' I ask him.

'Just a normal kid. A kid's a kid,' Brent says. James did the same as every other kid. He hung around. Went swimming. 'He was a good kid all right until he got mixed up with them.' He means the people living in the Mission houses, the blackfellas. 'They just ruined him. He spent all his time out there. Not with us, you know?'

'So what was it that took him down there then? What took James to the Mission? What was it?' I ask Brent.

'I don't know. It's a funny thing, mate, why do any of 'em go there?'

'You mean whitefellas?'

'Yeah. Why go there?'

'I'm guessing you don't go there much yourself.'

'No.' He laughs out loud.

James was a good worker, Brent says. Big enough to lift the cow hides ready for tanning easily enough. But the morning after Clinton disappeared, James was drunk at work and useless. Staggering.

Brent says his nephew did not murder the three children.

'Have you ever asked James about it?' I ask.

'No.'

'How do you know he didn't do it then?'

'Because I know he wouldn't do it . . . I believe he wouldn't do it, I believe he wouldn't be able to.'

Eric catches my eye and nods at the road behind us. There's Noel, driving slowly in a dirty station wagon, staring at us through the window.

Brent doesn't seem to notice. 'The police concentrated on James without even trying to look for anybody else or anybody else connected and it was all too late and they ended up with nothing,' he says. 'You don't know what this family has been through because of them.'

'How do you mean?'

'Well, I spent a year and a half at home, couldn't go to the pub, couldn't go to the club. They were out the front of me house calling me a murderer 24/7. Out on the road, driving up and down, yelling out, screaming,' he says.

We thank him for his time and leave, heading back to the pub in Bowraville to get some food. As we walk into the bar, Noel is sitting in the corner, staring back.

Still unsure of how much has changed in Bowraville since that first article appeared in *The Australian*, I drive up through the forest that shrouds the steep hillside above the town, between the angled bars of sunlight cast through the gum trees and the clouds of dust thrown up from the dirt road. Over the ridge and down I drive to meet Clive Welsh, who was one of scores of local volunteers who spent days in the heat of the summer of 1991 pushing through lantana and twisted, fallen eucalypts to search for the missing children. Today, he still farms the same 93 hectares of land carved out of the forest. His daughter lives further up the hillside. To the south a small river known as Welshs Creek carries his family name.

Following the dirt road through the forest, I feel lost among a vast and wild landscape. Around a sharp corner, overlooking a wide valley, I turn down the long, thin drive through cleared fields towards the farmhouse. In the distance a figure on a red quad bike

looks up and sees me heading towards him, then cuts the ignition
and walks towards where he knows I will pull up. We are the only
two figures moving in the landscape. When I arrive, Clive smiles,
shakes my hand, then invites me to sit with him on the veranda,
which looks back through the frangipani flowers towards the
narrow road down which I drove, twisting and turning to the solitary farmhouse. A wiry man, his hands flattened by work, Clive's
skin is sun-beaten though still shows pale beneath his shirt. It's
peaceful here with the cattle lowing and I find myself smiling.
I explain that I am here reporting on the murders. Clive brings me
a drink and speaks in a soft voice.

'I wouldn't be surprised if they're chasing the wrong bloke.'

I scramble for an answer. 'Who could it be?'

'Someone in the bloody Aboriginal community,' he says. 'The
feeling seems to be they think the Aboriginal community was
involved in it. Whether they were or not, it's yet to be proved.'

The cows in the fields are moving closer, advancing on the
house in time for next feeding.

'Listen to those cattle bellowing,' says Clive. 'They're just going
to bellow all night.' I doubt I could sleep, alone, in that isolated
farmhouse, surrounded by the lowing cattle, but Clive says he is
used to it. He's farmed here for forty years – roughly the lifetimes
of Colleen and Clinton, had they not gone missing – and is used to
the noise. He'll sleep just fine, he tells me. He's been through much
worse and not let it trouble him. After all, he was here when they
found the first of the children's bodies in the hills above his house.

Saturday, 2 February 1991

Detective constable Glen Jones was batting for the visiting Nambucca XI when two uniformed officers walked onto the cricket field in Bowraville and told him an Aboriginal was missing. This was barely five months after first Colleen and then Evelyn had vanished. Glen, a big man with broad hands and pale blue eyes, who'd moved to the area from Newcastle just three months earlier and was still adjusting to life outside the city, listened with a growing sense of worry as they told him about Clinton. At work, he'd seen the paperwork on Colleen and on Evelyn, or what there was of it. Both children had gone missing before he arrived at Nambucca Heads but, still, if he was being honest, he'd worried about how little was done.

Glen had hoped the move up the coast would save his marriage. The past few years he'd been in the regional crime squad working frauds and motor thefts mostly, everywhere from Newcastle to

Coffs Harbour and inland of them both, managing as best he could being constantly away from home, while his wife managed with the kids. He loved the job, and cared about it – his dad was a cop, as was his brother. People had joked that moving to Nambucca Heads, less than half an hour east of Bowraville, where the beaches were made of white sand and the cliffs overlooked the Pacific Ocean, would be his retirement, but that hadn't happened. Glen was the only detective based permanently in the region, which meant every serious case landed on his desk.

Reading through the records dealing with Colleen and Evelyn's disappearance, he'd seen that both were treated as missing persons cases. Both were dealt with separately and both of them were worked, as far as it went, by uniformed officers from Bowraville and Macksville. A few detectives up from Newcastle, where Glen used to work, had joined them in the days after Evelyn's disappearance, but had driven back down south again and were no longer involved. The feeling Glen got was people thought that blackfellas just went missing, went walkabout or simply wandered off. The police were barely speaking to the children's families. No one was suspected. Few, if any, statements had been taken. Not even from Colleen's mum.

As Glen spoke to the two police officers, the match around them faltered. There'd been some kind of party, two days earlier. Clinton was last known to have been sleeping in a caravan belonging to a local man, James Hide. Clinton's father had reported his son was missing and the two uniforms had been out and spoken to James, who told them Clinton had left early in the morning and he hadn't seen him since. Inside James's caravan, they'd noticed that the double bed had no sheets, pillowslips or blankets on it. Looking around, they found a bottle containing hundreds of cannabis seeds and, when they asked James about these, he showed them a bong, so they arrested him. James was now waiting in the cells at Macksville, the next town down the river.

Shouldering his cricket bat, Glen walked with them off the pitch.

Inside his house, Glen tells me to sit at the dining table while he makes a coffee. He's retired from the police but his phone number is listed and, when I had called him, he'd suggested meeting in the early afternoon, before his kids get home from school.

Like Clinton's father, Thomas Duroux, and Evelyn's aunt, Michelle Jarrett, Glen is wearing an old footy jersey, this one for the local Nambucca Roosters team. A gold chain around his neck catches the light spilling through the open window. Unlike the children's families, Glen doesn't want to be recorded, but says I can take notes. The coffee made, he brings it to the table, sits down and looks at me.

'Is this a witch hunt?' he asks, meaning – I think – am I looking to blame him for the failure to put someone in prison over what happened to the children.

'No,' I tell him. And I mean it. He nods and uncrosses his arms. You need to understand what Bowraville was like back then, he tells me. 'It was *Dodge City,* when I got there, it was amazing. How the cops let that get like that, I don't know.'

For one thing, there was so much drinking. It wasn't like Newcastle where you'd go to a job with fifteen other blokes behind you; up here you were on your own. If someone hit you, you hit back. As Glen talks, his eyes widening like two growing pools of water, I get the sense of a police force under siege, outnumbered

and exhausted. Who had allowed a wall to be built between themselves and the people they were supposed to be protecting, in order
to protect themselves.

Glen says he understood where people living on the Mission
came from; they endured broken windows, kicked-in doors and
wrecked or burnt-out cars, but that didn't mean they'd turn to the
police for help. As children, some of them had been members of the
Stolen Generations, taken from their parents and put in orphan-
ages by men wearing police uniforms.

When Glen arrived at Macksville police station following
Clinton's disappearance, he had James brought out of the cells
and into an interview room. They faced each other across the
table. Glen was thirty-four, he played footy as well as cricket, but
James was bigger, around 110 kilos, a lot of it muscle, and a decade
younger than the detective. James told him that Clinton and Kelly
Jarrett had spent the night sleeping in his caravan, but when James
got up to go to work the next morning, Clinton had already gone.

'He's plausible,' Glen says, remembering the conversation. And
what did the police have? No evidence. A sixteen-year-old girl,
a four-year-old girl, a sixteen-year-old boy, all missing but no
pattern. 'At that stage with Clinton and Colleen, they're just disappeared. Sixteen-year-olds gone off,' Glen says, cradling his coffee.
Sixteen-year-olds do that. Inside the police station, he asked James
a few questions. James made eye contact and answered. There was
no sign of guilt or panic. You couldn't even see his Adam's apple
going up and down.

Glen looks at me across the dining table and raises his hands,
palms upwards, as if in supplication – as if to say, 'What could I
do?' It's a good question. At that moment in time, James had been
arrested on a drug charge and Clinton was being treated as a missing

person. So no crime scene was established, no attempt was made to collect or preserve evidence, nor, while James was being questioned, did anyone conduct a search of his caravan – the last place, as far as Glen knew, that Clinton was seen before he disappeared.

Glen released James, arranging to speak with him again on the Monday, 4 February. James went home.

Glen's second interview with James took place at the Bowraville police station, and this time he was joined by a police constable who recorded what was said on a manual typewriter, which clattered as they spoke. The transcript of the conversation is brief, running to just four pages. James says that he met Clinton on the night of the party; that the two of them and Kelly Jarrett had been drinking; that he got some Jim Beam from the club; and that they went back to his caravan to keep on drinking, before falling asleep around 4.30 a.m.

'I got up when the alarm went off, reset it for a later time because I was going to have a sleep in,' James told the detective. 'I laid down, that's when I heard Clinton get up not long after that and leave.' Soon after, James himself got up and went to work.

'Did any of you have an argument that morning after the party?' Glen asked him.

'No.'

'Do you know where Clinton Speedy may be?'

'No.'

'Did Clinton Speedy mention to you about going anywhere at all?'

'No.'

'Is there anything further you want to say about this matter?'

'No.'

Once again, Glen let James leave after the interview. The next day, Tuesday, 5 February, five days after the night Clinton was said to have gone missing, the police did search James's caravan, taking a dog with them. Nothing was found. Of course they found nothing, said people living on the Mission. They'd let James go home before they searched it. Fear over the children's disappearance fed into the prejudice that existed between the police and the Mission's residents. The police hadn't helped them. All three of the children's families claimed that when they reporting their kids missing, a policeman told them that their children might have gone walkabout. Maurie Towers, the local police sergeant who typed out that first missing persons report when Muriel Craig reported her daughter missing at the Bowraville police station, insisted he never said that, but it didn't matter. Around that word, walkabout, or around the belief that Maurie said it, came to coalesce all the bitter feeling: the police didn't understand the Mission. They didn't try to. If the police wanted to solve this, they could have done, the Mission thought. But they didn't, because the kids were black and this man, James, was white.

It was the women living on the Mission who said that they still had to trust them. If they wanted to find out what happened to their children, they had to work with the police. On Thursday, 7 February, one week after Clinton disappeared, Glen watched as dozens of people from the Mission marched on the Bowraville police station, led by the mothers, grandmothers and aunties. The crowd were chanting out James's name.

The local police commander, Inspector Bob Moore, went outside in the rain to meet them, the confrontation captured by television crews attracted by the news of a third child going missing from the small town. A thin man in a blue uniform, the inspector stood alone, hands raised, palms outwards.

'Why did you stand there and say you wanted information from us when the black people gave you the information?' a woman in the crowd demanded.

The inspector said he had teams of police working around the clock to find Clinton. Already, they'd found witnesses who'd seen the missing teenager hitchhiking. Someone matching Clinton's description had been seen in Coffs Harbour. Even now, after three children had vanished, the police were still uncertain as to whether they were dealing with three separate missing persons cases or a homicide investigation.

'To do this investigation properly, we've got to have you people on side and working with us,' the inspector told the mass of angry people.

'We know there's a maniac in Bowraville!' a man shouted from the crowd.

Afterwards, back inside the police station, the inspector called for reinforcements. The closest forensic detective, Rob Wellings, got a call asking him to come down, quick, to Bowraville.

'What am I going to look at?' Rob asked. James's caravan, the inspector told him. It was still their best, and only, chance of finding any actual evidence. And Rob should bring his police-issue Holden station wagon, the one with 'Scientific investigation' written down one side. Make sure that was visible. They needed to be seen to be doing something.

By now, says Glen, sitting across the table, he knew that he would not get time to play cricket again that season.

When Rob, the forensic detective, arrived, he went with Glen to meet James for a third time at the Nambucca Hide and Skin

Processors factory where he worked, just outside of Bowraville. James agreed to go with the policemen to his mother's property on Cohalan Street in town, just a few hundred metres from the Mission, and showed them the yellow Viscount caravan in which he was living. His mother's house itself was unlike the others on the street in that it was set further back from the road and partially obscured by a stack of garbage bins and milk crates, a picnic table and a derelict green Ford station wagon that was infested with vermin. James's mother, Marlene Hide, lived there with her partner, Noel Short. James and Noel did not get on well with each other. When the police asked about James's father, Marlene told them that he was dead.

Inside the caravan there was a double bed with a purple vinyl headboard. In the centre was a kitchen and at the other end a lounge and fold-down table, which converted into a second bed, if needed. It didn't look like too much cooking went on in there, or too much cleaning, Rob thought. He took some photographs and did a quick search but found nothing unusual. But he knew that it was more than a week now since Clinton had gone missing, and there was no way of knowing what might have been removed, or washed, in that time. At least the bed had a sheet on it now, he noticed. That was an improvement. The sheet had a pink and brown design of overlapping circles that looked like butterflies.

Three days later someone smashed the window of James's mother's car.

On Thursday, 14 February – two weeks after Clinton's disappearance – a third, more senior, detective, Allan Williams, from the Child

Mistreatment Unit based at Coffs Harbour, was sent to Bowraville to join the investigation. His bosses told him to take charge, to poke around and look at things 'from a CMU point of view'. That meant investigating whether the children's disappearances were caused by someone in their families. Reports from social services had echoed some of the rumours running round Bowraville that some of the children's parents might not be up to the task.

But Allan was not a homicide detective. He'd never led a murder inquiry, and when he got to Bowraville, he felt unsure who was in charge and whether they were supposed to be treating this a murder inquiry, or still as a series of unconnected missing persons.

Whoever it was, they'd left a lot of work undone, he reckoned, and he now needed to catch up. Sometimes, the only records Allan could find were those kept on telephone message pads, giving names of people with whom the police had spoken. Even when he could find records, they were paper files and running sheets, often filled out by hand. Elsewhere in the state, the New South Wales police was using computers. Allan had three separate lever-arch folders, one for each of the children. Each new document would go into a file marked 'Colleen', 'Evelyn' or 'Clinton', and then he would go through these with the other two detectives, Glen Jones and Rob Wellings, looking for similarities or links. Allan could see that the police had spoken to Medicare and to the banks, trying to find any official trace to prove that the children were alive, but come up with nothing. But there was no easy way of knowing what might have been missed before he arrived.

Two local men, who claimed they were out collecting firewood, discovered Clinton's body on Monday, 18 February, lying on his back in the bush beside a faint walking track just over 80 metres from the dirt-track Congarinni Road, which climbs up into the forest overlooking Bowraville. Rob got the call in his office at Coffs Harbour and, when he arrived at the roadside, a couple of detectives from the regional crime squad who'd also been notified, told him to walk into the forest, down the steep hillside. Following their directions, Rob disturbed a mob of goannas and scurrying animals clustered near the body. Clinton was dressed in a t-shirt and shorts and skeletal to the waist. He was not wearing shoes.

Rob was sweating. The humidity and the heat – 35 degrees or more – gave the day a fierce intensity. Following procedure, he began a first, brief, search of the forest surrounding the body, discovering a blue- and pink-striped blanket a few dozen metres away. From the stains on the material, Rob thought it looked as if the body had been wrapped in it. It had been late afternoon when he arrived at the crime scene, so Rob called in the SES to set up generators, strung tarpaulins over what was left of Clinton's remains, then slept in his car on the dirt road, while a solitary policeman sat awake on guard throughout the night, listening to the animal noises in the surrounding forest.

Today, Rob sits outside at the Sawtell surf club, less than an hour's drive from Bowraville, staring out at the fixed line between the sky and the ocean. The waves crash and a school party chatter as they walk up from the beach towards us. Allan Williams, Rob says, still lives in the area also. No one, he suggests, can leave these murders behind them once they've been involved.

For years after the children went missing, Rob would find old bones left in his pigeonhole at Coffs Harbour police station.

Everyone in the small towns along the Nambucca River knew about the murders and knew that the police had not found Colleen's body. The local cops would get calls on Saturday morning from the sports grounds, saying someone had found a bone of some description and thought it might belong to one of the children. It happened so often that they'd just put the bone in an envelope and send it on to Coffs Harbour with a note for Rob.

Eventually, Rob was diagnosed with post-traumatic stress disorder. From behind his sunglasses, he tells me how, at first light on the morning after Clinton's body was discovered, a forensic pathologist arrived from Sydney and the two of them walked down the faint track to where the body lay upon the ground. A trail of cannabis leaves ran past the body, leading on a few hundred metres to a crop of freshly harvested plants. Tucked into the front of Clinton's shorts was a clump of material. Bending down, Rob pulled it out and saw it was a pillowslip, stained and dirty. Looking closer, he could still see the design.

'I've got to go back,' Rob said, feeling his heart beating. 'I've got to go back to that house at Bowraville, that caravan.' Back up the track to where his car was parked, sweating freely, tyres spinning, throwing up clouds of dust behind him, Rob drove back to Cohalan Street, and asked James's mother for another look inside the caravan. Inside, he saw the same sheet he'd seen the last time he searched it. The one with that pattern of pink and brown overlapping circles, which looked like little butterflies.

Just like the ones he'd seen on the pillowslip he pulled from Clinton's shorts that morning.

Tuesday, 19 February 1991

The police took James Hide back to his caravan and searched it again. This time, they took away the bed sheet as well as a butterfly knife found in a storage unit underneath the bed. The pathologist who'd examined Clinton's body found a narrow hole in his cheek, just below the right eye socket. It looked like a stab wound. This may have proved fatal, the pathologist believed, although he also found that Clinton's left jaw was broken. This fracture was caused by a powerful blow, spinning Clinton's head over to the right, and it also may have been enough to kill him.

Rob Wellings, the forensic detective, kept thinking about the pillowslip tucked inside Clinton's shorts. The teenager had been drinking, so maybe he had pissed himself while sleeping, woke up and stuffed it down there in a clumsy effort to soak up the mess. Or, Rob knew that when a person dies they lose control of their body. Their bowels empty or their bladder goes. He'd seen it at crime scenes, far too many times. Maybe whoever killed Clinton saw that this was happening and took the pillowslip and shoved it down there.

That afternoon James Hide was brought back for another interview, this time at the regional police headquarters in Coffs Harbour. Another round of questions. And, this time, detective sergeant Allan Williams was one of those involved in the examination.

'I understand that Clinton, Kelly and yourself all slept in your van that night. Is that correct?'

'Yes.'

'What time did you go to bed?'

'Be somewhere around half past four.'

'What time did you get up in the morning of the first to go to work?'

'I got up the first time about quarter past, half past five and reset me clock then got up again and left just before six,' James said.

'Was Clinton and Kelly still in your van when you left?'

'Only Kelly. Clinton had gone earlier.'

'Did you see Clinton leave?'

'No, I didn't see him leave but I heard him leave just after I laid back down.'

So far, James's account was consistent with what he'd told Glen Jones two weeks before. James said there'd been some confusion that morning about his normal lift to work. A mate had been supposed to pick him up, but when James awoke, he said, he thought he'd missed him, and ended up setting off to drive himself. Only then, he'd seen his mate coming to pick him up, so he'd gone back and had a cup of tea, then driven off again.

Allan changed the subject. They had information from another police officer who'd spoken to James that he had not had any sexual relationships with Aboriginal persons. Was that correct?

'No, it's not correct,' said James. 'I misunderstood the question.' Allan looked at him in silence. James continued: 'He said to me, "Are you rooting any of them?" meaning the Aboriginal women. And I said, "No." I thought he meant was I seeing anyone in a permanent relationship.' In fact, he'd been in a relationship with Colleen's aunt, Alison Walker, though that had ended. He'd also slept with Evelyn's mum, Rebecca Stadhams, he told the detectives. There had been others, too: 'A few, just one-night stands.'

After an hour and fifty minutes, the interview was over. Once again, James read through and signed the transcript in his neat, looping handwriting, then stood and left. He had not been arrested. He was free to go.

Allan, the Child Mistreatment Unit detective who, by now, had started to take charge of the investigation into Clinton's disappearance, sat back and asked himself where the interview had got them. What next? He had no real experience of leading a homicide inquiry but there was no doubt now that this was murder, which meant the investigation needed to be bigger. They needed to be careful. Everything had to be recorded. And if Clinton had been murdered, then what about the other children? Were they still only missing persons?

Allan felt as if his bosses weren't interested in helping him answer these questions. On paper, the regional crime squad had oversight of the investigation but on the ground, Allan was running the show. He didn't have much in the way of resources. Each morning, he'd drive from home to Bowraville in his old Chrysler Valiant with a manual typewriter in the boot of the car, which he'd use to take witness statements. The sheer amount of paper he was using soon proved too much for his three lever-arch folders, which burst out in a spill of running sheets and statements and reports. They tried using index cards to keep on top of the hundreds of separate pieces of information. Allan had no experience with the sophisticated information management system used in homicide investigations, let alone the computer index systems being introduced elsewhere.

Without an analyst to help them manage these reams of information they were dealing with, the three detectives, Allan Williams, Rob Wellings and Glen Jones bought a roll of butcher's paper and used sticky tape to fix it to the walls of the Bowraville police station. They used black texta to map out a timeline of the children's disappearances and the connections between their families. They realised how closely many of the black people in Bowraville were related. The grandmothers of the two missing children, Colleen and Evelyn, were sisters; while another of their sisters was the mother of Clinton's father's partner, Marjorie Jarrett.

But even then, they didn't really understand the complex family lives being lived on the Mission. An Aboriginal child could grow up in Bowraville calling his mother's sister 'Mother' and she, too, would help to bring him up. Sometimes one sister might give a child to another to look after. The words 'Aunty' and 'Uncle' were used as a sign of respect, often for elders. And while the white detectives would call their mother's sister's children 'cousins', on the Mission the same relation would be called 'brothers' and 'sisters'. The bonds that held second- and third-cousins together were also much more clearly felt.

With so many people who called Colleen, Evelyn and Clinton family, the trauma of their disappearance ran throughout the connections the three detectives sketched out on their butcher's paper.

Despite Clinton being last seen inside James's caravan, despite the pillowslip, they still spent weeks investigating whether somebody within those interlocking families had played some role in what happened to the children. Allan was particularly concerned about Evelyn's mother, Rebecca Stadhams. To look at her, she seemed to still be partying and drinking. She was not behaving as you'd expect a grieving mother to behave, he thought. This doubt was fed by confidential information sent to the police from the Department of Family and Community Services, saying 'Rebecca drinks heavily and is not caring properly for the children . . . Parents have not been approached by FACS as yet. Possible they have got wind and removed Evelyn to another location to prevent her being taken.'

Other scraps of gossip also sustained their suspicions. One police running sheet, used by individual officers to keep track of information coming in, or what that officer is doing, records:

INFORMATION: *That the missing Greenup girl is alive and is presently in the Uranga or Coffs Harbour area and being well looked after and that she is better off there than with her mother who is not looking after the child and that the child would end up a neglected and an unkempt child as at the time before going missing the child was able to wander and no one seemed to care about her. I was advised that she would be better off wherever she is now, and leave the situation alone.*

Another potential witness claimed that Evelyn's mother and grandmother had come into her shop to buy some clothes and 'indicated her suspicion that Evelyn Greenup may have been sold on the black market for monetary purposes'. Someone else claimed

the four-year-old was still alive and living with relatives ten hours'
drive west of Bowraville, in Bourke, so the police put a house there
under surveillance and took photographs of Evelyn to all the local
infants' schools, in case somebody knew her. They found no evidence Evelyn was, or had ever, been living in the city. Despite this,
and despite the discovery of Clinton's body in Bowraville, the
police pursued the child's relatives, asking about information they'd
received 'concerning the selling of Evelyn by the family'.

Weeks were spent chasing rumours. One witness said he'd seen
a stranger making an approach to three young Aboriginal girls during the first week of the school holidays; another that she'd seen a
white man in his late thirties driving a 'late model, white four-door
vehicle' with a dark-skinned girl sitting in the front passenger seat
with something tied around her mouth. The police were also getting calls from pyschics offering to help, or local people demanding
that something be looked into. One call reported that graffiti had
appeared under a bridge near Macksville that read 'I like fucking
little black hairless (4–10 yrs) cunts! Do you??' All of these reports
had to be logged, followed up, the results typed out, and organised
using index cards by Allan, Glen and Rob.

The three detectives also struggled to get time away from other
cases. Rob Wellings was the only forensic detective assigned to a
huge stretch of the coastal region reaching all the way from Ballina
to Port Macquarie, and inland as far as Armidale, meaning any job
could mean travelling hundreds of kilometres there and back. After
spending five days straight in Bowraville following the discovery
of Clinton's body, he got home to Sawtell in the mid-afternoon,
showered and went to the RSL next door for a cold beer. His pager

went. There'd been a double murder–suicide: a husband who'd caught his wife with her lover and had killed them before turning the gun on himself.

Glen Jones was also still working other cases across the region. Clinton's murder was the second he had dealt with in the months since he moved to Nambucca Heads. Having made the move from Newcastle, in part, to save his marriage, he saw it fail completely as he spent so long at work, away from home.

But the three detectives kept working. James's neighbours told them how they had heard his mum's car, with its distinctive loud exhaust, leaving the property just before 5 a.m. on the morning Clinton went missing, and how they'd seen it coming back at speed, with James driving, around 6.30 a.m. If true, that contradicted what James had said about that morning when they had interviewed him. One of James's workmates, who called to collect him on his way to the hide factory that morning, also told the police that he'd arrived at around 6 a.m. and seen an Aboriginal girl asleep inside the caravan, but no one else.

On Friday, 1 March, two months after Clinton disappeared, the police seized James's caravan and Rob went back inside it to conduct a more detailed forensic search. This time, a month after Clinton had gone missing, he found a tiny bloodstain on the headboard, too small to be able to test which blood group it belonged to, and yet another bedsheet with the same butterfly pattern of overlapping circles. Rob sent the sheets for laboratory analysis. It came back saying they had found the same flaw in the printing of each, as well as on the pillowslip found stuffed in Clinton's shorts. 'The three items have been printed on the same machine, and could well have been part of the same set of linen,' the scientists concluded. On Monday, 8 April, Glen and Allan questioned James again.

'Yeah, I have spoken to a solicitor, I know me rights,' James told them when they met him at work in the factory, and asked him to come with them for questioning. They waited for him to shower all the muck off from heaving around the heavy hides and then they sat in silence during the hour-long drive from Bowraville to the regional police headquarters in Coffs Harbour. James was wearing a crumpled t-shirt, a dirty pair of shorts, and thongs. Once inside, there was no emotion. James sat across the table staring at them like a boxer watching his opponent before the bell is sounded.

'Have you discussed the disappearance of Clinton Speedy from your caravan with anyone?' Allan asked him.

'Just popped up around the table at home, that's all.'

When pressed, James said he'd spoken to his uncle. 'It was just something on the news or in the paper. We talked about it for a while and once he asked me if I did it. I said "No." That's it,' he said.

Watching, Glen didn't get the sense that James was lying. Or maybe James was just smarter than they thought. He met each question calmly.

'Can you give me a reason why you invited Kelly and Clinton back to your caravan?'

'No.'

'When you went inside your caravan who sat where?'

'I have no idea, I don't know.'

'Did you take Kelly Jarrett's pants and underpants off through the night?'

'No.'

'When Kelly Jarrett woke up the next morning she found her pants and underpants underneath the shirt you had left out for her. Would you care to comment on that?'

'That's bullshit.' His indifference was growing.

They pushed a photograph across the table. It showed the pillowslip Rob had found with Clinton's body.

'Does that pillowcase come from your bed?'

'Doesn't look familiar,' James told them. If they thought he was guilty, it was up to them to prove it. And the truth was they couldn't. After two hours, Allan left to find some cigarettes. Coming back in, he asked, 'Did you think it strange that Clinton got up at five o'clock in the morning and left your caravan, considering he had only been in bed a short time?'

'No. Because I have brought people up there before and nine times out of ten they have been gone when I got up.'

The detectives knew they needed something better. Without any direct evidence – something forensic; a witness who saw the murder happen – all they could prove was that Clinton had been inside James's caravan. They hadn't landed a punch on him. To do that, they needed to find something that would tie James to Clinton's murder, or at least to the site up in the forest where Clinton's body had been dumped.

'How long has it been since you have driven a car along the Congarinni Road?' asked Allan.

'Wouldn't know.' James's answer gave them nothing.

'Did Clinton Speedy wake up and catch you sexually interfering with Kelly Jarrett the night they stayed in your caravan?'

'I didn't touch Kelly.'

'Did you punch Clinton Speedy in your van that night?'

'No.'

'Did you strike Clinton Speedy with any object that night?'

'No.'

'Is it correct to say that you have had sex with numerous Aboriginal women?'

'Not going to answer that one.'

'Is that the reason why you invited Clinton and Kelly to your caravan?'

'No.'

The interview was over. Despite failing to land a blow, they still had the pillowslip, and James's neighbours who said they heard him driving out and back on the morning Clinton disappeared. Allan charged James with Clinton's murder.

In Bowraville, Maurie Towers, the desk sergeant who'd been on duty when the first of the children was reported missing, heard about the decision. He wondered if Allan might have gone too soon. Maybe they did have the right person, but that didn't mean they had enough to prove it; maybe there was something, or someone, who had been overlooked.

After James was cautioned, a police running sheet records that he was asked if he was happy to be questioned about Evelyn as well.

'What do you think?' James replied, according to the running sheet.

'Are you prepared to be interviewed?'

'You gotta be fucking joking. I've already said too much.'

Wednesday, 17 April 1991

Nine days after James Hide was charged with Clinton's murder, a preacher for the Assemblies of God Pentecostal movement was fishing in a tributary of the Nambucca River when he hooked a pair of jeans with a black vinyl belt and pulled them from the water. Police divers later found a plastic bag weighted down with rocks containing Colleen's purple jumper, a white t-shirt with the words 'Surfers Paradise', her underwear, shoes and socks.

A little way upstream from where the clothes were recovered, a bridge across the river led to the dirt-track Congarinni Road, which headed up into the forest and, if you followed, past where Clinton's body was discovered.

Ten days after the preacher's discovery, on Saturday, 27 April 1991, Evelyn's skull was found lying among a scatter of bones in the forest beside the same stretch of Congarinni Road. Clive Welsh, who'd told me 'someone in the bloody Aboriginal community' might have murdered the children, was among those who found her body, lying on the dry leaves in the bed of a gully. The four-year-old's remains had been dumped close to a walking track leading away from the road between the trees, as had Clinton's body. Her skull also clearly showed the mark of a penetrating wound to the right temple, which a subsequent post-mortem found could have been caused by the same implement that was used to kill Clinton. A child's pink sandshoe was also found in the forest about 12 metres further up the track from where they discovered Evelyn's skeleton.

Detectives Allan Williams and Glen Jones went to tell Evelyn's parents that they had found her body. Her mother, Rebecca Stadhams, wept. Her father, Billy Greenup, was furious.

'If you cunts had done your job when Colleen went missing, this would never have happened,' he shouted at the policemen. As the detectives left, they knew their worst fears had been confirmed: they were dealing with a serial killing.

Sitting at his dining table, Glen watches as I write in shorthand, trying to keep up with his description of what happened. Now the police had to go back and reconsider their previous missing persons investigations into the disappearances of Colleen and Evelyn. They had to find and establish crime scenes – the bedroom where Evelyn was last seen by her mother, the house where the party took place at which Colleen was last seen; they had to search for forensic evidence, or at least anything that had not been lost already, and interview anyone they hadn't spoken to at the time the children disappeared. All of this had to be done quickly, and all of it should have been done months before.

But the information that they got only confused them. Some witnesses said Colleen had been seen sitting in a white Holden Commodore driving away from the party on the Mission. One said that on the night following the party, Colleen stayed over in James's caravan. Another said that she'd met Colleen in Bowraville two days after the party happened and Colleen sang out, asking for a cigarette: 'Cookie, can I have a smoke?' Someone else said she believed that Colleen was dead and it was actually her spirit they'd spoken to during this conversation.

On the Mission, word spread that a pink cigarette lighter and two bottles of Passion Pop had been found where a nearby timber mill dumped its offcuts, which the blackfellas used for firewood. Colleen had a pink cigarette lighter and had been drinking Passion Pop on the night of the party, people told each other. Another rumour was that an elder from another Aboriginal community could bring back Colleen spiritually, and did manage to bring her back, with Colleen coming as close as if she'd been in the same room as you, before she vanished between two telegraph poles.

The different accounts of what happened to Colleen were one thing, says Glen, shaking his head slowly. But with Evelyn, it felt like they were chasing spirits.

Evelyn's mum, Rebecca Stadhams, told them her daughter went missing sometime during the night following the party, when they were sleeping in the same room. But the detectives spoke to several people who said they'd seen Evelyn on the day after her mother said that she'd gone missing. Two boys from the Mission said she followed them to town, where they bought some lollies. Others said they saw Evelyn playing on swings in a vacant block at the Mission. Evelyn was seen walking down towards the cemetery. Evelyn was at the Lanes Bridge waterhole. Evelyn was playing at James Park.

Months after her daughter's disappearance, Rebecca moved away from Bowraville, leaving behind her the house on the Mission where Evelyn went missing. Its new occupier was tidying when she found a child's pink sandshoe in one of the cupboards and took it to one of the detectives, Glen Jones. It was the same shoe Rebecca had found lying in the front garden on the morning after her daughter disappeared and the pair of a shoe recovered near Evelyn's remains several kilometres away on Congarinni Road. One shoe at home and one found with her body, Glen thought. Evelyn would not have walked from the Mission into Bowraville, and then to all those different places, wearing only one shoe, surely? Sitting watching me make notes of what he is saying, Glen shakes his head again.

Their attempt to build a case against James over the murder of Clinton had run into a similar thicket of contradictory witness statements. One claimed Clinton got into a fistfight with Kelly Jarrett's ex-boyfriend shortly before he disappeared, meaning someone other than James might have a motive to hurt him. People claimed to have seen Clinton standing on the roadside hitchhiking out of Bowraville on the morning after he disappeared. If that was true, and he had been alive that morning, then the fact he spent the night before inside James's caravan meant nothing. They needed to establish who was right, who was wrong and who had misremembered. Looking up from my notebook, my eyes meet Glen's and hold them.

'Could the investigation have been better?' I ask.

''Course it could have been better,' he says. 'You do an investigation on a portable typewriter in the boot of the car and three detectives.'

There's an idea among criminologists called 'ideal victim' theory. It holds that not all victims of crime are equal in terms of the response they get from the media, and sometimes from law enforcement too. Working in different newsrooms, I've seen how some missing children – often white girls, from good homes, and good looking – seem to get more attention than others.

The victims who are not ideal – because they'd run away from home, or were in care, or poor, or black – receive less attention from the media. It's as if they go missing twice, first in real life and then in the public reaction to their disappearance. At times, I've run this sorry calculus myself while reporting on a murder, knowing that this death or disappearance will provoke less interest among my bosses because of who the victim is or how they look in photographs.

Media attention can also have an impact on how the police respond. A case that's on the front pages or the nightly TV news may get more officers assigned to work on it. Six months after he was first arrested, in October 1991, the police charged James with killing Evelyn. The decision led the local news. A year later the detectives, Glen Jones, Allan Williams and Rob Wellings, sat in their respective homes on the mid-north coast watching the news, and saw the tsunami of media attention that followed when Ivan Milat's victims were discovered in the Belanglo State Forest in southern New South Wales. Yes, Glen says, there were more victims than in Bowraville – five foreigners and two Australians, all aged between nineteen and twenty-two – but, still, the reaction was different. At its height, a dedicated task force of around thirty detectives were pursuing the backpacker killer and several hundred uniformed and plain-clothes officers searched the forest where he left his victims, over several months. Another couple of hundred were involved when they raided Milat's home to arrest him.

In Bowraville, at different times, after Evelyn went missing or when Clinton's body was discovered, a few other detectives or a couple of police analysts had been sent up from Newcastle or

Sydney to help with the investigation, but that was all the help that they'd been offered. It was mainly just the three of them doing all the work, says Glen.

After the police charged James with killing Evelyn in October 1991, his lawyers applied to have the cases separated, meaning that even though he had been charged with killing both the four-year-old and Clinton, evidence about the two murders would be heard separately, in different trials. The lawyers argued that the legislation guiding how such trials were conducted prohibited the use of what was known as 'similar fact evidence'. This meant any evidence that implied the two killings were so alike they must have been carried out by the same person, unless that evidence was good enough to prove that the same person, in fact, was the killer in both.

James's lawyers said the evidence gathered by the police did not pass this test. It suggested James was the connection between the murders, without actually proving that he was involved.

The judge agreed, and ordered that the trials be separated. Yes, there were similarities between the murders, the judge accepted, but said, 'It does not seem to me that the fact that in each case the killer chose to dump the body on a track off Congarinni Road rather than in the bush adjacent to any other road out of the town can be regarded as contributing much, if anything, to the proposition that the killer was the same in each case.'

His decision would have devastating consequences. To the police, James was the only person present at the place where each of the three children went missing – the parties on the Mission after which Colleen and Evelyn went missing and the caravan from which Clinton had disappeared. But the law said that, if the trials were to be separate, then the jury in each could be told only about one of the murders. When the jury assembled in the old courthouse in Grafton in January 1994, more than three years after Colleen was first reported missing, for the trial over Clinton's murder, they were not told that two other children had also disappeared from Bowraville. The children's families were disgusted.

Sitting at his dining table, Glen closes his eyes and sighs.

'That was a miscarriage of justice as far as I'm concerned,' he says.

The trial over Clinton's murder also revealed other problems with the prosecution case. Witnesses were called who said they'd seen someone, who could have been Clinton, hitchhiking out of Bowraville on Norco Corner, named after the North Coast Dairy Company store that operated there, on the same morning that the police were saying the teenager had been murdered. One woman who'd been heading out of Bowraville to work that morning said she'd seen a hitchhiker and when the police had shown her Clinton's photograph, she was certain it was him.

Part of the confusion, Glen says, was the way the police responded at the time of the children's disappearance, treating them as missing persons, not a homicide investigation. He says there is a difference in the way you ask your questions between the two types of inquiry. With missing persons, you go around with a description, or often with a photograph, asking people if they have seen that person. With a homicide, you ask people only where they were at a given time and what they saw.

The reason for the difference in approach is that memories cannot really be trusted. Spend enough time knocking on doors in Bowraville, asking people if they have seen an Aboriginal teenager with a muscular build and shoulder-length hair, particularly if you're actually carrying a photograph, and you're going to prompt their memory. As a result, it's likely that you will find someone who thinks they've seen that person. Maybe that woman who saw the hitchhiker that morning did in fact see a goori, Glen says, but he doubts that it was Clinton.

Before the trial, he went up and asked if she was certain.

'Yes,' she told him. She gave the same evidence in court.

'She killed us,' Glen tells me, looking past me, through the window. If Clinton was alive and hitchhiking that morning, then there was no link between his murder and the night he spent sleeping in James's caravan.

Despite this mess, he still thinks that the police were right to charge James with the murder, but there were other problems with the case, these of their own making. To disprove James's version of what happened, in which he was still asleep when Clinton slipped out of the caravan early in the morning, the police relied on the evidence of his neighbours, who said they'd heard James's mother's red Galant leave early and seen it return around 6.30 a.m., with James at the wheel. During the trial, the jury were taken to visit Bowraville and shown the property on Cohalan Street where James lived. One juror spotted a red car leaving the house next door and passed a handwritten note to the judge, asking, 'Did the owner possess that car at the time of the incident?' If so, it might not have been James who was seen driving out that morning. If it was not, then maybe he was still tucked up in bed, inside his caravan, like he claimed.

The owner of the red car was called to give evidence. Despite living there at the time that Clinton went missing, he said that the police had never been to ask him about the disappearance, or what he'd seen, or what he was doing on that morning. It introduced an element of doubt into the prosecution, and into the work of the police.

Sitting on the wooden benches of the courthouse, Glen watched James when he was called to give evidence. James swore to tell the truth, confirmed that he had been at the party with Clinton Speedy-Duroux and Kelly Jarrett and said that, as he had previously told the police, the three of them then went back his caravan.

'In telling the police your movements, how would you describe what you told them in relation to what happened?' James's barrister asked him.

'It was the truth.'

'And then afterwards you also gave an account of what happened from the time you left the caravan until you went to work, do you remember that?'

'Yes.'

'And what was that, in relation to what happened?'

'That was the truth as well,' James said.

What happened, he told the court, was him and Kelly and Clinton fell asleep. James had to be at work for 6 a.m. but, when his alarm went off somewhere around 5.30 a.m., he reset it and tried to get more sleep in. After he lay back down James said he heard Clinton get up and leave the caravan. He woke up again just before 6 a.m., thinking that he'd missed a lift with a mate, Provost, who had been due to pick him up and drive to the hide factory.

'He normally came to pick you up, as we have heard,' the barrister continued, leading James through his evidence. 'Is there any reason why you thought you'd missed him?'

'Well, normally he would just pull up out the front. If I didn't come straight out he would come and knock, and if there was no reply or anything he would just leave.'

'What did you do?'

James said that he went into his mother's house, shook her awake and asked for her car keys.

Promising to return the car before 8.30 a.m. so she could drive his brother to school, James finally left for work, turning left onto Cohalan Street, then left again and through the intersection.

Listening to this, Glen says he thought James's account only provoked more questions. As he was driving to work, James said that he then noticed Provost's car behind him, heading towards the caravan. James said he pulled his car over to the side of the road and waited. After a couple of minutes, James said he turned around and drove back home, arriving at 6 a.m. with his alarm still ringing unattended in the caravan.

'What did you find there?' his barrister asked.

'Provost was walking back down towards his car.'

'Did you speak to him?'

'Yes, I told him something along the lines to go to work and I would take Mum's car.'

'Why did you do that?'

'Well, I wanted to go inside and have a cup of tea, coffee or whatever . . . I thought it would make me feel a bit better than I was at the time.' After all, he'd been out drinking until a few hours before.

'How were you feeling?' his barrister asked.

'Pretty sick,' James told him.

But why, says Glen, did James assume he'd missed his lift to work? His mate Provost had given evidence himself saying that, actually, he normally woke James up when he arrived to get him. And why, when James saw his mate drive past, did he pull over and wait rather than turning his own car around? Why, when he did return to the caravan, did James send his mate on to work without him while he hung back to drink a cup of tea or coffee, knowing that he was late already? Why, if James had been dead drunk and sleeping, did he wake up the second time before his alarm? And why was James's alarm still ringing when he drove back to the caravan?

The prosecution lawyer told the jury that, in fact, James was lying. James actually had spent that morning dumping Clinton's body, he said, which was why he wasn't there when the alarm went off, as normal, just before 6 a.m. James then drove back, the prosecutor argued, just too late to catch his normal lift to work, and so he told his mate Provost to go on to work without him, using his need for a cup of tea or coffee as an excuse because he wanted to be alone at the caravan.

To find James guilty, the jury had to be certain that the prosecutor's version of events was right. If they had any doubt, the judge warned them, they had to find James not guilty.

When the jury retired to consider its verdict, the prosecutor told Glen that he was feeling confident.

On Friday, 18 February 1994, three years to the day since Clinton's body was found lying in the forest outside Bowraville, James was found not guilty.

He took the news quietly, sitting alone in the dock in the middle of the courtroom.

As Clinton's family made their way outside following the verdict, his grandmother collapsed. Clinton's father, Thomas

Duroux, took off his shirt to wet it and wipe her face but the sheriff's officers surrounded him, thinking that Thomas had lost it.

Glen says that he spoke to the prosecutor afterwards.

'Well that's the way it goes, Jonesy,' he says the prosecutor told him.

'That's bullshit,' said Glen.

In Bowraville, following the verdict, the women from the Mission led a march up Cemetery Road, then right, then left, then right again, wailing, throwing rocks and threatening to burn down the house belonging to James's mother. From there, they headed for the police station, smashing windows and picking up glass bottles to use as ammunition. One of the local officers who worked there lived in a house next to the station building and lay awake in bed that night, with his family around him, listening to the shouting coming from the crowd and fearing what would happen next.

Three weeks later, the New South Wales public prosecutors' office announced they would not pursue the charges laid against James over the murder of Evelyn Greenup. The judge's decision to separate the two murder cases, meaning that each jury would be told only about one of the children who'd been murdered, made prosecuting James much harder. If that decision had led to a not-guilty verdict over the murder of Clinton, where the evidence was stronger, then there was little chance of getting a conviction over the killing of Evelyn. Better then to not attempt another prosecution.

As a result, the police investigation also faltered. Whoever the killer was, they would not face jail.

Friday, 19 February 2016

The not-guilty verdict rankles. Two decades later, and twenty-five years since the children first went missing, Michelle Jarrett is sitting in the passenger seat beside me, giving directions as I drive out of Bowraville past the Norco Rural service station, following the road through farmland, crossing small tributary streams that run down towards the Nambucca River, and then up, over the crest of a small hill, where she tells me to take a sharp turn to the right. Ahead of us in the forest is the place where the body of Michelle's niece, four-year-old Evelyn, was found.

I turn the car onto a narrow, bitumen road leading up into the forest, our car passing between the bars of shadow cast by the eucalypts that surround us on either side.

'This is Congarinni,' says Michelle. Down here, closer to Bowraville, a few isolated homes have been constructed. Back when the murders happened, Michelle says, it was more wild, dark and lonely. The trees crowd in closer, blocking out the sunlight. 'She was a princess, always gentle, clean and pretty and very delicate,' says Michelle, talking about Evelyn. Then, looking at the shadows, 'Back then, this was a dirt road.'

For a moment, the forest clears and we pass men working in wide-brimmed hats on rusting farm machinery. Then the gum trees return and the road climbs towards the tall, narrow ridgeline, the sound of the car engine rising as we drive up into the hills.

'So now you can go to your left here,' says Michelle. The road forks at a small quarry where dusty stone has been gouged out of the forest. The right-hand track leads steeply up but, following Michelle's instructions, I take the other track and the car leaves the bitumen behind us as the Congarinni turns back into a dirt road.

Earlier this morning, I went with Eric George, the producer, to the Bowraville cemetery, just a few hundred metres from the Mission, where Evelyn is buried. Just like the Congarinni, the cemetery was built on a steep hillside carved out of the forest. A simple fence, a gate, the air thick with the noise of insects. Inside, on the flat ground at the top of the cemetery, I saw ranks of solid, stone memorials marking the graves of Bowraville's white population. Beneath them, at the bottom of the hill, were the other graves, clustered together near the wire fence that marked the divide between the cemetery and the dark shadows of the trees.

Down there were a few, smaller, gravestones but many more white wooden crosses. Each had a person's name written out in black paint or, sometimes, black pen. These names were those of people living on the Mission: Buchanan, Ballangary, Greenup. Evelyn's grave was decorated with white angels and ceramic teddy bears and scattered with plastic pink and purple crystals of the sort a little girl would love.

Walking among these graves, I'd found others with no monument or cross above them. No name, just piled rocks. For the first time, Eric had turned on the microphone he'd used to record my interviews with the children's families, and asked what I was thinking. Up to this point, on his recordings, I'd been the reporter, listening to what other people told me; now he was expecting me to talk.

'What's surprised me is how much it's starting to get to me, how much it's starting to eat at me,' I told him. Before I came here, the murders had seemed abstract, like a puzzle. What happened? Why had no one been sent to jail as a result? But the people I had spoken to in Bowraville had described living with the killings. How they were still caught up in the eddying trauma. How they could not move forward.

'It cannot be allowed to continue, it can't go on without some kind of resolution to this,' I told Eric. As a reporter, I was used to ignoring my emotion but this was different. 'This is just people we are talking about, real people, like my children, like your children.' Standing amid the jumble of wooden crosses, I'd looked back up, over Eric's shoulder, at the neat, stone memorials to Bowraville's white people standing on the hilltop above them. A pain rose up inside me.

'Frankly there is a part of me that really wants to leave because it would be easier to leave and there is a part of me that wants to not leave, to not be the person that can just walk away,' I said.

Michelle signals to stop the car. We sit in silence. Down there among the trees, she says.

*

The car doors slam. We cross the road, our feet rustling in the carpet of dead leaves. Michelle points to a faint track running off the road, downhill, among the undergrowth. On either side, the trees reach up like pylons.

'We've got friends who live not far up here,' says Michelle, pointing with one hand further along the hillside while staring fixedly at the place where Evelyn's body was discovered. 'We drive out this way thousands of times.' A sob catches in her throat. She's trembling as she raises a hand towards her mouth in grief or horror. 'She was just there all the time and we didn't know.'

Eric George and I stay silent.

'We just drove past her all those times, and how she would have been, and just left alone, thinking no one loved her or cared.' Michelle is crying gently now. 'Only four, she was a baby still.'

I say nothing, hoping I will never know how much this hurts.

Eventually, because there is nothing we can do here, we walk back to the car, sit inside it and I gun the engine, as if that will dispel the silence. Michelle says to drive on a few kilometres to where Clinton's body was discovered. The road twists a little through the forest before, at the top of another steep hillside, we pull up beside homemade memorial to Clinton, built from a metal sheet fixed to the top of a scaffold pole. On it is a stencilled painting of Clinton done in black, yellow and red, along with his name, his nickname 'Bubby', his date of birth and the date he disappeared. Beneath the painting of Clinton, someone has painted the word 'Justice'. It's not the first memorial his family put here, says Michelle, but someone ripped the last one up and burned it, so they made this one from metal and cemented it in place.

Michelle says to keep following Congarinni Road. We've crossed the ridge itself now and are driving downhill, past a few homes largely hidden from sight and marked instead by letterboxes cut from a plastic tub, a microwave and a beer keg nailed into place on a fencepost. Fording a stream, where cattle feed in a small forest clearing, the road flattens then heads back into the trees before crossing a river. Michelle says to follow this downstream, to where Colleen's clothes were found and dragged to shore from the water. Driving this road is like standing on the Mission, looking at how close together are the homes in which Colleen, Evelyn and Clinton were staying when they disappeared. These murders have to be connected: three Aboriginal kids, in one small town, all staying in houses on Cemetery Road, all disappear within five months. Two of their bodies are found lying beside the same dirt road and the third's clothes are recovered near where that track crosses the river. It's hard to see how they could be treated as anything other than three connected crimes. But that didn't happen. Not when the children were first reported missing, nor when Evelyn and Clinton's killings went to court.

'Basically, the law is saying that three different people just happened to come into Bowraville and just happened to take three different kids from the same town,' Michelle says, her voice rising inside the car. 'Statistically, how is that possible? Tell me, how is that possible?'

I cannot find an answer and we drive on in silence. Later, I learn that statistics gathered by the Australian Institute of Criminology from every murder in Australia dating back to the year that Colleen went missing do answer her question. The killing of three children in a small town over such a short period of time by different offenders has never occurred.

*

Michelle believes that the decision to separate the trials over Clinton's and Evelyn's murder meant the jury was never given all the evidence they needed.

The decision to separate the murders also had another consequence, which Michelle describes as she directs us home. Once the jury had found James Hide not guilty of Clinton's murder, the law prevents him from being tried over that killing again. It's known as double jeopardy, an ancient law that exists to protect the accused. But double jeopardy is not a Gumbaynggirr law; it can instead be traced back to the Greeks and Romans and was imported to Australia from England along with the people carried on the First Fleet. Michelle understands it, but questions whether this is really justice. In Gumbaynngirr law, if you take a life then you will suffer in return.

'We are never going to get true justice because we wasn't accorded the right of a proper investigation and respect, like any other family in Australia,' Michelle tells me. 'If we were treated right from the beginning, but we wasn't. We wasn't listened to. We was disrespected. We were treated like blackfellas on the Mission.' She directs us away from the river where Colleen's clothing was discovered and back onto the road that runs through the farmland to Bowraville. Here, some of the scattered houses have Australian flags hanging in their driveways, or beneath a window. Stencilled on a sign tied to a tree out the front of one of these homes are the words 'True blue'.

Allan Williams, the senior detective who had led the investigation that led to James being charged, got blamed when it collapsed and his suspect was found not guilty in court. In March 1996,

more than two years after James was acquitted, Allan sat down
in Grafton police station and typed up a report that laid out his
troubles. The five-page document describes the murders and the
state of the investigation when he took over:

> Very limited resources . . . were provided for me to actually carry
> out the inquiry. To put it mildly I was met with much hostility from
> the Aboriginal Community. This was due to the fact that no inves-
> tigation had been conducted into the disappearance of three of their
> children. Police were generally not trusted as the Aboriginal com-
> munity saw the role of the Police as one of Law enforcement and not
> one of actually caring for what had happened to their people.

The report asked for money and permission to do more forensic
testing. This would 'reconfirm my standing with that community
and reflect on any future investigation conducted.'

Allan wanted to keep going. He wanted all the paper files,
which by then were piled up in a cell in the Macksville police
station, to be put onto computer and analysed. 'From that process
I am sure that many new questions would need answering and a
Task Force would be needed to meet that need,' he wrote.

But Allan could not know what would happen. A task force
meant new people coming in. If he led it, then that was one thing.
If he didn't, then they would go over everything that he had done
to look for failures. It would feel like a witch-hunt. Detectives get
warned against this, but Allan had started to take the investigation, and its failure, personally. His colleagues thought he'd begun
to withdraw into himself.

'This is going to come back and bite me on the arse,' Allan
told his boss when he submitted his report on the murders. It was

passed to another, senior detective who had years of experience in working homicide cases. This detective spoke to Allan, who told him there were parts of the case that were confidential. He'd done everything he could to solve the murders, Allan told the senior detective, but there were aspects of the investigation that he could not discuss.

The second detective wrote up his own report on the killings in Bowraville, which was passed through the ranks above him until it reached the desk of the police commissioner, Peter Ryan.

'In my opinion there is certainly no question that all efforts should be made to investigate these very serious criminal matters to a successful conclusion,' this report concluded. Whoever had murdered the children 'is a "serial killer" who may escape prosecution for these crimes if no further effort is made'.

In Bowraville, the children's families were also telling local journalists that the police had failed them, news of which was reaching back to Sydney. The police commissioner was new and wanted to make a difference. That December, six years since Colleen first went missing, he flew up to Bowraville and announced that there would be a new investigation into the children's murders.

Tuesday, 22 March, 2016

Gary Jubelin is fighting.

The police have built a boxing gym in the old cells beneath the fortress-like Sydney Police Centre, their main outpost in the city centre. As I tape my fists, ready to join him, Gary stalks out of the furthest cell, the walls and bars of which are painted in a chipped and tired white. A row of punching bags hangs along one wall and in the other stands the heavy metal door that still clangs shut and still has its sliding bolt in place. Beyond this stands the ring. On the walls are stuck old boxing posters advertising fights: Floyd Mayweather versus Manny Pacquiao, Kostya Tszyu fighting Ricky Hatton. Real fighters, including Kostya himself and the Australian world champion Danny Green, have been in here before me. Kostya wrote 'Always in your corner' on the wall in black texta.

'I love the feeling of being hit. I love hitting,' says Gary, after a round on the heavy bag, the metal chains of which complain as it swings. 'If you've got anger, and I do, there's nothing more humbling than coming into a boxing gym. You can win in here, or lose. Either way it's just you and your opponent.'

It's now a month after my visit to Bowraville. At *The Australian*, Eric George and I have largely been left alone to make the podcast as we want to. I've been given a day a week to work on it, spending the rest covering terrorist attacks, paedophile priests and the internal politics of the police force. Inevitably, during the constant rush of working on a daily newspaper, that day a week is swallowed by these other stories. Working on the Bowraville murders means fighting to find the time and much of the work ends up being done at home rather than the office.

Working through the interviews recorded in Bowraville, we settle on a five-part structure as a way of trying to explain what happened; the first episode will focus on the details of the murders, the second on the police investigation. But to understand this, I need to spend more time with Gary, the detective who leads it. Our first meeting outside the police headquarters in September 2014, when he told me about the children's murders, was only a beginning. This is where he enters the story.

Watching, you can tell Gary is a practised fighter. He's working short, two-minute, training rounds and sweating freely, but still light on his feet and fast for a man in his fifties. Beneath his black t-shirt, a tattooed Sanskrit 'Om' is visible on his right biceps. He also has the words 'Better to die on your feet than live on your knees' tattooed on his left flank. The balance is important, Gary says, when the buzzer sounds for his one-minute rest. It's a yin-yang thing. He likes to fight but, outside the boxing gym, he also meditates.

The buzzer sounds again and Gary steps forward, crouches down and curls a fist into the heavy bag. For two minutes, I watch the frown lines on his face relax. When the time is up and he lowers his fists, he starts to scowl again.

Gary says that people reckon he's aggressive, but he doesn't see it. When people take a shot at him, he says, he cops it. He got into a lot of fights when he was younger and grew up hating bullies. His father was a bully, Gary offers. Maybe that's what made him so hard on himself as an adult. That's why he gets up early and comes down here to train, pushing himself harder. Once again, the buzzer sounds.

When Gary was growing up in Epping, on the northern edge of Sydney, his best mate was a boy called Anthony, who lived across the road. Anthony was a few years older, an Aboriginal kid who'd been adopted, and the two of them ran wild together, sitting up trees or crawling through caves in the bushland near where they were living, fishing in ponds where they weren't meant to, or stealing cigarettes for an illicit smoke.

Gary was white but naturally dark-skinned, and people sometimes thought he, too, was Aboriginal. One of his earliest memories is him, sitting with Anthony, watching the Aboriginal boxer, Lionel Rose, win a world title on a black-and-white television. Gary was five years old at the time of that memory. The two of them were so excited. When Gary was sent to Bowraville as a detective, he stood watching the children laughing on the Mission, and remembered his childhood. He saw their excitement, their smiles, their wild innocence and thought to himself, That's Anthony.

I watch Gary drive an uppercut into the heavy bag, forcing it up into the air, unable to fall back down before he throws another. The buzzer sounds and Gary lies on his back, throwing a medicine ball repeatedly into his stomach. It teaches the muscles to deal with an impact, he says, the same way boxing teaches you to get hit and keep on fighting.

In December 1996, a police task force was established to re-investigate the children's murders, with eight detectives, two full-time analysts, and an experienced commander, who himself had been involved in catching Ivan Milat, the backpacker killer. Detective superintendent Rod Lynch had learned lessons from that serial killer investigation and stressed the need in Bowraville for a coordinated task force this time round, with a clear leadership structure, as well as the importance of investigating and discounting false witness sightings, which had led the Milat inquiry in the wrong direction, chasing claims the victims had been seen alive after they were killed.

Gary Jubelin was in his thirties, had been working as a detective for five years give or take, and recently completed a course in homicide investigation when he was assigned to the task force. Working homicide meant something, Gary thought. It was the NRL, the AFL, the centre ring, the finals. It was the first crime listed in the New South Wales *Crimes Act 1900*, or at least the first after Offences Against the Sovereign. In the *Sentencing Bench Book* that all judges kept close at hand, it was described as 'the most serious offence'. Take a life, get life imprisonment in return. That counted. Gary found he liked the work.

But he didn't over-think it. In fact, he had only joined the police by chance. Before signing up, he'd been working as an electrician and, one afternoon was sitting with his girlfriend in a northern Sydney park when two police officers ran past them, chasing another person. That looks good, thought Gary. He'd been getting too comfortable as a sparky, so he went to the police station the next day and applied. And Gary was right – he enjoyed the pursuit. He also grew to like the way, as a homicide detective, people looked at them when they turned up at a crime scene, as if they were thinking, The A-Team have arrived.

With Bowraville, the task force would reinvestigate the murders, meaning they'd go back over the work of the original investigation right from the beginning. During their early briefings upstairs in the Sydney Police Centre, on the floors above the boxing gym, the bosses emphasised the other lessons of the Milat investigation, including the importance of looking for potential links between the murders rather than treating them as isolated events, and the importance of a central computerised information management system. In short, their task force was to be everything the first police investigation lacked.

The plan was to start at the edges, assessing the work done by police in the months after the children's murders, teasing out the individual strands and following them until they found their suspect. Only, as they unpacked the boxes of documents, which had been brought down from Macksville, Gary began to worry about what he was reading. This was unexpected. The written statements of interviews with witnesses, particularly the early ones, were short; sometimes just a single sheet of paper. He also didn't like the way the police had targeted the children's families as potential suspects.

Gary himself had been working in Coffs Harbour, just north of Bowraville, around the time the three children went missing, dealing with armed robberies. There had been more detectives in his squad than worked on these murders, he thought. Maybe, if the police had done a better job after Colleen went missing, the other children would not have disappeared. Slowly, his worry hardened into shame.

As the weeks passed, the reinvestigation involved long stretches spent in Bowraville, which was like leaving one world for another. At home in Sydney, Gary had married the girlfriend who'd been sitting beside him when he saw the two police officers chase their suspect across the park. When he came home after weeks away working on the reinvestigation, he sometimes seemed a stranger to her. All told, Gary spent about six months of 1997 in Bowraville working on the case.

To understand the work they did there, Gary says, you have to know about Aunty Elaine Walker. She was Colleen's aunty, a sister to Colleen's mother, Muriel Craig. Aunty Elaine had been there when the murders happened, and been in the middle of protests outside the Bowraville police station. She was also an elder, meaning she had respect on the Mission. But the first thing she'd said to Gary when he approached her was, 'Why should I trust you? You're a cop.'

He couldn't offer her an answer.

'You've got so much to learn, whitefella,' she laughed. Slowly, because at first he did not know better, Gary came to realise that people on the Mission had grown used to seeing the police as aggressors. The way the police responded to the early reports that the three children had gone missing only made this worse.

He could see that, if they were going to solve this, then the police needed those people living on the Mission. Over months, the task force tracked down and re-interviewed dozens of the people who'd been at the parties after which Colleen, Evelyn and

Clinton went missing. But nothing came easy. 'Traditional methods of investigation did not necessarily extract all the relevant evidence from Aboriginal witnesses,' Gary wrote in an internal report. 'This is due in part to the fact . . . a large majority of witnesses interviewed during this investigation are not comfortable dealing with police.' It had now been more than six years since the first of the three children disappeared.

'There's memory loss . . . people draw conclusions,' another of the detectives involved in the re-investigation said during a radio interview. That meant the police found it difficult to interpret fact from what had been discussed, or suspected or feared. Sometimes, without thinking, people build memories from emotions or rumours. 'It becomes fact to them', the detective continued. Some witnesses refused to deal with the detectives, or laughed at them, like Aunty Elaine had when Gary first approached her. Others had left the town or died.

Despite this beginning, Gary kept on trying. In time, he says, Aunty Elaine came to notice his commitment. He'd sit under the old tree on the Mission for hours, sometimes, just talking to people. He encouraged them to call him, at any time, if they had a problem, if a family member was in trouble, or if they were simply grieving and wanted to talk. He'd take their phone calls at all hours, no matter if he was at work, at home or in bed, which didn't help his home life. Gary had two kids of his own by now. But this was three kids who'd been murdered.

Eventually, Aunty Elaine softened. If the children's families were fighting to get justice, then Gary was a combatant, and her community could use him. She taught him to spend time with people without asking questions, so they could decide if they would trust him. And when he did ask questions, Gary learned not to look directly at people's faces and not to put them in a position where they had to answer 'Yes' or 'No'. Do that, Aunty Elaine taught him, and you might get a 'Yes' just because they're saying what they think you want to know.

Aunty Elaine also encouraged those living on the Mission to work with the detectives. People started to open up.

Among them were new witnesses. These disputed the evidence gathered during the first investigation that each of the children had been seen alive in the days after their families insisted they'd disappeared. One of these old accounts had put Colleen in a white Commodore driving away from the Mission on the night of the party. But the detectives working the reinvestigation spoke to the people who were in the car that night, who said that she was not with them. Another account, that Colleen had been drinking in James Hide's caravan on the night after the party, also started to look unconvincing. The detectives spoke to the witnesses who said this. They admitted they'd maybe got the date wrong. Maybe it was the night before the party took place.

Similarly, the detectives went back and spoke to several of the witnesses who claimed they saw Evelyn on the day after her mother said that she went missing. They asked one, who had been only seven at the time of the first investigation, 'Would you have been able to recognise exactly the day you saw Evelyn?'

'No,' this witness told them. Another had been eleven when she gave a witness statement saying that she saw Evelyn at the waterhole on the Friday morning after the night of the party. She was asked who first suggested that she saw the missing four-year-old playing on that date, Friday, 5 October 1990. Was it her or the policeman who'd been asking the questions?

'He told me,' she said.

If the reinvestigation couldn't trust the evidence that the three children were alive in the days following the parties, then James Hide came back into the picture. He'd been there at each of the parties held on the nights the children's families said that they'd gone missing. Clinton disappeared from his caravan.

Gary spent time talking with Patricia Stadhams, Evelyn's grandmother. She'd seen Colleen alive on the night of party, walking down the left side of the house at 3 Cemetery Road. In 1991, the the detectives on the first investigation asked her if she also saw James that night. She had, she told them, outside the front of the same building. A week later, she said she'd seen James coming from the party and Colleen was heading down the side of number 3 and 'that's the way [James] was walking'.

Gary was certain Patricia was important. She was the only witness who put Colleen and James together, outside on the Mission late on the night of the party. She was also at the second party, when her granddaughter Evelyn went missing three weeks after Colleen. Gary spoke to Patricia again, and she told him that she saw James's mother's red Chrysler Galant parked behind number 3, where Colleen was walking. She told him that she watched James leave the footpath and walk through the gate to number 3, then down the right side of the house, towards the car. She saw him do this, Patricia said, because she was suspicious and turned around to watch.

Gary also asked Patricia about the night Evelyn went missing. The party had been at her house on the Mission, number 6, and Patricia had been one of the last people awake, going to sleep only after most people had left or crashed out drunk. In 1991, during the original investigation, she'd told police she woke up in the night and heard Evelyn making 'weird noises'.

'Can you tell me the full details?' Gary asked her.

'I can't. I can still hear it, it's just not like her to stop screaming that sudden.'

Gary waited.

'She was just screaming and she stopped,' Patricia continued. 'It was like a thud or something.'

A thud. And then the screaming stopped.

Gary asked Patricia why she had not mentioned this before.

'I was thinking about it,' she told him. She took a breath. 'I can just hear her screaming and screaming every time I think about it. I could tell by the sound of her voice that she was scared.'

'Why didn't you tell police this?' Gary pushed her. Finally, the wall between them broke.

'I told my people that I just heard them crying but didn't tell them all that I knew and they put me through hell,' Patricia told him sadly. 'They accused me of having something to do with it. If I told them all that I knew, if I told them how she was screaming for her mummy, they would have blamed me.'

A screaming child. A thud. The screaming stops. As if someone had struck her. Patricia's evidence suggested something happened in that room to Evelyn. And yet, she'd never told the police about this before. There was also the evidence from Fiona Duckett, who had seen James come out of that room after everyone was sleeping.

All of them had too much to drink and to smoke at the party, Patricia told Gary. She was Evelyn's grandmother. She should have done something.

'I do feel guilty,' Patricia said.

*

Inside the boxing gym, Gary says I lean too far into my punches. He wants me to stand back a little. It's about watching your opponent, he says.

'I'm playing with you, watching the way you move, and then —' his right fist crashes in. The heavy bag shakes dumbly — 'There's a sting,' says Gary. 'Get that right, that hurts.'

He suggests we leave the heavy bag and do some drills, him wearing boxing gloves and me with thick, protective pads, simulating something closer to real boxing. We walk through the old cell door into the room decorated with boxing posters and climb through the ropes into the ring.

'You do have doubts,' Gary says about the Bowraville reinvestigation while I strap the pads on. 'When you have been working on something for twenty years, you think, Am I the only one that sees this?' He takes a few practice shots against the pad on my left hand, which land with a dull clap. 'And then I speak to the families and that sort of recharges me and I think, No, let's go. We're going to fight again.'

'Who are you fighting?' I ask. He looks at me, puzzled.

'I suppose the justice system,' he says. 'We are trying to get justice. We are fighting some racism, we are fighting some cultural ignorance, we are fighting poor practices from the past.'

This jars. Gary is a policeman, a part of the justice system, and yet he seems to see himself outside it. He hunches down, fists raised, ready for me to call out which punches he should attempt in combination.

'So in terms of who are we fighting with, it's a system,' Gary tells me.

'Jab,' I tell him. His fist slams into my pad. 'Cross.' His right fist powers past my face, knocking my pad backwards. 'Hook.'

The left follows beneath it, curling in at chest height, looking to make contact. I turn, forcing Gary to circle. Jab follows hook, follows cross. The sound of each impact echoes from the stone walls around us. The buzzer sounds but Gary ignores it, the sweat running off him freely now. I keep calling out more punches, curious to see how far I can push him: jab, cross, uppercut, hook, jab.

Gary shows no sign of stopping, the smack of each punch now striking before the echo of the one that went before has faded. I watch his face, again empty of expression, leaving only his determination to keep going. I've pushed him further than I could push myself, I'm certain. I start to fear that he might keep on pushing until he does himself some damage.

I call time, dropping my pads, and Gary stands there swaying. His gloved hands hang downwards as he looks at me across the boxing ring. He outlasted my challenge. His breath is ragged but exultant.

December 1997

Now that the threads of the first investigation had led again to James Hide, Gary Jubelin was convinced they only needed time. Among the stacks of old documents collected in the years after the murders, the detectives found a pair of witness statements saying James was involved in a fight on the Mission in the months before the children went missing. According to these witnesses, James started smashing at the front door of their house with a golf club, saying, 'I'll get youse, you two fuck heads, I'll take youse out to Congarinni Road and use youse for fertiliser, under the ground.'

The reinvestigation also made other advances. They spoke to another woman on the Mission, who told them how she'd woken one night years earlier to see James standing in her bedroom. He seemed to be watching her and her sleeping children. Another witness, Hilton Walker, said he'd been drinking with James in the months after the children's disappearances when James had whispered something to him. Something like, 'I've got bodies. I've killed people and their bodies are out on the Congarinni Road near my crops.' Clinton's body had been found near a marijuana crop.

When the detectives asked Hilton why he'd kept this information to himself over the years since the murders, he said that he was scared, and he feared the police would not believe him, because he was Aboriginal and James was white.

Despite this, as the months passed without a clear breakthrough, interest in the reinvestigation among the senior ranks of the police force began to wane. Rod Lynch, the task force's commander, was promoted out and another detective stepped up to replace him. Then he, too, was promoted and not replaced. Gary was convinced they had the evidence. It was an injustice that no one had been jailed over the children's killings. This was something that was solvable, he told himself. Something that could already have been solved. Yet, as he watched the thinning ranks of the task force's members, it also felt like a war of attrition, and it was the numbers on their side that were falling.

Nor did all of Gary's comrades share his confidence in what they had discovered. A police running sheet, made during the early stages of the reinvestigation, records another meeting with Hilton Walker. Two detectives had gone to talk with him about the disappearance of four-year-old Evelyn. They reckoned he was drunk at 11.30 a.m., and had no memory of anything from around the time of the murders. 'Walker has been a very heavy drinker for some time and cannot assist with this matter,' the running sheet recorded. Gary believed they were wrong and that Hilton could help them, but he had to fight to make his case, even to the other detectives.

At the low points, when he was sitting under the Tree of Knowledge, exhausted after failing to convince another potential witness to talk to him, Gary felt like no one wanted them to solve the murders. People on the Mission didn't trust them. People in his own police force didn't seem to care.

Eventually, with their bosses seemingly reluctant to commit more time, money and detectives, the task force was reduced to Gary and a junior detective, Jason Evers. Jason was a decade younger, a smoking, swaggering guy in his mid-twenties who'd joined the police looking for excitement. Like Gary, he was from the northern suburbs of Sydney, meaning they had something in common, but the two of them were different. Jason was a joker. Gary, despite his restless determination, found the reinvestigation was beginning to weigh heavily upon him. He came to rely on Jason to provide him some balance as much as the younger man looked up to him.

For a year, from one hot December to another, at the end of 1997, the two of them kept working, leaving their families behind for weeks and staying in a serviced apartment outside Bowraville in Nambucca Heads. Each day, they'd drive to the Mission along the river, feeling the murders hanging over them like the storm clouds that gathered in the summer. It was an old town, bound up in its suspicions. People on the Mission talked about a gumburr, a spirit who stole children. Jason felt like the spirit was still wandering the town and that he and Gary were on their own, trying to chase it away.

They kept finding new reasons to be hopeful. In the years since the first police investigation, DNA evidence technology had been introduced in New South Wales, promising the ability to identify individual people from tiny, biological traces left at crime scenes, such as fallen hairs, or drops of sweat, or blood. Thinking it might offer them some answers, the detectives looked again at the forensic evidence gathered from James's caravan. There was the bloodstain found on the headboard of the bed in which Clinton had been sleeping. The first investigation had confirmed the blood was human, but the technology at the time had been unable to say anything more. Let's retest it, the detectives decided. If DNA can prove the blood is Clinton's, then that could be evidence he was in the caravan when he was killed.

But when they checked, they learned the bloodstain had been destroyed during the first testing process. There was nothing to retest.

Going through the records detailing the other evidence gathered during the first investigation, they found two exhibits listed as still being held in storage: a clump of black hair found on the blanket recovered close to Clinton's body, and a part of the blanket itself, which previous tests had shown was likely stained with blood or body fluids. The detectives approached the state government's Division of Analytical Laboratories, asking for these old exhibits. They were told the facility had moved buildings in the years since James was acquitted. Worse, following a not-guilty verdict, they were told that old exhibits were often thrown away to make space for new ones. Whatever the reason, a search of their storage unit found neither the hair nor the scrap of blanket were there.

In Bowraville, Aunty Elaine Walker tried to lift the detectives back up from their corners and convince them to keep fighting. Her husband, Larry, took the two men to the stretch of white beaches and blue water where the Nambucca River meets the ocean, where in the Gumbaynggirr story the local gooris chased the handsome stranger, and told them to sit, and wait. They were here for a reason,

Aunty Elaine told them. The children's families needed them, she said.

In May 1998, seventeen months after the reinvestigation was announced and more than seven years since the children's bodies and clothing were recovered, the police collected the evidence they had gathered together and sent it to the New South Wales director of public prosecutions, Nicholas Cowdery, asking whether James could now be charged with murdering Colleen and Evelyn. They argued that the law itself had changed over the years since the not-guilty verdict. When James was put on trial over the killing of Clinton, the judge ordered that no evidence about the other missing children could be heard by the jury. The police said the law would now allow evidence about the similarities between the different killings to be heard in court.

Here you had a suspect, they said, who knew all three of the children before their disappearance. Who was with them or seen near them at around the time each of the children went missing. James was also big and strong enough, they argued, to inflict the head injuries that killed Evelyn and Clinton. And after James was charged with Clinton's murder no other murders had occurred in Bowraville.

It took a year to get an answer from the DPP and, when they did, Gary felt it as a blow to the body. The prosecutor's office said the charges were unsustainable, meaning the evidence did not justify charging James with the murders. That decision meant the task force was formally disbanded and Gary and Jason were returned to working other jobs in Sydney, the older man with the Homicide Squad and the younger as a senior detective in Gladesville in the city's northern suburbs.

Neither of them gave up on the murders, however. They found time outside of work, borrowed it from other investigations, or in Gary's case walked into his bosses' office and demanded to be allowed to keep trying to solve this triple murder. Somehow, they stitched together a way to keep the investigation going. The children's families needed them, Aunty Elaine had said.

If the DPP said the evidence they'd gathered so far was not enough, then they'd need more evidence, more witnesses. They found them in two former prisoners who'd been inside with James when he was awaiting trial over Clinton's murder and who had since approached the police, saying he'd spoken to them about what happened to the children.

The first, who was in the next cell to James in Grafton prison, claimed that their suspect told him, 'If I had done a proper job burying the cunt I would never have got pinched.' That sounded like a reference to Clinton's body, found dumped among leaf litter and undergrowth in the forest off the Congarinni. 'I didn't put it deep enough and the dogs got to it,' this man claimed James said.

The second prison informant, who had also been in Grafton, came forward after watching an episode of *Australia's Most Wanted* featuring the murders in Bowraville. 'I stabbed the bastard,' he claimed that James told him. 'I took Speedy out in the bush, he had been drinking. I'm going to do the girlfriend too.'

Both of these accounts had problems. Neither of the conversations they claimed happened were recorded, while prison informants were also, almost by definition, unreliable. After all, they were criminals, so how much could you trust them? And even if Gary and Jason trusted them, what chance was there they would convince a jury in court?

But it gave them an opening. Working through prison records, the detectives started calling other former inmates who had known James in prison and found two more who claimed James had discussed the murders. One said James would often talk in detail about the children's killings, but always insisted he was innocent; the other said James 'specified about the boy being knocked in the caravan and the girl's body just outside of town'.

The fourth of these informants was tall, tattooed and physically intimidating. They'd found him by going through the letters that James had sent and received after being moved to Maitland prison. He claimed James told him Clinton was killed as a result of a drug deal taking place in the caravan.

'Clinton came at him with a knife, he took it off him, give it to him in the head and wrapped him in a blanket,' their informant told them. He said James had a patch of yarndi plants growing on the hillside above Bowraville, close to the Congarinni Road. James 'took him out to the patch, that's where he left him, on the patch and pulled up the plants.' Their informant claimed James had trusted him as a result of their time in prison, which explained why he would have made this confession. Only, this new witness himself had a criminal record, including for perjury – lying in court.

He was also nothing but work. Needing to maintain a working relationship, Gary and Jason put him up in a motel close to Jason's home. They paid for his food and washed his clothes when he asked them, and even lent him some of their own. At seven in the morning, when they left for work, he'd be sculling a bottle of bourbon, and when they returned in the afternoon, he'd be floating round the motel swimming pool, still drinking.

Twice, they had him wear a listening device and visit James where he was living in a small town west of the Great Dividing

Range, twisting the truth only slightly to give their informant a cover story where he was trying to warn James that the police were still digging into the murders. On the first occasion, James refused the offer of a beer together and though they still sat and spoke for hours, the detectives listening to the tape were disappointed. James admitted nothing. The second time was different. This time, somehow, James worried that the police were listening. When he was in prison, he said, he didn't ask anyone else their business and didn't tell anyone about his own.

'I'd be even more worried if I was fuckin' guilty of something and had to be careful what I said in my own house,' James told the informant. He explicitly denied having anything to do with Colleen's disappearance. And yet, their bourbon-swilling, tattooed giant of an informant kept insisting James admitted to killing Clinton when they were in prison. Nothing was straightforward.

At night, their informant would call, trying to stand over the detectives, telling them they had to do what he told them or they would get nothing. They didn't want to cut their ties with him because both Gary and Jason still believed he had brought them evidence, but eventually, he said something stupid on the phone to Jason about his wife and kids. Gary had to stop the younger man getting in the car and driving over to finish the argument in person. Their informant also had a reputation for having beaten a murder charge.

Eventually, these blows started to get through their defences: the witnesses who would not talk to them, the lawyers who would not believe them, the bosses who would not give them time to work the case. Both Gary and Jason were also working other cases, including other murders. Often, they worked together, which brought them into conflict. Gary kept demanding more of Jason, wielding

his authority as the senior officer, refusing to accept any weakness
or mistake.

Jason, in turn, would needle Gary, asking why he needed to be
angry, or joking about Gary's fractured relationship with his father.
On long drives together, to crime scenes or to track down a witness,
Gary had opened up to Jason about growing up in the sixties and
seventies, when kids got belted. He could handle being hurt, the
more bitter memories were those where Gary brought his school
report home and his father said that it was shit, or when his dad
watched Gary playing soccer and, afterwards, said only, that he
should not have let a goal go in.

It became a joke between them, they talked about it so often –
the joke being that Gary's father didn't love him and that was the
reason he was so hard on himself and everybody else.

On one of their cases, the two detectives were driving through
the dry, exhausted landscape of the state's interior, feeling like they
were going absolutely nowhere, when Gary stopped the car, got out
and walked into the bush, staring at the horizon.

Jason was tired. He waited. Gary stood there.

'What the fuck are you doing?' Jason shouted.

'I'm listening to the silence and you're wrecking it,' Gary told
him. Jason exploded.

'I don't know what the fuck's wrong with you, I really don't,'
he shouted. 'I don't care if Daddy didn't take you camping,
I don't know what your issue is, but you can get back in the fucking car, drive like a normal human being so we can get to where
we're going.'

Gary found his own way to relax. He meditated daily.

*

At work, boxes of documents relating to the Bowraville investigation sat constantly beside Gary's desk, while other boxes containing evidence of other killings moved constantly across it. At home, he was always on the telephone, talking about the children's murders. His children would turn down the television volume and listen to what he was saying. They followed the investigation by watching their father's reaction: smiling and exultant when something had gone right, or taking out his frustration on the punch bag hanging from the back deck.

The years passed with little progress. In 2003, nine years since James was found not guilty and thirteen years since Colleen went missing, Gary and Jason took the evidence of their prison informants and went to see the state coroner, to ask if he would hold an inquest into Colleen and Evelyn's deaths.

Gary knew that he could argue doing so was following the proper procedure – the director of public prosecutions had declined to prosecute and the police investigation had formally been halted, so the next step would be for the coroner to investigate and establish a cause of death. But both he and Jason were hoping the coroner could do more to help them. They wanted to make public the evidence about the similarities between the children's disappearances. They wanted to show the lawyers working for the DPP they were wrong to dismiss the evidence that they'd collected. Holding an inquest would mean the details of all three children's murders would be heard together. It would also put pressure back on the DPP.

The coroner agreed.

An inquest meant that James would be served with a court order to give evidence. Gary and Jason decided to deliver it in person.

'You guys think I've done something I haven't done,' James told them when they knocked on the front door of the house where he was living. Gary explained about the inquest and the court order, then decided to push him.

'I'm basically accusing you of being a serial killer,' he said. 'Where do we go from here?'

'I just need to be left alone.' James said he had already been found not guilty. They stared at each other. Gary scowled and bit his teeth together. James was straight-faced and smelt of cigarettes. At forty-one, James was no longer the young man who'd first been charged with murder. The muscles on his arms and shoulders, which he'd put to use in the hide factory, had wasted. He had children of his own now in the house behind him.

The inquest began in February 2004, held in Bellingen's Federation courthouse, less than an hour's drive north from Bowraville itself.

Wednesday, 11 August 2004

James Hide came alone to the inquest. When asked, he confirmed his name and that his address was known to the police.

'Have you had legal advice in the matter?' the coroner, John Abernethy, asked.

'By phone, yes,' James said.

'We'd like to hear from you but is the legal advice to the effect that you've been advised not to answer any questions if the answers you give may tend to incriminate you?'

'That's right, your Honour.'

'And do you want to exercise that right?'

'I do, your Honour.'

James had also chosen not to attend the court during the two weeks of evidence that had preceded his appearance. With nothing to gain from asking him more questions, the coroner watched as James stepped down and then adjourned the court for a month to make a decision about what he'd heard.

The records of those inquest hearings are contained in thick paper stacks of transcript and witness statements, stored in two cardboard boxes in the archives of the NSW Coroner's Court. These show how, at the beginning of the hearing, the coroner explained that an inquest was not a trial, its purpose was not to establish guilt, and instead his role was to make a formal decision about the nature of each of the children's deaths.

The legal counsel assisting the coroner, police sergeant Matthew Fordham, argued that James had good reason to kill the children. On the face of it, he said, the victims were quite different – Colleen and Clinton were different sexes and both nearly adults, while Evelyn was a preschool-age girl – but there was a thread that bound all three.

'There is evidence before this court that James Hide was keen to have sexual relationships with several young Aboriginal women from the Mission,' the police lawyer told the coroner. He 'pursued them by providing them with alcohol and drugs to overcome their inhibitions'.

Seven different witnesses said they believed James spiked alcoholic drinks with pills or powders before giving them to women on the Mission. The evidence suggested he had done this to Evelyn's mum, Rebecca Stadhams.

Rebecca was called to give evidence. 'That drink that James gave me, I went out like a light,' she told the inquest.

Following the thread of the police lawyer's argument, if James was the killer, then he was motivated by sex rather than murder for its own sake. Clinton's girlfriend, Kelly Jarrett, gave evidence, saying that she woke up inside James's caravan with Clinton missing and with her shorts and pants removed. Rebecca also described how she had woken after the party to find that Evelyn was gone and her trousers had also been pulled down. James had drugged Rebecca at the party, the police lawyer told the coroner. 'The obvious inference is that Rebecca Stadhams had been drugged to the point of making her incapable of refusing sexual advances.' One witness claimed she'd seen James put a white pill inside a bottle of Jim Beam bourbon, and that a friend of hers claimed James had chased her across the golf course – where Muriel Craig once dreamed of her daughter Colleen being chased. One of Colleen's friends described how she and Colleen once spent the night in James's caravan. She said James had got into bed with the two girls when they were sleeping and the next morning, Colleen had seemed worried.

'James mauled me all night,' Colleen had said, her friend told the inquest. 'He touched me down below and up the top as well. This morning I had to pull my pants up when I woke.'

'James Hide must know more about the manner and cause of Colleen's death,' the police lawyer told the inquest.

Follow this argument and the children become not so much the killer's targets as potential witnesses who needed to be silenced. Another witness, Fiona Duckett, who I'd spoken to in Bowraville, told the inquest that she'd seen James late at night, leaving the house following the party at which Evelyn went missing.

'This evidence . . . establishes that the time that Fiona Duckett saw James Hide leaving Rebecca Stadhams' bedroom was after the time that Patricia Stadhams heard Evelyn Greenup crying inside the bedroom,' the police lawyer argued. 'This means James Hide was inside Rebecca Stadhams' bedroom at the time that Evelyn Greenup was crying.'

Perhaps he was in the process of removing her clothing when Evelyn woke up. Perhaps James then attacked the four-year-old, picking her up and bashing her head against the wall to silence her. Evelyn's grandmother had said she heard a thud that night, after which the little girl's crying stopped.

The detectives' fourth prison informant, the one Jason Evers had almost come to blows with, was called into the witness box. Known only as Witness X to protect his identity, he was asked why, as a criminal himself, he agreed to give evidence?

Witness X claimed to have changed since he'd been in prison. He was now married, with two kids of his own. 'I've received nothing and I want nothing,' he told the inquest. Responding to the lawyer's questions, Witness X said that he was watching TV in his cell when James came back to the prison after being charged with killing Evelyn in 1991. They spoke about what happened. 'He went into . . . a bit of detail and I had to cut him off but she'd had her head smashed against the wall.'

'Did he talk about how old the girl was?'

'Four-year-old.'

Evelyn's family sat in silence, listening to this new evidence.

Witness X also said that James told him that Clinton had 'pulled a knife on him and he took the knife off him and, yes, he dealt with it'.

'Did James talk to you about what he'd done with the knife?' asked the lawyer.

'No, apparently it was left at his mother's and his mother got rid of it out of the house.' The knife, said Witness X, was buried at the Bowraville racecourse. James had told him that he wanted to get out of jail and find it.

*

James's mother, Marlene Hide, was not called to give evidence at the inquest, though she is a vital witness. There are transcripts of several brief interviews she gave to the police in February and April 1991, during the months after Clinton's body was discovered and before Evelyn's remains and Colleen's clothes were found.

James was her eldest son, she told the police. 'I do his cooking and if there is room at our table he eats at our home otherwise he eats in the van.' This was the caravan from which Clinton had gone missing. 'He cleans his van himself. I insist that he drops his washing in my laundry. That includes all his clothing and bed linen. I wash and iron it and he picks it up from my place.'

'How often do you do his washing?'

'Every Friday. I get his work clothes and undies and the odd item through the week but generally I just do the one wash.'

Marlene also backed up James's account of his movements on the morning Clinton went missing: her son woke her up shortly before six, asking for her car keys so he could drive to work. If true, this means James could not have driven her car up to the forest earlier that morning to dispose of Clinton's body, as she kept all the car keys in a pink purse, stashed inside the pillowslip that she slept on in bed.

During the interviews, however, the police returned to the question of James's laundry. When would have been the first time she washed his clothes after Friday, 1 February, the day Clinton went missing? It would have been that night or the next morning, on the Saturday, Marlene told them.

'Did you notice any stains similar to blood on any items of clothing belonging to James?'

'Well, I've got to say yes. He works on the hides and he always brings home clothes with blood and hair on them.'

'Did you notice any stains that were unusual to the ones normally found on his clothing?'

'No.' Nor were any of James's clothes missing, that she knew of, Marlene told the policemen.

They showed her a photograph of the pillowslip that had been found down Clinton's shorts. In the picture, the material was still stained and crumpled.

'Do you recognise this pillowslip?'

'Not from that I can't.'

'Is it similar to any linen belonging to James?'

'I can't say looking at that.'

'Do you wash James's linen?'

'Yes, I do,' she told them. But by the time of the inquest, scientific testing had proven that the pillowslip and James's linen were a match.

Reading through the stack of curling paperwork relating to the inquest, I find a nine-page document on which the coroner typed up his notes about the different witnesses themselves. Before now, I've never seen one like it. These notes reveal what the coroner thought, not only about their evidence, but about the people who delivered it as they sat before him in court.

Evelyn's grandmother Patricia Stadhams, who said she heard Evelyn crying late at night at the party, then a thud, 'was a very good witness . . . she adhered to what she saw and would be unlikely to be shaken.'

Others, like Clinton's girlfriend, Kelly Jarrett, were more troubling. Asked when she had last seen Colleen, or about when she had been drinking with Clinton, Kelly tended to answer with silence, a nod or shake of her head. When she did speak, Kelly often answered with a word, either 'No' or 'Yeah'. This silence was troubling.

'I was not satisfied that she was telling the inquest all she knew,' the coroner noted. 'There are many reasons for this, perhaps related to the Speedy trial, guilt, the community pressure. She tended to say "No" when she really didn't know.'

Reading his notes, you see how the coroner is weighing whether a case can be constructed from the evidence heard at the inquest. One witness, who claimed he heard Colleen arguing with James on the night of the party and saying, 'No, don't touch me,' was 'very important but it may not be the truth'. Hilton Walker, who'd come forward claiming James said he had bodies out on Congarinni Road 'was a very heavy drinker but was brave enough to adhere to the version in his statement'. Another was 'badly ravaged by drink'. In court, it is not so much what is true that matters, but what you can prove.

On Friday, 10 September 2004, the coroner delivered his verdict. James was not in court to hear it.

Colleen had been the victim of a homicide, the coroner decided. 'As to the nature of that homicide or the identity of the person or persons who carried it out, the evidence adduced does not enable me to say.'

With Evelyn, the evidence was stronger. 'A known person has been given every opportunity to make submissions before me and has chosen not to do it,' the coroner said. He would suspend his inquest, and write to the state's director of public prosecutions, Nicholas Cowdery, asking him to reconsider whether there were grounds to charge James with the four-year-old's murder.

This letter was sent in October 2004, thirteen years since James was first charged with killing Evelyn, a decade since the DPP decided not to go ahead with it and five years after Gary and Jason failed in their first attempt to get the state prosectuor to reconsider this decision. In it, the coroner asked the DPP to look again 'at all three cases which occurred over a very short period of time in the environs of that tiny village'.

In his notes, the coroner wrote that Colleen's death 'on its own will never get to the stage of a prima facie case. However if it can be linked to Evelyn Greenup and Clinton Speedy, it might.'

Leaving the coroner's court after reading through the inquest transcripts, I think this is no way to get justice. By this point, James has been charged twice with different murders, been tried over one of those alleged killings and acquitted, seen the second charge abandoned and been the subject of an inquest in which he declined to play a part. The police, one part of the state government, had asked another part, the director of public prosecutions, that he face trial a second time on the previously abandoned charge of murder, only to rejected, before finding an ally in a third part of the justice system, the state coroner, who seemed to think that the police were right.

Just the language of the letters these official bodies sent to one another – 'the environs of that tiny village' – seems a world apart from that of the people who called home either 'Bowra' or, if they lived in one of the houses on Cemetery Road, 'the Mish'.

That night at home I listen again to one of the interviews we recorded in Bowraville. It's with Colleen's aunt, Alison Walker, who told us that she'd lived with James on the Mission and had a child with him, a son. These tangled small-town interconnections meant that Colleen herself had known the man who the coroner suspected may have played a part in her murder. Colleen had called him 'Uncle'.

Alison said that James was 'a big man, quiet, very quiet, especially when he was sober. When he got alcohol into him, he was different.'

'How different?' I asked.

'He'd change.'

'In what way?

'He became the devil.'

She said they'd been together for nearly ten years, on and off, because they were fighting.

'What do you hope will happen?' I had asked her.

'White law won't get up, black law will get them.'

Not understanding her meaning, I asked Alison what black law meant.

'If black law got them they wouldn't know, they'd just go silly.'

'Can black law get James?' I asked her.

'Yes.'

'What would happen to him?'

'He'd never be able to rest. He won't be able to rest,' she told me.

Seven months after receiving the coroner's letter, on Wednesday, 25 May 2005, the DPP overturned its previous decision not to take James to court over the murder of Evelyn. Eleven years, two months and twenty-one days had passed since the prosecutor's office first decided to drop the prosecution of Evelyn's suspected killer, following the not-guilty verdict over Clinton's murder. It was six years to the day since the police asked the prosecutor to reconsider this decision. Resentment at this delay ate away at Gary Jubelin. But there it was. James was going to stand trial.

Tuesday, 7 February 2006

Evelyn's mum, Rebecca Stadhams, was the first to give evidence at the trial over her daughter's murder. By now, sixteen years had passed since that killing – a childhood – but Rebecca was still recognisable as the thin, haunted woman caught in the newspaper photographs taken at the time.

She looked small in the witness box. Isolated. Even after all these years, she still suffered nightmares about her daughter and carried around with her a fear that the killer would come back and take another of her children. As a result, Rebecca drank and took antidepressants. James Hide's barrister smiled at her as he began to test her memory.

'This is what you told the police, is it not?' he asked, reading from the statement Rebecca gave to police after Evelyn went missing. Back then, caught up in fear and confusion, she'd said that other people had seen Evelyn alive after the party: someone said they'd seen her daughter at the Reibels store in Bowraville; someone else said they'd seen the four-year-old at Lanes Bridge; someone said Evelyn was on the Mission.

Rebecca wanted to explain that what she'd told police was just what she was told by others, not what was true, but in the witness box, surrounded by judge, jury and the tall, questioning, defence barrister, it was hard to find the words to do it.

'Okay, now I read out, didn't I, what is in that piece of paper?' the barrister asked Rebecca.

'Yeah.'

'And that is what you told police, did you not, when you saw them on the day you made this statement?'

'I can't remember.'

'Well, you would not have told the police any lies though, would you?' A pause, waiting for an answer. 'You would have told them the truth as best you could remember?'

'It's been that long,' Rebecca answered.

'But when you talked to the police back in 1990, two days after Evelyn disappeared, you would have told the police the truth, wouldn't you? What you could remember?'

Rebecca said nothing.

Looking down, the judge asked her, 'Can you answer the question?'

Rebecca did not answer. The jury watched her sit in silence. This time, the trial was being held in Port Macquarie, a sprawling town at the mouth of the Hastings River, over an hour's drive from Bowraville. No one had told the jury about the differences between how Indigenous and non-Indigenous people might answer questions; how long silences might be seen evasive in one but not the another; or how a white person looking at the ground might seem to be hiding something, but to a black person it might be a politeness to avoid confrontation. None of the white people in the jury box could share Rebecca's fear and misunderstanding at that moment.

They could understand the lawyer's point, however. If Evelyn had been seen alive after the party at which James was present, then there was no connection. The case against him shattered into pieces. James's barrister tendered Rebecca's police statement into evidence.

Outside the court, Gary Jubelin argued with another witness, who ran the Reibels store in Bowraville and who insisted she'd seen Evelyn inside her store on the day after the party. How could she be certain? Gary asked her. She'd not spoken to Evelyn, nor could she remember what the four-year-old was wearing. She'd claimed Evelyn had been in the store with some other children, but the police had checked, those boys weren't in town that day.

The woman was adamant in the face of Gary's anger and, when called into the witness box, insisted that she had seen Evelyn that day.

Gary's anger at the shopkeeper disguised a deeper worry. The state prosecutor's office, who'd dropped the prosecution of James over Evelyn's murder, then refused to reconsider that decision before finally overturning it, assigned a barrister to run the case, and Gary didn't trust him. The two sides, police and prosecution, were supposed to work together, with the lawyers asking the detectives to clarify their evidence, or do more work on some part of the case: 'That's good, I see why you've done that but I want this tightened up,' or, 'Can you strengthen this part of the evidence?' With any other murder, there'd be a stream of such questions but so far they had not received a single such request.

The silence gnawed at Gary. He began to doubt the prosecution lawyer. Before the trial started, Gary was sure that he'd heard him say, 'We're not going to win this case.' Maybe it was an off-the-cuff remark. Maybe Gary misheard it. What Gary didn't know, although he suspected, was that it reflected a current of opinion running through the state prosecutor's office, where others felt the trial was being run only for political reasons.

For the detectives, Gary and Jason Evers, who'd spent years working on the investigation, it was a deadening experience. To get justice, Gary thought, you had to put the effort in, and he couldn't see it happening. Watching from the public gallery, Evelyn's aunt, Michelle Jarrett, sat there watching the prosecution and thinking to herself, Why aren't you fighting harder? Why don't you call more witnesses? At one point, she imagined herself walking up to the lawyers' bench, slapping one of them on the head and asking them, 'What are you doing?'

Gary's answer was to keep on working, harder. He insisted that he and Jason write another report summarising the key points in the evidence and give it to the prosecution barrister.

'What's the purpose?' Jason asked him. 'He's not going to listen.'

'Fuck you, I'm the inspector,' said Gary. 'This is what we're fucking doing.'

As the days passed, Evelyn's family sat in court and wondered why the jury were once again not being told about the other children's murders. That first judge's decision to separate the cases still bedevilled the prosecution. It was as if this bad spirit had returned to throw confusion over this trial also. When called to give evidence, witnesses who'd been on the Mission at the time of the murders wanted to talk about what happened to all three of the children. But their instructions were strict: they were not to mention Colleen and Clinton's names.

That Saturday, following the first full week of evidence, an Aboriginal teenager died while riding his bicycle through Redfern, in inner-city Sydney. One version of what happened had him being chased by police, although the force denied it. By nightfall, rioters strung themselves across Eveleigh Street in Redfern, throwing bottles, fireworks and petrol bombs. The train station burned. On Monday, one of Gary's bosses called him, worried the trial could be another flashpoint. The families weren't violent, Gary told him. The trial dragged on throughout the heat of February. Again, James exercised his right not to answer questions.

'The death of Evelyn Greenup, there is no doubt that it was a tragedy,' James's barrister told the jury before they retired to consider their verdict. Yet, when you looked at it objectively, the evidence they'd heard about her murder did not amount to a hill of beans. The prosecution case relied on 'the evidence of a large number of people who were extremely drunk at the time' – those people at the party after which Evelyn's mother claimed that she went missing. Drinking was endemic on the Mission, and it could surely ruin people's perceptions and memories. Evelyn's grandmother Patricia Stadhams – who claimed to have heard the four-year-old crying in the night, followed by a thud, then silence – had been asked about this drinking when she was called to give evidence. 'Talking about everyday blackfellas' life,' she'd said.

Worse, James's barrister continued, the prosecution case 'includes the evidence of someone who could only be characterised as being a drunk now, and he has been for many years' – that was Hilton Walker, who claimed that James admitted having killed people and leaving their bodies in the forest by Congarinni Road. And it 'includes the evidence of a prison informant who has been convicted of perjury and, in my submission, has clearly lied to you in court' – that was Witness X.

Compared to this, the evidence of the shopkeeper who claimed she saw Evelyn in her store the morning following the party was 'absolutely like a beacon'. In his own summing up, the judge reminded the jury that James, as the defendant, had to prove nothing. It was the prosecution who had to prove that the case against him was true. Fail to do that – if any reasonable doubt existed – then, the jury had no option but to find James not guilty.

On the day of the verdict, riot police appeared inside the courtroom, dressed in black uniforms. Gary and Jason had little warning of this and were furious at the decision; Evelyn's family felt they were being treated like the criminals. When James was found not guilty, there were tears and screams and howling.

James walked out a free man, smiling.

After the not-guilty verdict, the detectives met with the children's families. Gary and Jason were exhausted, defeated and unsure what to tell them. During the trial, some of the Bowraville elders had invited the detectives to a smoking ceremony at nearby Valla Beach, near where the gooris chased the shining stranger in the old Gumbaynggirr story, and where a small headland faces out towards the Pacific Ocean. The smoke was meant to drive away any evil spirits. The policemen were told to stand at the edge of the water and look past the breakers to where it met the horizon. Jason thought they were supposed to see something, but he couldn't and it left him feeling guilty.

Now, with the court verdict, his bosses had told him to pack his stuff up, put the exhibits in storage, then drive home and get to work. Both he and Gary were told not to speak to the media. It seemed that no one in the police wanted to talk about the murders either.

Two years later, Jason would be diagnosed with post-traumatic stress disorder and leave the police force. He was no longer the joking, swaggering detective. He felt shit and he was feeling sick, and sick of feeling sick, and sick of fighting.

He felt that they had failed the families. That he and Gary encouraged them to put their trust in a justice system that was more likely to treat them as suspects than victims. According to the Australian Bureau of Statistics, Aboriginal people were thirteen times more likely to be prisoners than other Australians. He and Gary had told the families they would be treated fairly, only to watch as they struggled in an ocean of court ritual and laws of evidence and cross-examination which had ultimately drowned them.

After the verdict, staring at the circle of sad faces as the children's families waited for he and Gary to explain what happened, Jason felt as if he was in the water with them. He was the policeman. He was supposed to be on the shore, helping them to safety. But he was in the ocean, floundering.

'What now?' asked Leonie Duroux. Hers was the one white face among the children's relatives. She wasn't Aboriginal, did not grow up in Bowraville, but had got together with Clinton's brother, Marbuck, and they'd had children – Clinton's nephews. She'd been in court when James was found not guilty over Clinton's murder in 1994, and again for this result over Evelyn's killing in 2004.

'Nothing,' the detectives said. The law says you can't be put on trial twice for the same crime. It was called double jeopardy, they told her, one of the pillars of the legal system. As far as Gary and Jason knew, it meant the end of the investigation. You can't change the law, they told the families. There's nothing you can do now, unless you were to topple double jeopardy itself.

'Let's do that then,' Leonie said.

The families agreed with her. Someone had killed Colleen, Evelyn and Clinton. No one had been found responsible. They didn't want another generation to grow up with the trauma of these unsolved murders. They were not going to be silenced.

For years now Leonie Duroux had been writing letters, at first to local politicians, then the state governor, the Ombudsman, to newspapers, to senators, to ministers, to the leaders of the federal opposition and the prime ministers themselves:

'I ask for your assistance . . .'

'Would you be able to be of any assistance to our family . . .'

'I have been writing letters in relation to Clinton's murder for nearly two years now . . .'

'I sincerely hope that you may be able to assist us in some way.'

Even after Marbuck was diagnosed with motor neurone disease, Leonie kept on writing. Among her letters was one faxed to the NSW Police Force commissioner, but she got no answer. So Leonie sent it again. The third time, Gary called her.

The two of them, Leonie and Gary, became allies. The families supported his attempt to get an inquest into the children's murders, which led to the trial over Evelyn's murder, while she appreciated having someone in authority who understood the system and spoke plainly. Someone she could trust. In that way, Leonie's letters opened up a new front in the murder investigation. Not only was Gary now cooperating with the children's families in the search for evidence and witnesses, he was also quietly encouraging their campaign to lobby politicians and journalists.

It was just a different method of achieving justice, Gary told himself. The louder the families' protests, the more people paid attention. More attention, especially from politicians, meant he'd be given more time and resources by his bosses in the police. Both he and the families wanted the same outcome – a guilty verdict. If they were not going to be given one, then they would have to take it.

Following the not-guilty verdict in the trial over Evelyn's murder, Leonie used the computer in the Aboriginal health centre on the Bowraville Mission to write to her local member of parliament, Andrew Stoner, and then to the state attorney general, asking for a change to the double jeopardy legislation. Stoner wrote back, which encouraged her. Leonie then wrote to every member of the New South Wales parliament. When she didn't get a reply, she wrote to them again.

Leonie knew that such change was possible; in the United Kingdom the law had been changed in 2005, following an inquiry into the murder of a black teenager called Stephen Lawrence. There, the police investigation was found to have suffered from incompetence, institutional racism and a lack of leadership. Local politicians were now asking if the same reform should happen in Australia.

Leonie spoke to others in the children's families, including Michelle Jarrett, Evelyn's aunt, and Aunty Elaine, who was Colleen's aunt, and had helped Gary when he was trying to uncover new witnesses for the reinvestigation. It wasn't always easy to bring the three families together, particularly for Leonie who was not a part of the community by blood but only through her relationship with Marbuck. She learned quickly that one family could not pretend to speak in place of the others. It had to be all three families speaking together, or nothing.

A campaign group was formed. They called it Ngindayjumi, meaning 'Truth be told' in the Gumbaynngirr language. The truth was what had happened to their children. So far, the courts had not heard what they were saying, because the judges had ruled that each jury would hear only about the murder of first Clinton and then Evelyn alone, rather than about all three of the children. To the campaigners, that mattered. If double jeopardy prevented the truth from being heard in court, they told themselves, it did not seem too big a thing to ask for the law to be rewritten.

Like Gary, I have formed an informal alliance with Leonie. During the process of writing the podcast scripts and editing the audio we speak often on the phone. I lean on her to check facts or dates or names, or to help understand the connections of blood and marriage that bind the three children's families. Out of these conversations, we have agreed to launch the podcast next month, in May 2016, to coincide with a protest by the children's families outside the state parliament, of which Leonie is one of the organisers.

I understand that she sees what I'm doing as an extension of that protest. The podcast, to her, is a way to have the families' voices heard. I understand also that this is what Gary wanted when he first suggested I cover this case for the paper, and when he introduced me to Leonie. As a reporter, I know I still have to be independent.

I'm telling this story because it is worth telling, not because they want me to, I tell myself.

The campaign to change the law around double jeopardy is a part of this story. After speaking on the phone, I decide to meet Leonie to ask her how it ended.

It's late April 2016 when I drive up to Kempsey, a sprawling, hardscrabble town about an hour south of Bowraville. Leonie suggests we meet at the town's pastel-coloured, one-room court-house, where she works for the local domestic violence court advocacy service. Oranges hang from the trees along one side of the building. Inside, a thin Aboriginal man sits in the heavy wooden dock while a white lawyer sprawls at the bar table, scrolling through his mobile phone. Leonie turns and smiles from her seat in the front row of the public gallery. She has an impish smile.

I sit and wait for the court to adjourn, watching a succession of Aboriginal suspects brought in by the sheriff's officers. One young woman wearing a white vest and patterned shorts sits with her hands clamped between her knees, rocking back and forwards and mouthing something at Leonie, who shakes her head. The cases are mostly about drugs and Apprehended Violence Orders. The suspects look mostly broken after their short hearings finish as they are led away.

Above them, the New South Wales coat of arms hangs on the court wall with its Latin motto, Orta recens quam pura nites, which translates as 'Newly risen, how brightly you shine'. I think about a line I once read in a Helen Garner book about a trial that might be better suited: Dura lex sed lex, 'The law is hard but it is the law'.

At lunch, Leonie leads the way along a path beside the orange trees and into a small room at the back of the courthouse.

'We're still doing it. Still fighting,' she says, opening a cupboard where tea, coffee, sugar, biscuits and lollies are all laid out neatly.

In 2006, while the families were campaigning to overturn double jeopardy, at home her partner Marbuck was getting sicker. His motor neurone disease prevented the messages carried through his nerves from reaching his muscles, which were wasting as a result. During the trial over Evelyn's murder, Leonie had pushed him in his wheelchair to the Port Macquarie courthouse every morning. He started to lose the ability to talk, while she spent hours helping him to eat and get dressed.

They both knew it would kill him but Marbuck had always said he wanted to stay alive long enough to see justice over his brother's murder. To him, justice meant somebody in prison. Handing me a cup of tea, Leonie says that she and Marbuck, as well as Marbuck's father, Thomas, went to meet their MP, Andrew Stoner. He helped arrange for the three children's families to go down to Sydney and meet with the head of the state premier's department. By now Leonie had sent hundreds of letters and emails, copies of which were stored in boxes inside her wardrobe and out in the garden shed. Overturning double jeopardy would not be simple, the experts and politicians had told the families. The defence lawyers were all against it and most of the judges were also reluctant to alter something so fundamental to how the legal system worked.

But the Ngindayjumi campaign had caught people's attention. That September, the ABC's *Australian Story* series ran a program about the children's murders and the families' attempt to overturn double jeopardy. Conversations were happening inside parliament that were sympathetic to the idea.

Soon after the television program, the New South Wales Premier, Morris Iemma, stood up in parliament and argued: 'There will sometimes be cases where diligent police and prosecutors will still fail to find all the possible evidence. Perhaps it is being concealed from them deliberately, or perhaps developments in forensic technology will reveal new evidence or new conclusions to be drawn from existing evidence.' In these cases, said the premier, not bringing someone back and putting them on trial again would itself be an injustice.

In October 2006, eight months after James was found not guilty of killing Evelyn, the Crimes (Appeal and Review) Amendment (Double Jeopardy) Bill was passed by the New South Wales parliament. The campaigners had succeeded. The politicians had voted to accept the premier's argument and the new law made it possible that a person who'd been found not guilty of murder could be retried, if 'fresh and compelling' evidence were found.

Andrew Stoner, who'd received one of Leonie's first letters, stood up in parliament and spoke about the Bowraville murders. He hoped the changes to the law would 'give some hope to those families that justice may eventually be done'.

Leonie finishes her tea and stands. The court's lunch adjournment is almost over and there will be other cases, other witnesses and victims of domestic violence for her to speak with this afternoon.

'Did you ever think, This is too big, this is massive that we are going to get a government to rewrite the law?' I ask her, handing her my cup.

'No.'

'Why not?'

'Because it was just wrong and it had to be fixed up.'

She turns away to run the two empty cups under a tap to clean them. Turning back, she says, 'Let's go.'

After saying goodbye to Leonie, I drive out of Kempsey between flooded paddocks where the river has burst its banks, drowning the trees and everything that stands upon the ground. At the junction with the Pacific Highway, a sign points south to Port Macquarie, the town where the trial over Evelyn's murder was held. The road north leads to Sawtell, where Muriel Craig lives in the house where she last saw her daughter; to Macksville, where James Hide was arrested; to Grafton, where the trial over Clinton's murder took place; to Nambucca Heads, where the detectives Gary Jubelin and Jason Evers lived while working on the case; to Bellingen, where they held the inquest; and of course to Bowraville itself. There is a dark geography along this stretch of coastline, I think, looking at the sheets of silent water on the roadside. As if some violence is also seeping out across the farmland and forests, swallowing the little towns.

I turn the car north, away from my home in Sydney, towards Bowraville again.

Friday, 8 April 2016

With Jason Evers gone, Gary Jubelin fought to keep the reinvestigation going. He kept working on the children's killings, often in his own time, determined to come back with the 'fresh and compelling' evidence they would need to have another chance of taking James Hide to trial.

People told him to forget it. Some warned he would damage his career if he kept trying to roll this boulder back up the slope. At home, in recent years his marriage had ended and Gary began a long relationship with another detective, only that, too, foundered. Following this break-up he got married again, this time to an Aboriginal psychologist he met while working on the Bowraville murders.

At work, Gary's frustration reared up. He clashed with his bosses in an attempt to get other detectives assigned to work on the murders. Once, he marched into the Homicide Squad offices and demanded he be given two detectives, telling a senior officer: 'I'm sick of fucking around with you trying to get staff.'

'You can't speak to me like that,' she told him.

'Fuck you. I'll speak to you any way I want.'

She told Gary there were other cases, other murders, ones that the police had a far better chance of solving than the three deaths in Bowraville. Those cases needed the resources. He threatened to take it up to level nine – senior management – and complain that he wasn't getting help to work on a triple murder investigation. That afternoon, he was given another detective, as well as an intelligence analyst to manage the huge slew of information gathered over the years. But the three of them were not to focus entirely on Bowraville. They would still work their other cases, he was told.

Gary didn't care. He'd got what he wanted. He also had some 'fresh and compelling' evidence, or so he thought.

One early morning in the summer of 1991, Michael Scafidi was riding in a truck loaded with meat for the Bowraville butchers, watching the silhouettes of trees whip by his window as the driver gunned the engine through the pre-dawn darkness, the truck doing 120-something kilometres an hour along the swooping, empty roads.

At the edge of town, on Norco Corner, where the road kicks up and left, Michael spotted someone lying on the bitumen. The truck had to veer at speed in order not to hit him, before coming to a halt around the corner. The prone body was in his late teens, wearing jeans but with no shoes on, his head facing down the road.

Twenty-five years later, Michael meets me at Macksville District Hospital, where he works. He swings into the passenger seat of the car I'm driving, and directs me along the route they took in the truck that morning. Rumours that he had seen something important started to spread after James was found not guilty of killing Evelyn. Different people claim to have first told the police about him but, eventually, Leonie and another woman from the Ngindayjumi campaign group, Vivienne Tedeschi, helped to track him down.

I pull up where Michael tells me that the truck swung to a halt on Norco Corner. Then, as now, the corner is deep in shadow. There was no street lighting back then, he says, and it was only their powerful headlights that meant they saw the body in the road.

'All of a sudden, a guy comes here,' says Michael, pointing through the windscreen. 'He just walks across the front there, comes around to the driver's side window.' Michael leaned across to talk.

'Mate, what's going on? We could have hit that guy,' he told him.

'It's all right,' the man replied. 'He's asleep and I've called the police.'

Remember, Michael tells me, this is years before people had mobiles and there are no payphones near Norco Corner.

'All right, but are you sure you don't want a hand to get him off the road?' Michael asked the man standing at the truck window.

'No, no,' he replied, refusing the offer. 'You'll be right mate, you'll be right,' he said.

Ahead of them, Michael says they could see a mucky-coloured station wagon standing with its boot open. He didn't see a number plate. It was dark, I say, but could he see the skin colour of the guy lying on the road?

Aboriginal, he tells me.

And the guy who spoke to you?

'Caucasian, white . . . fairly solid built, in his late twenties maybe, something around that stage. Had scruffy kind of shoulder-length hair, not very tidy-looking.' Michael says this meeting happened on Friday, 1 February, the morning that Clinton disappeared.

This evidence, that a white man was seen standing over the body of a black teenager on that morning in Bowraville was not heard at the trial over Clinton's murder. Norco Corner itself is not far from where Clinton had been sleeping in James's caravan on Cohalan Street, and lies between Cohalan Street and Congarinni Road, where his body was dumped. On the face of it then, this information is both 'fresh' and 'compelling'.

As I drive Michael back to Macksville, he says he told the police about what happened at the time they were first investigating Clinton's murder, but no one followed up on it. I worry how that report can have disappeared into silence during the first investigation and then he tells me something else, which makes me pull the car over, switch off the engine and ask him to repeat it.

'Couple of years later, I worked at the hospital and . . . someone was passing me a photograph of some event at Bowraville,' says Michael. 'It could have been a football carnival, I can't remember.' He's frowning at the memory. He says he recognised one of the faces in the photograph as the white man he'd seen at Norco Corner on that morning, and asked who it was.

No one was certain, so they looked at the back of the photo, where several names were written out, and told him:

'They said "Oh, that's James Hide."'

*

Gary Jubelin also thought the Norco Corner evidence sounded 'fresh and compelling'. It was enough to bring new life to the reinvestigation. He also now had new people to pursue it; a homicide detective, Jerry Bowden, and a civilian intelligence officer, Bianca Comina, who had been assigned to the case after Gary had threatened to complain about the way the case was being treated by his bosses. Gary knew them both – Jerry, with his broad-shouldered, wide-smiling, easygoing attitude, and Bianca, who was neat, precise and had proved herself working on other complex and demanding murders. What's more, Gary liked them.

Together, they started to search again through the old boxes and folders of evidence collected about the case, looking for more about this meeting between the two truck drivers and the white man on Norco Corner. To their disquiet, they found a set of handwritten notes dated 1 February 1991 – the day Clinton went missing – describing a conversation between the drivers and the detective who led the first murder investigation.

Bianca also found other documents showing these notes had also been examined during the reinvestigation, when Gary had been working the case as a junior detective, although he had known nothing about it at the time. On both occasions the drivers' claims had been disregarded. What happened? Why had the evidence not made it into the trial over Clinton's murder?

Gary and Jerry decided to ask the detective in charge at the time, whose name was on those handwritten notes: detective sergeant Allan Williams.

*

'I wasn't sure if she would like you,' says Allan, looking down at the Jack Russell twisting itself around my legs as I walk into his kitchen, 'But she seems to.'

Square-set and balding, the former detective takes a seat at a table covered in a pink and green decorative tablecloth. The house is decorated with his wife's artwork and stacks of jars containing coloured stones. Lying on a counter is the printout of a newspaper article with the headline 'Child protection is the hardest job in NSW Police Force'. Allan says he was working for the Child Mistreatment Unit when he was put in charge of the murder investigation. He says it gave him nightmares.

'I'd get home and I wouldn't sleep because it was child murders and I'd dealt with so much child abuse.'

Two plastic boxes of documents lie open on the table. They are filled with newspaper clippings, old police reports and letters relating to the Bowraville case.

'I didn't hide it, didn't steal it,' says Allan, unprompted, about the contents of the boxes. He shows me a formal invitation, received in 1993 and still pinned to its envelope inside a plastic wallet, sent by the families of the missing children and asking him to join them at the opening of a memorial park in Bowraville. Another handwritten note which does not have the name of its author reads: 'To Allan, may we be friends always. You are one of us now. Wait for your initiation. We the family LOVE you very much. Stay well till the road is clear. But stay with us always.'

Allan says he has another six boxes of documents stashed elsewhere in the house.

Gary came here, years ago, with Jerry to talk about the Norco Corner evidence. Allan says that the reinvestigation hurt him. 'I was supposed to be the dill and couldn't track a bear through snow and I got ridiculed.' Digging through the boxes, he pulls out a photograph taken on the day he arrested James over Clinton's murder. There is James, with thick legs and shoulders, a towel covering his head. There's Allan, in a creased suit that sags off him and hangs too long over his wrists. He had a moustache back then but has since shaved it off, which makes him look vulnerable. 'I've got two mates left, including police,' he says. 'Everyone has just walked off and left me because of this.'

I start to record the interview and Allan says he wants to clear up a couple of things, particularly about the Norco Corner evidence.

'This is just a quick list I've made,' he says, pulling out another scrap of paper. 'You're welcome to take any notes.'

Firstly, he says, there's issues with the truck drivers' version of what happened. For example, Michael Scafidi said the Aboriginal teenager they saw lying in the road had his shirt tied around his waist and was wearing jeans.

'I'll take your word for that,' I tell him.

'Clinton didn't have jeans on,' says Allan. When his body was found, he was wearing football shorts.

Allan says he spoke to the two drivers during his investigation of Clinton's killing and showed them six photographs of white men, including James, but they did not recognise him. He says he showed Michael a photograph of Clinton and asked if he could say that was the black teenager he'd seen but Michael couldn't. I wonder why Allan seems so keen to knock holes in this evidence.

'Look, I'm not going to try and blow it out of the water,' he tells me.

He digs again into one of the plastic boxes and show me the formal statement taken when Gary interviewed him about the Norco Corner evidence in 2006.

'Detective Jubelin asked me if I recalled any information about witnesses seeing an aboriginal male lying in the middle of the road with a white male standing over him around the time that Clinton Speedy went missing,' the statement reads. 'I have no recollection of any information like that.' This is confusing. A decade ago, Allan told Gary he had no memory of speaking to the truck drivers, but now, to me, he's talking as if he does.

I start to question everything that Allan's saying. It is impossible not to think that it was him who led the first investigation, which led to James being acquitted. Did Allan charge James without having the evidence to back it? Could he have waited? Why was the truck drivers' account of what happened on Norco Corner so quickly disregarded? Given all the different witnesses who claimed to have seen both Evelyn and Clinton after the parties on the Mission, could Allan have done more to make certain of the evidence before going to court?

Allan shows me how, attached to his 2006 police statement, are a few sheets of paper covered in a neat, old-fashioned handwriting – the tails on each 'f' and 'y' curl around to join up with the letter that follows. Gary brought the sheets of paper with him when he came to interview Allan about the Norco Corner evidence. Gary told him they were notes found in the archives of the first murder investigation.

'I can say that the handwriting on those pages is definitely my handwriting,' Allan's statement records him as telling Gary. 'I have no memory whatsoever of making these notes.'

Today, Allan watches in silence as I read through the documents. At the top of the first page, in his handwriting, it reads '3.30 – 4.30 a.m. on 1-2-91' – the morning that Clinton went missing. Beneath this is an account of a conversation:

I: What's going on mate
H: Oh this bloke is blind drunk asleep here in the middle of the
road.
I: You want a hand to move him
. . .
H: Don't worry about it mate I have rung the Macksville police.
They are on the way out here.
I: See ya later mate – left area

There are also two descriptions. The man is described as:

5-10 – 6´
Solid build – towards fat
Slight beard – few days growth
Round face
Blue type 'T' shirt
Darkish hair, collar length – but shorter – full face
25–35 old

The teenager is described as:

Dark skin
Dark straight hair
No shoes
Laying on his side
T-shirt

And beneath that the words: 'Car. Galant – Mustard.' James's mother owned a Chrysler Galant, I think. He drove it that morning. Clinton's shoes were left behind after he went missing. Another witness said James was wearing a blue t-shirt on the morning Clinton disappeared.

On the final page are the names of the truck drivers, along with their addresses and telephone numbers.

'I had a look at it and I did ask for a statement to be taken,' Allan tells me. He means that, at the time he was investigating Clinton's murder, in the months after it happened, he asked for a formal witness statement to be taken from the truck drivers about what they'd seen.

'Why didn't it happen?'

'Well, I actually marked with a tick that it had been done,' he says, pointing to another handwritten sheet of paper, without a date or a title. This time, the handwriting is different. Block capitals. It reads:

Running sheet last interview
Statement of Levett
Statement of the 2 witnesses
My evidence would be hearsay

Next to each of these there is a little tick in pencil.

'The boys were supposed to get a statement off them, but they didn't,' Allan tells me, as if the list absolves him.

I say, 'But it was never done.'

'It was supposed to be done but I've never seen it. But there was a lot of paperwork.'

This list, I think, is useless. It's not dated, nor contained in an official notebook. It could have been written before or after James was put on trial.

The question of responsibility swirls around us at the dining table. Had formal witness statements been taken from the truck drivers, had this evidence been used during the trial over Clinton's murder, maybe it would have changed things. As it is, James was found not guilty, and the rule of double jeopardy prevents any challenge to that verdict. Double jeopardy can only be overcome if you have 'fresh and compelling' evidence. Only, this evidence is not new because it was known about at the time – Allan took notes of his conversation with the truck drivers. Only, no one took a formal witness statement and it was never heard in court.

It is a clusterfuck.

Whose job was it to make sure this material got into the brief of evidence?

Allan's police statement, from when he was interviewed by Gary, says, 'As officer in charge of the investigation I was responsible for delegating the tasks.'

There is another piece of paper contained in Allan's plastic boxes, which might explain what happened: a one-page statement given by a police constable who was stationed at Bowraville and dated 10 June 1991 – six months after Clinton disappeared. It says that six months earlier, on 25 January, exactly one week before Clinton went missing, the constable was woken at 3.15 a.m. by a telephone call saying someone was lying on the road between Bowraville and Macksville. Norco Corner is on the edge of Bowraville, and the road there heads to Macksville.

In their account, the two truck drivers said the man they saw standing over the black teenager claimed to have called the police.

'You assumed it was the same call?' I ask Allan.

'Yes,' he answers. If it was, then that would mean the truck drivers' meeting with the white man took place a week before and could have had nothing to do with Clinton's murder. The drivers' evidence about how there was a black teenager lying on Norco Corner on that morning could have been dismissed.

Allan had no experience at that time of leading a homicide inquiry. 'Do you think you should have been the person in charge of the investigation?' I ask.

'Look, I was a competent investigator. I'd done a lot of investigations, obviously. It's not that I shouldn't have been in charge.'

I think about everything I've learned about that first investigation: three detectives, all also working other cases. Allan as the commander. No computer. Using a typewriter to take statements. Sketching out their timeline of what happened on butcher's paper stuck to the wall of the police station.

Mistakes were always going to happen.

If he'd been given the resources, Allan says, that would have made a difference. He pulls out copies of old newspaper articles, each preserved inside a plastic wallet and highlighted in pink. One – 'Police probe murder links' – is from a local newspaper about the murder of a white woman in Coffs Harbour, about an hour north of Bowraville. It's dated Tuesday, 12 March 1991, the month after Clinton's body was discovered, and Allan has highlighted the words 'Detectives from the Newcastle Homicide Squad joined the police in their investigations'. To get to Coffs Harbour from Newcastle, he says, those specialist detectives would have driven up the Pacific Highway, past three turn-offs to the town where he was working on a child murder and the disappearance of two other children, but they didn't come to help him.

He shows me another newspaper clipping, again dated from the weeks after the children's murders. March 1991, when he was leading the investigation. The headline – 'New district commander' – has been highlighted and a pink box drawn around the article. It says the new commander 'would like to focus on improving relations between police and the community . . . eradicating drugs, improving family safety, property protection, and road safety.' Allan has scrawled 'No mention of Bowraville' beside it in green.

Tuesday, 6 February 2007

So the Norco Corner evidence was hardly new, but maybe it was 'fresh'.

There was, it seemed, a mischief in the new double jeopardy legislation, which defined evidence as fresh if 'it was not adduced in the proceedings in which the person was acquitted' and 'could not have been adduced in those proceedings with the exercise of reasonable diligence'. The legislation was silent on what the word 'adduced' itself should mean.

Gary Jubelin found different dictionaries provided different meanings. 'Adduced' could mean evidence was tendered, meaning a lawyer asked the court to accept it during a trial, or it might mean that evidence was both tendered and admitted, meaning a judge agreed the evidence would form part of the proceedings. During meetings with the lawyers to ask whether the Norco Corner evidence might still be enough to warrant an attempt to have the not-guilty verdict over Clinton's killing overturned, Gary sat in silence, feeling under water as they rowed back and forth above him.

Finally, after an hour of one such discussion, the lawyers asked Gary for his opinion.

'It seems quite strange,' he told them, 'that I am talking about convicting a serial killer and we are here arguing about the word "adduced".'

What frustrated Gary further was that neither the police nor the children's families could themselves present their evidence to the state's Court of Criminal Appeal, which had the power to over-turn James Hide's not-guilty verdict and order that he face a trial again. To get to the CCA, according to the double jeopardy leg-islation, the case had to be referred to the court by the director of public prosecutions. It was unfair, thought Gary. Murderers, who had been found guilty, didn't need to go to the DPP to ask if they could appeal their conviction. They went straight to the appeal court. Why should the victims of murder not be able to do the same themselves?

Eventually, in February 2007, fifteen years after James Hide was first charged with killing Clinton, the police wrote to the DPP, Nicholas Cowdery, describing how they now had two wit-nesses claiming to have seen a white man standing over the body of a black teenager at Norco Corner, possibly on the morning Clinton disappeared, and asking whether there was now enough 'fresh and compelling' evidence for him to send the case to the appeal court.

Four months later the DPP wrote back saying no.

'Even accepting that any admissible evidence concerning the Norco Corner incident is fresh, in my view it is not compelling in the required sense,' the one-page letter told them.

This was the same office, thought Gary with some bitterness, that had previously charged James with killing Evelyn and Clinton, then dropped the prosecution over Evelyn's murder, then refused to resume this when the police first asked them back in 1999, then overturned its own decision six years later, following the inquest, before putting up a prosecution lawyer who failed to win the case at court.

Although the letter made no mention of the fact, the lawyer who'd been asked by the DPP to review the new evidence and recommend whether or not there was a case to go to the Appeal Court was the same prosecutor who'd led, and lost, the trial over the killing of Evelyn. Gary only learned this later. He couldn't understand it. He didn't believe the lawyer had fought their case hard enough the first time – few people can fight hard enough for Gary – and now here the same barrister was again, saying it could not be won.

The one relationship on which Gary depended was with the children's families. They wanted what he wanted. When Gary broke the news of the DPP's decision to Leonie Duroux, they didn't talk about defeat, they talked instead about who they could find to help them challenge the decision. She wanted to keep fighting.

Leonie started calling lawyers, asking them to help. One of her calls was answered by a volunteer working for the Public Interest Law Clearing House, an organisation that put those who need help but cannot afford to pay legal fees in contact with lawyers who offer to do that work for free. Leonie started to tell the volunteer, Enda O'Callaghan, the story. Enda, a trainee lawyer who'd previously spent years working for TV companies typing up the closed captions for news programs across the country, was amazed he'd never heard about the murders before.

'So where is the case up to?' he asked Leonie.

'You can ring Detective Jubelin and he'll tell you that story.'
Enda did so. Within a year, PILCH had organised for a barrister,
Chris Barry QC, to advise the families.

He wrote a nine-page memorandum, which Leonie passed to
Gary. It said that if the DPP would not refer the case to the appeal
court then they should try the attorney general.

The attorney general also had the power to refer the case to the
Court of Criminal Appeal, the memorandum argued. 'In this case
the murder of three children in what appears to have been serial
murders is a matter which I think would weigh heavily in the minds
of the judges.'

As for 'fresh and compelling' evidence, they had the Norco
Corner evidence, but also the similarities between Evelyn and
Clinton's murders, which had never been mentioned in a criminal court due to the judge's decision to separate the two trials.
They also had Hilton Walker and the prison witnesses, who all
claimed James had told them different things about the killings.
Based on what the barrister had seen of Gary's reinvestigation, he
was satisfied there was enough evidence for the court to order a
retrial over the murder of Evelyn and Clinton. James could then
also be charged over the murder of Colleen, and the three cases
heard together.

'I have more confidence in the jury system and the capacity of
jurors to reach a just result,' the barrister wrote.

Throughout 2008 and the year that followed, Gary and Leonie
spent hours on the telephone together, working out how to mount
their attack. For Gary, this was dangerous. He was out in no-man's

land already, seeking legal advice outside of the police, getting involved with a family's campaigning, way outside the normal lines of police work.

Both he and Leonie knew they needed allies. The process of applying to the attorney general meant going back over years of evidence, analysing the exact wording of the new double jeopardy legislation, as well, ideally, as that of the parliamentary debates during which it was brought into effect. It meant studying legal precedent from both Australia and overseas, then drawing up a formal, written application. Neither he nor Leonie were lawyers and, as Gary looked at the swollen boxes of witness statements, running sheets and court transcripts stacked in the Homicide Squad offices, he realised it would take them months, or years, to do it.

Leonie turned again to the Public Interest Law Clearing House. In August 2009, they put her in contact with a law firm, Allens Arthur Robinson, who offered to do the work.

Leonie's partner, Marbuck, died a month later, on 15 September 2009. He'd lasted longer than the doctors had expected, five years since his diagnosis, but not enough to see anyone convicted of the murder of his brother, Clinton. By the end, as the muscles in Marbuck's throat began to fail him, even his family had difficulty understanding what he was trying to tell them. At night, Marbuck could no longer turn himself in bed. Leonie would wake up six or seven times a night to roll him over. So she was awake around 1.40 a.m. to hear him taking his last breath.

*

In February 2010, nineteen years since the three children went missing, Allens Arthur Robinson wrote to Attorney General John Hatzistergos asking him to refer the murders to the appeal court.

The attorney general consulted the DPP, the crown advocate and the solicitor general. After eight months, he wrote back, saying, 'While there may be similarities and connections in the evidence, I am unable to agree that these are striking and establish a conclusive nexus with James Hide.' As a result, he said, there was no reasonable prospect that James would be convicted should a retrial happen, and so he would not refer the case to the appeal court.

The following year, a state election saw the government defeated. There was a new attorney general, a former deputy director of public prosecutions, Greg Smith. Allens Arthur Robinson wrote to his office again. The children's families also packed into cars and drove the six hours from Bowraville to Sydney to protest outside the state parliament. They stood on the footpath, holding up photos of their murdered children. No one working inside the building came out to talk to them.

This official silence sickened Gary. He started to see every delay and disappointment as evidence that the whole system – the courts, the lawyers, the politicians, the newspapers and television stations who'd thrown themselves at other cases like the Beaumont murders or the killings of Ivan Milat but failed to turn up to cover the Bowraville families' protest outside parliament – was either against them, or simply didn't care. The months, the years if you added them all together, that they had spent waiting for the DPP, or the attorney general, to read their applications and get back to them was offensive. It was as if government officials seemed to think it was right that the killer of three children go unpunished, rather than the courts hear all the evidence they'd gathered in the case.

Whether these politicians and lawyers' fault lay in being too fearful or too formal, Gary didn't pretend to understand them. The repeated experience of being knocked back, and of having to fight his bosses for the resources to work on the murders, made him look at himself differently. He was a cop, but he was at war with the justice system.

To those around him, Gary's reaction seemed predictable. His first response to any problem was to put up his hands and fight.

Gary knew that some of the children's families, the men mostly, thought about other ways to deal with the murders. If it were up to them, they'd told him, all this would be done with. But, instead, they had waited. Wiser voices, the voices of the women, had won out. Revenge is not the same thing as justice, they said. Nothing was going to bring the children back, so they had to believe someone would be brought to justice for the killings instead.

And so the families put their faith in Gary. He'd proved himself. And, as much as Gary felt he was fighting a running battle with the justice system, he was still a policeman. So he told them to do what was right; given the first attorney general they'd consulted had refused to send the case to the appeal court, then they should wait to see what the second attorney general said.

It was a long time waiting. Greg Smith took more than a year and a half to respond to the request that he refer the Bowraville murders to the appeal court. Late in the afternoon of Friday, 8 February 2013, Leonie got the phone call and had to break the news to each of the children's families. In a letter that followed, Greg said the decision had weighed heavily on him but there were 'significant issues . . . relating to inconsistencies in witness' evidence, the effect of the effluxion of time on memory, issues

in credit in circumstances where numerous witnesses had con-
sumed alcohol, the possibility that evidence in the two decades
has been contaminated and the fact that juries in previous trials
have rejected evidence of many of the witnesses whose evidence
is crucial.'

James had already twice been tried and acquitted, the letter
from the attorney general continued. Although you could argue
the Norco Corner evidence was 'compelling', the police had known
about it at the time of the trial over Clinton's murder, which meant
it was not 'fresh'.

'I sympathise with the argument of the families that a retrial
is in the interests of justice, however the legislation does not spe-
cifically address the interests of the families of the deceased,' the
attorney general continued.

Gary looked at the letter and didn't understand it: in 2007 the
director of public prosecutions had said the Norco Corner evidence was 'fresh' but not 'compelling'; now it was 2013 and the
attorney general was saying the same evidence was 'compelling' but
not 'fresh'.

The families responded by organising another protest outside the
state parliament, only this time, rather than huddle on the footpath, they marched up the road from Hyde Park, blocking the
traffic and shouting. For years now they had been inviting government officials to visit Bowraville and talk to them, to no effect. So
this time, they called out, 'You wouldn't come to Bowraville, so we
brought Bowraville to you.'

They made the television news. Soon after, the families were
invited back to Sydney to meet Greg Smith in person.

The meeting went badly.

'I'm afraid there is a lot of imperfections in the law and I'm sure you'd think that this is one of them,' the attorney general told them, talking about the Norco Corner evidence.

'I think we understand that,' said Leonie. But did he understand what the children's families were saying? 'As a white person you can't take away from them what they are feeling and what they have gone through.'

'No, that's right,' Greg told her.

'Are we just supposed to walk away and forget about it?'

'In some ways that is the best thing to do.'

'Some ways!' shouted Jasmine Speedy, one of Clinton's cousins.

'Yes, in the sense of being able to let go.'

'You can't do that when it's three kids!' She stared at him across the table. 'No, that is unrealistic. We can't walk away and forget about these three kids.' Her anger was loose.

'But that's what happens to other people. They have to.' The attorney general had walked into a minefield.

'No!' Jasmine exploded. 'It does not happen to other people. People fight for justice for their families and that's what we want to do.'

'Yes.'

'There is no way in hell we are walking away,' Jasmine told the attorney general. What if it was his three kids who were murdered?

'It would be dreadful, I know. I'd be bitter and twisted and all that, but I'd have to try and let go to get on with my life.'

Thomas Duroux, Clinton's father, had been silent throughout the meeting. He found the whole thing patronising. 'I want fresh evidence, real, fresh evidence, then I would do something,' the attorney general told them as the meeting came to a conclusion.

It had taken Thomas eight hours on the train to get to Sydney that morning. After their time was up, he would travel eight hours to get home again.

Following the meeting, the children's families staged a third march on the state parliament building. This time, a Greens MP, David Shoebridge, came outside and invited them to come inside.

The families sat in the Legislative Chamber, watching as David spoke about the children's murders. He'd seen the families' previous protest outside parliament and been troubled that, despite their raw grief, no one seemed to be doing anything to heal it. Since then, David had worked to establish a parliamentary inquiry into the murders. The families had asked Gary, and he told them this was worth pursuing; anything, he said, that got them some public attention and helped convince the government to act. The inquiry was announced a week after the latest protest, on Tuesday, 26 November 2013.

In May, the inquiry members – seven politicians, from different parties – travelled up to Macksville to hear evidence, including from the murdered children's relatives. Leonie gathered each of the family members around her. 'Make these people cry,' she told them. It worked.

In November 2014, the inquiry reported. It was now three years since the families' first protest outside parliament, eight years since the reform of the double jeopardy legislation, almost two decades since James was found not guilty over Clinton's murder and twenty-four years since the first of the children disappeared. The inquiry recommended that any new application for a retrial over the murders be dealt with independently of the state government;

that the police review how they deal with Aboriginal people; that the government provide funding for memorials to the murdered children and that medical services be provided for their traumatised community. It also recommended yet another review of the double jeopardy laws themselves.

'Further delay,' warned the inquiry's report, meant risking evidence. Witnesses' memories could fade as the years passed, or witnesses might die themselves. Indigenous Australians, like those living on the Mission, die a decade earlier on average than do white Australians. 'Any additional delay is also likely to further exacerbate the pain and frustration already experienced by the three families,' the report concluded.

On the day the inquiry tabled its report in parliament, I sat watching the proceedings on a small closed-circuit television in the media offices on a floor deep beneath the Legislative Council chamber. It was shortly after my first meeting with Gary, who convinced me to start working on the murders. I'd already had a few conversations with the children's families by telephone, and written two articles for *The Australian*. Ahead of me lay my first visit to Bowraville, the decision to make a podcast and the work of researching the first and second police investigations.

That work will make my feelings harden. I will start to find it perverse that it is politicians and their appointments, the attorneys general and the director of public prosecutions, who get to make the decision about whether the appeal court will hear the evidence, rather than a judge. I will also quickly grow to like the children's families. I'll sit with Colleen's brother and sister beside the wide Nambucca River, along the banks of which their family still walk, searching for her body. Evelyn's aunt will clear a space for me at her kitchen table beneath the framed photograph of the murdered four-year-old. I'll look at Clinton's father, Thomas, who always seems to have a grandchild or a great-grandchild in his arms, and ask him how many of both he has.

'Oh dear, now you're asking me. I'd have to sit down and count them all,' he'll tell me, smiling.

Spending this time with the children's families will make me less willing to forgive the official silence they've encountered. The long delays, the rejections, the repeated refusal to find a way to provide justice over the murder of their children, or even to hear the evidence about all three murders at the same time. I will grow angry that so few people have heard about the murders, or that they are not featured every evening on the television news.

In doing so, I will become less of a reporter. I will start to see my reporting and the podcast, when it launches, as being something else. Not quite a campaign, perhaps, but an attempt to answer the silence. I'll become convinced that evidence about all three murders should be heard in court together. Without that, no one is listening to the facts of what took place.

In April 2016, at *The Australian*, as Eric George and I edit the third and fourth episodes of the podcast ready for their launch, I'll ask to interview the former DPP and two attorneys general, who each decided not to send the murders to the appeal court. The former DPP, Nicholas Cowdery, will write back saying he's retired, does not have access to his files and 'my memory is not such that I could usefully contribute to a discussion'. John Hatzistergos will send a message through a press officer saying he 'politely declines your interview request'. Greg Smith will also refuse to talk on the record. I'll call his office and leave a message, then call again a few days later. That time the woman who answers the phone will tell me, 'I don't think he plans on calling you back.'

But on the day they tabled the report of the parliamentary inquiry, Thursday, 6 November 2014, I sat alone, watching that small closed-circuit television as a series of politicians took the floor of the Legislative Council chamber to tell the children's families:

'We have been dismayed by your predicament.'

'Let us ensure that justice is achieved from this inquiry.'

'I believe the families will get justice for their children.'

One politician, a former police minister, got to his feet and said that 'injustices can be recognised and corrected'. Later during his speech, he said, 'My final message is to the person responsible for these murders: sleep with one eye open.'

Only, nothing changed as a result.

Wednesday, 4 May 2016

The coach on which I'm riding pulls off the Pacific Highway, throwing up a cloud of dust. It's now eighteen months since the parliamentary inquiry reported and twenty-five years – a lifetime – since Colleen, Evelyn and Clinton disappeared.

Tomorrow, their families will protest again in Sydney. They've agreed to march down the middle of the road to the state parliament building, holding up traffic through the city centre. Gary has also been working to prepare another application to the current state attorney general, Gabrielle Upton, asking her to overturn the decision of her predecessors and send the case to the appeal court. At *The Australian*, the first four episodes of our podcast are written, edited and ready to go, the fifth still being put together. I want to launch the series on the morning of the protest. As the coach slows and stops inside in the barren lay-by, I watch a small group of adults and children pick up their bags and run towards us through the slanting bars of sunlight. This is no longer just about reporting the murders, I admit to myself. The three of us, police, families and the newspaper, want to make as loud a noise as possible. We all want to be heard.

Which is why I am sitting on the coach. The new arrivals climb on board and find a place to stow their bags and sit. Like almost all of those on board, they are members of Clinton's family, for some of whom this journey to take part in tomorrow's protest in Sydney began at six-thirty this morning, over the state border in Queensland. The other children's families are travelling separately, on planes, trains and cars from across the country. There's not room enough on this coach to fit them. Many of those who have found seats on board have brought food and blankets with them, for it will be night before we arrive.

As the coach swings back into the flow of traffic, I post a series of short updates and photographs of the journey on Twitter. Most of the few followers I have on the social media platform are other journalists and will, I think, either be unaware of tomorrow's demonstration or unconvinced it's worth covering. If I can show them *The Australian* is covering the story, maybe they will convince their own newsrooms to take an interest, too.

Amid the rush to get the podcast finished, this stretch of time as the coach barrels down the highway is the first moment of calm in weeks, and in it I ask myself what I am doing.

Have I been coopted? Have I done nothing more than Gary wanted me to do when we met that first time outside the police force headquarters?

Not yet, because I do not believe that James is guilty. Nor do I believe that James is innocent. His voice is missing from the podcast. The little I know about him has been picked up instead from speaking to different people, or from the transcripts, witness statements and police running sheets I've read. His date of birth – 10 January 1966 – would make him twenty-four when Colleen became the first of the three children to go missing. It would make him fifty now. I know he was born in Sydney and was fourteen when he moved to Bowraville. I know he lived in a caravan on his mother's property and owned a blue Holden Kingswood but didn't have the cash to get it fixed.

As much as I do want the courts to reconsider the murders, reporting this story also means accepting there are weaknesses in the case against James: the lack of actual, direct proof that he attacked the children; the lack of an eyewitness, or any forensic evidence dating from the time.

Is that enough? I ask myself. We are about to launch this podcast and the accompanying newspaper coverage tomorrow, telling the story of the murders, yet I have not spoken to the suspect. I've tried, leaving messages on a landline number, but heard nothing. Do I have only half the story? If only James would talk.

Around me on the coach sit different generations of Clinton's family, some sleeping, others nursing babies who lie sprawled on blankets. Clinton's father, Thomas Duroux, stands in the centre aisle to stretch his legs, one hand dragging down his stubbled face, fingers brushing the darker bags of skin that have collected beneath his eyes.

This will be his fourth protest outside parliament. 'We get pushed back and we still keep going,' he says softly. 'We've got to make the government take notice.' He just wants justice. Outside, the yellow sun sinks against a red sky into a black horizon, as I walk to my seat at the back of the coach, next to one of Clinton's aunties, Dolly Jerome, who is wrapped in a doona and drinking a vodka premix from a six-pack she brought with her for the journey.

'I come down because I'm hoping that this will be the last effort for our family to finally get justice,' she says, when I ask why she chose to make this journey.

'What do you mean by justice?' I ask. To me, justice is a court being able to hear evidence about all three murders together. Dolly doesn't need that. She doesn't need a jury to tell her what happened, she just needs a jury to to say her nephew's murderer is guilty. To Dolly, justice means a killer being sent to jail for life.

Thursday dawns bright and clear and certain. The first episode of the podcast, called 'The Murders', has been published. The newspaper is running an article I filed yesterday from on board the coach, under the headline 'Serial killer probe "tainted by race"'. This quotes the assistant minister for health, Ken Wyatt, saying, 'If this had been three children in Sydney's Point Piper, then would there have been a different approach? . . . There would have been an outcry.' ABC Radio National ask to interview me about the murders along with Evelyn's aunt, Michelle Jarrett, and also play a short section from the podcast. In the excerpt, Michelle is standing in the forest above Bowraville, looking at where her niece's body was discovered, dumped beside the road:

> Her skull and one of her shoes, some bones, some — the shoe and that, but not much of her. It was all mainly skeletal . . . It just kills you that she was just there all that time and we didn't know. We just drove past her all them times and how she would have been out here in the hot and just left alone, thinking no one loved her.

As I leave the radio studio, messages scatter across my phone like stones thrown over concrete. People are listening to the podcast in their thousands. Listening to Michelle describe what happened to her niece.

I hurry to Hyde Park to catch the families' protest. Dolly Jerome is marching in the first line of demonstrators advancing up Sydney's Macquarie Street towards state parliament. She's singing out 'What do we want?' – to which the mob answers 'Justice!' – and holding up her raised fist and forearm, which have been painted white.

Behind her, others among the children's families carry empty lever-arch files representing the folders of evidence about the case that have previously been sent to the the attorneys general. Colleen's mother, Muriel Craig, is there among the crowd in the demonstration. So too is Michelle and Clinton's father, Thomas. Gary Jubelin is watching, wearing a tie decorated with a dot painting, which the families gave him. Outside the locked gate of the parliament, the television cameras circle. A few of the reporters say they'd seen the messages I posted yesterday on Twitter.

Back at *The Australian*, the editor-in-chief Paul Whittaker is listening to the podcast. I file a report for tomorrow's edition of the paper:

> *NSW Police will present an 18-volume submission to the state's Attorney-General calling for a retrial of the man alleged to have carried out the unsolved murders of three children in Bowraville 25 years ago.*
>
> *The submission, drawn up in co-operation with lawyers acting for the victims' families, details similarities and links between the killings as well as evidence uncovered by police that has not been heard in court.*

Later, Paul himself walks past my desk and says, without stopping, 'We're going to put this bastard back in court.'

I stare after him as he heads into his office. I don't know what convinced him. I later learn he had sat all morning with the door closed listening to the four podcast episodes that we have edited, without stopping, while the newspaper's other executives waited for him to chair the morning news conference. My guess is this was the first time he had heard the families speak about their children's murders. It was very hard, I knew, to hear the choke in Michelle's throat as she stood looking at the bush where Evelyn's body was discovered and not want to help her, somehow.

In that moment, Paul shifted *The Australian*'s position from reporting on the murders to campaigning. He wanted a new article about them every morning. I write about the experience of visiting Bowraville, about the details I'd found in old transcripts and witness statements and about the twenty-four alleged similarities between the three children's killings outlined by the police in their submission for the attorney general.

Paul ran these articles, often on page one, under a series of lurid headlines: 'How kids' deaths killed town's spirit'; 'Police list murder links'; 'Cellmate says Bowraville accused admitted killing two children' and, when the relentless press of stories provoked a reaction and the New South Wales Premier Mike Baird publicly committed to refer any application for a retrial to someone independent of his government, 'Baird vow to act on murders retrial bid'.

Amid all this, Eric and I work at editing the fifth and final episode of the podcast. In it, I want to look at the flaws in the police case. Partly, we've left this to last so we can address the balance.

But mostly, I'm still hoping James will talk to us. We need him, innocent or guilty. This story is not complete without his voice. I call James again, but get no answer.

I decide to visit him at home.

The car is pulled over in the shadow of a boat hitched up on a trailer, which I'm hoping will provide us some cover, but I already suspect this stakeout isn't going to work. This tired suburb reminds me of the Mission: single-storey, brick houses. An empty, pitted road. Plastic toys in the front gardens. A community where people know their neighbours, I think. It was a mistake this morning to pick out a car from the work fleet that is too new and too expensive. It was another to wear a collared shirt.

We've been told James is living under a different name in one of the houses opposite, a low-slung building with three staring windows and a carport standing empty. The plan, as best we have one, is to wait until he arrives or leaves, then approach him in the open to ask if he will talk and get a photograph. I'm reluctant to walk up and knock on his door as it would be too easy for him to stay inside and avoid the confrontation. So we wait, relying on the fact that he does not know that we are here.

Two men leave one of the houses, start to cross the road then stop and point in our direction. A woman leans over her broken fence and looks right at us, sitting in the car.

'How long can we sit here before someone gets a message back to James?' asks Eric, who's sitting in the passenger seat with his recording equipment. I don't know, I tell him, but not long. The woman has now walked out of her garden and is standing, hands on hips, still staring, in the middle of the road.

Other people walk out of their houses and stand together, their eyes following where she is pointing at us. One man rolls towards us on a skateboard and slams his hands down on the bonnet of the car.

'What are you doing?' he asks, peering through Eric's open window.

'We're journalists,' I tell him.

'You're not coppers?'

'Not coppers, mate.' He spits. Eric stares straight ahead.

'You look like coppers,' he says.

'Yeah, I know.' I'm thinking about the collared shirt I'm wearing. 'But we're not coppers,' I tell him. 'We're journalists.'

'I'm just saying it's not fucking any good. Someone will be doing something soon if you sit here too long.' Is that a threat? He rolls off on his skateboard. Watching him go, I glance up to the rear-view mirror and see someone standing right behind the car and peering in.

Another man shoves his face through Eric's open window.

'Proof of ID,' he demands. 'Who you are and who you work for.' I show him my work ID-card.

He looks at it for a second, then hands it back and looks instead at the equipment resting on Eric's knees.

'Youse got fucking cameras and just sitting up here,' he says. 'So what are you doing?'

By now, they have the car surrounded. One man shouts that we've been taking photos of his house. A woman shouts out, 'James! James Hide.' I'm startled.

'You know James?' I ask her.

'His daughter and me went through school together so, yeah, I do know the neighbours,' the woman tells me. 'He's quite the lovely man.' I'm thrown.

We want to talk to him, I start to say, but she interrupts me. 'They're very well respected.' An older woman pushes her way from the back of the group and leans down to the window.

'Ah yeah, we know all about it,' she says. 'The Bowraville. Yeah, we know, we know.'

How does she know about the murders? I don't have time to ask. Instead, the older woman is saying James has been her neighbour for twenty years — which would mean since shortly after he was found not guilty of killing Evelyn. 'This guy's been a neighbour of mine and I've never heard boo from him yet, right?' she tells me. 'Always been quiet, well mannered, everything, righty-ho.' Through the gaps in the crowd pressing closer all around us, I look around at the family houses, the children's toys, the swing set in the garden of the house next to James's, and wonder what exactly they knew about the murders, whether they didn't believe it or whether they did not want to know.

Some police who came here once told her what James had been accused of, she says, answering my unasked question. 'I just looked at them and gone, "Him? Oh, you've got to be kidding." I said, "Him next door? One of the quietest people in the street."' She's pointing at different houses on either side of the road surrounding James's house. 'They're all about as quiet as each other.' She gives me a smile.

'Tell me one thing,' I ask her. 'Have you ever asked him about it?'

The younger woman, who first spoke to us, answers, 'No.'

The two women are now the centre of the crowd's attention. The younger stands in the road, hands still on hips. It's not their place to pry into someone's private life, she tells me. 'My daughters play with his grandson.'

My mind is reeling. She takes out a mobile phone. If her daughters were out here with us, she says, she would march them into James's house and wouldn't have any dramas with him being around her children. The crowd around her is now staring at me, blank-faced and hostile. How quickly we've become the target of suspicion. She starts to make a call.

She's trying to tell James we're here, I think. Our cover blown, there's nothing left to wait for. We may as well just go and knock on his door.

As we push through the crowd of James's neighbours, one of the men shouts out, 'You won't get him now, I guarantee it. He don't come out. I've been here seventeen years, I seen him twice.' I open the gate and walk up the little path to where the screen door is standing open. A dog barks. I knock.

'We're not interested,' a woman shouts. The main door slams shut behind the screen. I knock, and knock, and knock. It goes unanswered.

Frustrated, I walk back to the car. The crowd disperses, casting glances over their shoulders as they drift back inside their homes. Once again the road is silent. The older of the two women approaches me and, in a low voice, says that she would like to ask James about what happened in Bowraville. They all have kids, she says.

'By the way.' She stops me as I turn to go. She starts to explain what happened on our arrival, when I parked the car outside one of her neighbours' and that wave of fierce aggression washed over us in moments. 'We've just had the 35-year-old up the road from where you was parked charged for being a child molester. Picked a little girl next door.' Then, she says, when people saw our cameras . . .

'Oh, really?' I say, smiling. 'You thought we were either cops or paedophiles?'

'Yeah. One of them two.' She grins.

The following week, we drive out of Sydney to knock on James's door again, without result. By now *The Australian* has been running articles about the murders daily for a fortnight. Other media have also picked up the story, and are running reports of their own. Having begun this, the absence of James's voice to answer the charges being made against him troubles me. I want him to talk.

Frustrated, we head back to the city and I spend the next day in the coroner's court, going through the old files relating to the murders. Always, the editor-in-chief wants something for the next day's newspaper. I head back to the office, worrying about what I can write to keep the story going. When I get back to my desk, it's early evening and the red light on the phone is shining, meaning someone has left me a message. Something else to deal with, I think.

The voice in the recording is heavy and dull, like stones.

'Hello Dan, this is James. I heard you're trying to speak with me. I think it was you that come to my house yesterday. If you'd like to arrange some time to speak, um, give me a call.'

Tuesday, 17 May 2016

'What do you want to ask me?'

James Hide is on the telephone.

For years until this moment, he's said nothing. The police interviewed him in 1991 about Clinton's disappearance and he gave evidence three years later at the trial over that killing, but he has since refused to talk in public about the children's disappearance. He declined to give evidence either at the inquest or at the trial over Evelyn's murder.

I imagine he is sitting inside the low, red-brick house we visited, where the thin curtains are hanging at an angle in the window and the air-conditioning unit is bolted to the outside wall. I picture him. His voice is heavy and emotionless. This is a chance to ask him everything. I want to know if he killed those children.

'You know what the questions are going to be,' I tell him.

'Well, most of them I can assume,' he says. He knows.

I ask about Colleen, the first of the children to go missing: 'You knew her?'

'Obviously.' She was the niece of a woman he dated on the Mission, the one he had a kid with. I tell him Colleen was last seen walking down the side of the house on Cemetery Road around midnight during the party on 13 September 1990. 'On the night of that party, did you walk down the side of that house to the back?'

'No,' he says. 'I was there at one point that night, but I left early.'

'Before midnight?'

'Well before.'

'Do you know what happened to Colleen that night?'

'No.'

'Do you say you had nothing to do with what happened to Colleen?'

'Absolutely.'

'Can I be blunt with you, James?'

'Yeah.'

'Why should I trust you, when other people say they saw you there walking down the side of the house around that time?'

Finally, he starts to really talk: 'Well, why should you trust that? See, that sort of stuff hasn't been tested —' he means not been tested in court — 'whoever said that has not been questioned, everyone is just assuming that they're right.'

I move on to Evelyn, the second of the children to go missing. She disappeared after another party on the Mission. I ask if he was there that night.

'Mm hmm.'

'You were at the party?' I repeat.

'Mm hmm.'

I say he was seen walking out of the room where Evelyn was sleeping with her mother, Rebecca Stadhams.

'No,' he says, putting the phone down to light a cigarette, then continuing. He says he's listened to the podcast, where we interviewed the woman, Fiona Duckett, claiming to have seen James that night. What she'd said in court was different, James says. In court 'she said that she didn't see me come out of the room. She said that she first saw me when I was about halfway down the hallway.'

I'm knocked back, firstly by the idea that he's been listening to the podcast and then by his command of the evidence in the case against him. It never occurred to me that James himself would sit there listening to the families and the police talking about the murders.

'So you were in the house in the early hours?' I say, trying to find my balance again.

His voice is calm, quiet and insistent.

'No, that's what she said.' She being Fiona Duckett, who said she'd seen James in the house where the party happened, after everyone had gone to sleep. 'I'm not agreeing with that at all.'

'Where were you?'

'Well, I don't know. I don't know what time it was, or what point of the party. We'd been drinking all day, we were all so drunk.' He takes a breath. 'You know, a normal person, an average person's idea of drunk doesn't measure up to what the level of drunk is on that Mission. So, we were all drunk. You know, it's twenty-five years ago. I've got no recollection of times now,' he says.

I'm unsure if I can contradict him. Working from memory, trying to remember the details of what different people told me about that night. Trying to keep James talking.

'Did you go into that room where Rebecca was sleeping with Evelyn?' I ask. Another reporter, sitting next to me, looks over and raises his eyebrows. He can hear what I'm saying and has started to guess who's on the phone.

'No,' James says.

'You're saying you had nothing to do with Evelyn's disappearance?'

'That's right.' If he is unafraid to say it, I ask why he declined to give evidence about her murder when he was put on trial.

'I was never asked,' James tells me. His barrister told him that it wasn't needed. James did not have to give evidence and his barrister didn't want him to.

'Why didn't you want to give evidence? Why not clear it up?' I ask him.

'At that point, it's not about clearing things up, it's about winning the case,' he says. It is a very honest answer.

'How would it not help for you to stand up and say, "This is truth, this is my account, I had nothing to do with Evelyn's death"?'

'I didn't need to testify,' he says. 'It's what it came down to. Because there was just no evidence against me.'

There is a rustling sound, as if James is selecting from a stack of papers. Does he have a stack of court transcripts and witness statements with him? How much of the evidence gathered by the police has he had access to over the years? At my desk I have only a few, bare documents about the case in front of me. No transcripts. I realise I am at a disadvantage. He knows much more about the detail of this case than I expected. He knows, I suspect, more than I do myself.

'I'd say the strongest evidence in these whole cases is the sightings of Evelyn at that shop the next morning,' James says. He means the Reibels store in Bowraville, where the owner and a few kids all said they saw Evelyn after the party on the Mission. The evidence the police now argue must have been mistaken. Because if it wasn't,

Evelyn could not have disappeared from the house where the party was held, and where James was seen.

I try to defend the evidence. When the police reinvestigation went back and checked with those witnesses, I say, it turned out many of them were unsure which day it was they'd seen the four-year-old.

'That's not true at all, that might be what Detective Jubelin's telling you, but that's just not true,' says James. This is the first time he's mentioned Gary. There's something in his voice that makes me think he very deeply dislikes the detective.

'So what did happen to Evelyn?' I ask him. This conversation feels like combat. One throws a punch, the other blocks it.

'I don't know. It's not my place to have a theory.' Like the judge told the jury, James says the defence does not have to say what happened. It only has to show that the prosecution has not proved its case.

By now, several other reporters in the office are listening to our conversation.

'Can we talk about Clinton?' I ask James.

'Go on.'

'Clinton was last seen in your caravan.'

That's not right, he tells me. Two witnesses saw an Aboriginal male out hitchhiking that morning, and the two delivery drivers saw a white man standing over a black teenager lying in the road.

'I've spoken to one of them,' I tell him. 'He thinks the white guy was you, James.'

'He's basing his identification on the supposed photos he's seen years later.' James is now quoting the interview with the truck driver Michael Scafidi we broadcast in the podcast back at me. 'You're a crime reporter,' he says. 'You have to know how sketchy that identification is.'

I know. Eyewitness evidence is often unreliable. Memory shifts and plays its tricks. James, I think, is arguing the evidence, not the fact of whether he committed the murders. But does *he* not have to say what really happened, if he's suggesting that the prosecution case cannot be proved?

'Are you telling me that you had absolutely nothing to do with Clinton's disappearance?'

'Absolutely nothing,' he says.

I ask about Clinton's girlfriend Kelly Jarrett, who woke up in James's caravan with her jeans and pants removed. 'Who took her clothes off, James?'

'It must have been Clinton.'

Then what about Evelyn's mum, Rebecca, who also woke up with her trousers around her ankles?

'I can't speak about that because that's something that I haven't been asked to give evidence on.'

'I'm asking you.'

'I can't speak about that. That's evidence that hasn't yet been entered in the court.'

We are still circling each other. What about the prison witnesses who say he confessed to the killings?

'That is so ridiculous.' One of them, Witness X, is lying, James says. As for the others, he's never heard about them before.

Then what about Hilton Walker, who came forward years after the murders claiming James told him he had bodies buried on Congarinni Road?

That was 'complete nonsense', James says. 'This guy took fourteen years to come forward with that?'

*

The one genuinely powerful piece of evidence to link James to the murders is the pillowslip. The one found stuffed down the front of Clinton's shorts when his body was discovered. The one with the pattern of brown and pink overlapping circles like little butterflies. The one that matched the set on the bed in James's caravan.

When James was questioned by the police in 1991, they had showed him a photo of this pillowslip.

'Doesn't look familiar,' he had told them. Twenty-five years later, I ask him about it again. Clinton's body was found lying in the forest near the Congarinni, I tell him.

'Yes.'

'He had your pillowcase down the front of his trousers.'

'Exactly. The last place when he left was my place. You could say he was looking for something to carry some pot in.' Clinton's body was found near a marijuana crop. 'That's the reason,' James says. This is surely nonsense.

'James, you reckon at four or five in the morning, he wakes up, hungover, walks several kilometres without his shoes on, with your pillowcase shoved down the front of his shorts to try and get some pot?'

'Have you seen the feet on some of them guys up there? They could walk across broken glass and they wouldn't even know it.'

'But that's your explanation?'

'It's not my explanation. It is a theory that's consistent with the evidence.' Again, we have circled back around to this point. He doesn't have to prove his innocence.

'Another theory that's consistent with the evidence,' I tell him, 'is that you killed him, shoved the pillowcase down the front of his shorts maybe when he starts to wet himself at the point of

death and then you carried him out and dumped him on the
Congarinni Road.'

People are now staring at me across the newsroom.

'But if you look at the law, and this is what the judge said in
the trial, if there is a scenario that fits the evidence and is consistent with innocence, you have to find not guilty. That was what the
judge told the jury.'

But James, I say, for what you're saying to be true, which is that
you had nothing to do with all three of these murders, then you
need all these different witnesses – Patricia Stadhams, who said she
saw you walk down the side of the house the night Colleen went
missing; Fiona Duckett, who said she saw you walking out of the
room from which Evelyn disappeared; Michael Scafidi, who said he
saw someone matching your description standing over the body of
a black teenager on the road outside Bowraville the morning that
Clinton went missing; Witness X, who claimed you confessed to
killing while in prison; and Hilton Walker, who said you told him
you had bodies buried out on the Congarinni – you need all of
these witnesses to be wrong, I tell him.

'You need all of those witnesses to have their evidence tested
and some have and come up short,' he tells me.

Talking of court, I ask if he would welcome a court hearing all this
evidence together?

'It's a tough question,' he says. 'Almost as tough a question as
me ringing you this afternoon, whether to talk to you or not.'

Over the years, James says, he's thought about this issue.

'If it wasn't for the strain that it puts on the family, emotionally
and financially, as well as the celebrity —' an odd choice of

word, I think, as if you can call being accused of child murder 'celebrity' — 'I don't want none of that,' he says. Nor, living on welfare, could he afford the motel bills he'd run up to attend the court. 'But then again, I want the actual evidence to be all heard and seen that it wasn't me.'

'You're saying there's a part of you that would like to see this go to court?'

'A small part. We'll put it that way.'

The account of this conversation would run on the front page of *The Australian*. Under the headline 'Trial would clear me: accused killer', it begins:

> *The man suspected of serial killings that have gone unsolved for a generation says he would like the case to be sent back to court, with evidence about all the murders heard for the first time since they took place.*
>
> *James Hide, who was found not guilty during separate trials of two of the three Bowraville murders, said: 'I want the actual evidence to be all heard and seen that it wasn't me.'*

When James and I hang up, I realise the conversation has changed the way I think about the murders. For months, he has been an abstract figure, a suspect, sustained only through rumour, allegation and the evidence contained in yellowing police reports. Now I've spoken to him, asked him questions and heard his answers. I've listened as he spoke about his family. He has children and grandchildren. He has a voice.

For a moment, I stare mutely at the telephone. Why did he call me? Was it because he wanted to tell the truth, or just his version of the story? Truth-telling is all anybody in this story has wanted.

Only later do I realise what James did not say during our conversation. He never asked me to believe in his innocence. He never got offended and told me to go fuck myself when I asked if he was a killer. Nor did he express any sympathy for Colleen, Evelyn and Clinton.

My eyes stray up from the phone to a newspaper cartoon of Lady Justice, pinned to the partition behind my desk. In the drawing, she is blindfolded and carrying her scales in one outstretched arm. The other, the arm that normally holds her sword up ready to punish an offender, holds a child to her chest instead. I realise I am now part of something bigger than a podcast or a newspaper story. The police are trying to convict a killer and I've just spoken to their suspect. It's not just an interview, it's evidence. I pick the phone up again to tell Gary about the call.

Wednesday, 18 May 2016

The morning after James Hide calls me at the office, Gary Jubelin wakes up at 4 a.m. to spend a last few hours re-reading the 150-page outline of the case he plans to submit to the attorney general, calling for the murders to be sent to the appeal court.

Gary and the other two members of the task force, Jerry Bowden and Bianca Comina, have also put together a brief of evidence that fills eighteen lever-arch folders detailing everything they've discovered: how the children all went missing following parties on the Mission; how James Hide was at the parties; James's previous sexual relationships with black women; the allegation that he mauled Colleen when she was sleeping; the way Evelyn's mum, Rebecca Stadhams, and Clinton's girlfriend, Kelly Jarrett, both woke up with their pants around their ankles; the allegations James that would spike people's drinks. It also includes the testimony of the two drivers who saw a white man standing over the body of a black teenager at

Norco Corner. And a statement from a police forensic psychologist arguing all three murders were likely the work of one person, motivated by a lust for sex rather than a desire to kill for its own sake.

We've had most of this evidence for the past decade, Gary thinks as he read through it. We've just been waiting for the politicians to let us take it to court.

The first two pages of the submission contain a list of names and empty spaces. Today, Gary needs to carry this document from one office to another, getting it signed off by those at every level of the police hierarchy, from Homicide Squad commander to assistant commissioner, then deputy commissioner and finally the commissioner himself. So far, the only signature is that of the manager of the NSW Police Operational Legal Advice Unit, who says there is sufficient 'fresh and compelling' evidence to justify a retrial.

For around a fortnight now, *The Australian* has kept the children's murders in its news pages, coming out every morning with more on the story, like a fighter who keeps going, round after round. At the same time, the podcast has grown beyond all expectation. At the beginning, I'd hoped, at best, that a few thousand people might hear it. It passed that on the first morning. Now it has been downloaded over half a million times, across the country and beyond it. People are listening in the United States, in Europe and in China. It's to the point where the podcast has itself become a story. The ABC and Sydney's conservative commercial radio stations call me daily for interviews, sometimes four or five times between the breakfast and drivetime shows.

Together, the newspaper, the podcast and the radio interviews seem to amplify each other. *The Australian*, a broadsheet and a Murdoch newspaper, lands on the desks of the Liberal state government politicians. The podcast is being downloaded by a younger audience, and being talked about on Twitter and Facebook. After I am interviewed by Ray Hadley on Sydney's 2GB radio station, I get a call from within the ranks of the police force to say they listened to the interview. Between the three, it seems, we are being heard.

Though I would be reluctant to admit it, by now, I am really only thinking about an audience of one, the attorney general, Gabrielle Upton. I want her to find the Bowraville murders to be unavoidable. There when she reads the papers in the morning. There on the radio on her way to work. On Twitter when she looks at her phone. My editor-in-chief, Paul Whittaker, is also deliberately targeting Gabrielle, running articles in the newspaper about the murders written by other reporters that accuse her of being 'missing in action' and, worse, needing a 'crash course in how to be colour blind'.

The reason is straightforward. She has the power to refer the case to the appeal court. When Gary hands her his submission calling for the court to reconsider James's not-guilty verdicts, I want her to know the decision will be made in the spotlight. Elsewhere, the constant reporting of the murders has been working. The police commissioner, Andrew Scipione, has said he will go to Bowraville to meet with the children's families. But, in public at least, the attorney general has so far been silent.

Outside Gary's apartment, the sun rises over Sydney Harbour. This early in the morning, he is the only figure moving on the dead-end road that leads to his unit block. Hurrying against the cold, he thinks how, when he started as a detective, it was simple. At work, he chased criminals. Outside of work, he was naive, not racist but he'd make stupid comments, like calling somebody a wog. Bowraville taught him that he was being ignorant. Working homicides taught him about the weight of responsibility placed on you by each grieving family who expected you to find and jail the killer. This work has defined him. He catches killers. You're told not to make it personal but, of course, it becomes that. If you're going to do something, get involved.

Inside his car, the sun dances across the rear-view mirror as Gary joins the stream of traffic heading for the freeway. He thinks that he's become a better person from working this investigation. Perhaps the work contributed to the fracture of his first marriage, and perhaps his second has also now ended in divorce, but he accepts what he has done.

In Parramatta, western Sydney, Gary carries the 150-page submission into the Homicide Squad offices and he asks the commander to sign it. Then he looks at the morning papers. They still contain no word from Gabrielle.

Across the city the offices of the attorney general, a slight, bright woman in designer glasses overlooks the rooftops and roads at the heart of Sydney, near to the state parliament. As a child, Gabrielle Upton was taught by nuns at a Catholic school in the city's wealthy eastern suburbs and she still has something of their earnest, Christian, perspective. Placed on her desk, beside the computer, are three rubber bracelets given to her by the murdered children's families. The black band is for sixteen-year-old Colleen, the yellow band for four-year-old Evelyn, and the third bracelet is red for sixteen-year-old Clinton: the three together making up the colours of the Aboriginal flag.

As a result of the families' relentless campaigning, Gabrielle met with them in the weeks after she took office in April 2015. She wanted to hear their account of what happened, and said little herself during the meeting. Perhaps you could count the words she uttered on two hands. When it was over, Leonie Duroux, whose late partner was Clinton's brother, Marbuck, gave her the three bracelets.

'Don't forget us,' Leonie told her as they left.

Gary gets his signatures. The following day, Thursday, 19 May 2016, he arrives at the Department of Justice offices in central Sydney carrying two cardboard boxes containing the eighteen-volume brief of evidence that accompanies the application for a retrial.

At the front desk, he is greeted by smiles, although he doesn't trust them. Both he and the children's families have got their hopes up too often and been disappointed, he thinks, handing the boxes over. Heading back to his apartment, he changes into running gear and heads out along the edges of Sydney Harbour, driving himself forward kilometre after kilometre, trying to cauterise the anger he's already feeling at how he is sure they are only setting themselves up for yet another disappointment. Afterwards, I call him from the newspaper office.

'I gave a commitment to the families,' he says. 'Not just to myself. That we will continue and take this as far as we can.' I wonder whether this sense of personal commitment might lead him to be mistaken. In the twenty years Gary has now spent working on the case, he's seen the murdered children's parents bent low with age and grief, and watched a generation of children on the Mission who weren't born at the time of the murders grow up to be older than the victims. Has his professional judgement of who carried out the murders been influenced by the families' belief in who is guilty? Has Gary's head-down, fists-up approach meant he has spent so long advancing towards his opponent that he's forgotten to look up and see there's someone else he should be chasing after?

It is now twenty-five years, one month and fifteen days since the police first charged James Hide with Clinton's murder. On the phone, Gary says that Aunty Elaine Walker, Colleen's aunt, told him something at the start of the reinvestigation.

'Justice comes in many ways,' she'd said. He'd kept coming back to that over the years since, turning it over, trying to understand. Now, with the podcast, the newspaper, and the radio stations all talking about the Bowraville murders, he hopes that James is listening. He hopes that James is worried. He wants James trapped inside his house, afraid to leave it, watching reports of the retrial application on the television news. That's a kind of prison, Gary thinks. Perhaps that's a kind of justice. Aunty Elaine never lived to see this moment, he says. They buried her on the anniversary of Colleen's disappearance, on Saturday, 13 September 2014. Gary has kept the funeral notice stuck to the fridge in his apartment.

After speaking with Gary, I start to think about what I can offer for tomorrow's paper. The editor-in-chief wants another story. He wants to keep the campaign going. It's not me driving this anymore, it's him.

Now the attorney general has to make her decision. When Gabrielle Upton met with the murdered children's families in 2015, the sorrow she'd seen in their faces sitting round the table made her fear how she'd feel if the same thing happened to her family. After the meeting she asked the lawyers in the Department of Justice to look again at the case. The three rubber bracelets representing the children continued to sit beside her computer. And, following the state parliamentary inquiry, other politicians, backbenchers and cross-party delegations also came to see her about the killings, all of them asking that a way be found through the tangle of legislation and the decisions of her predecessors that prevented the murders being sent to the appeal court.

Against this, Gabrielle weighed her responsibility to uphold the law itself. The law was like a golden thread, she thought. You can't just break it. If the law said there were not the right reasons to send the case to the Court of Criminal Appeal, then she could not do it. There were many wanting, needy cases that would go unanswered because the law or a lack of evidence said that they could not be helped. She had to do the right thing.

In public, Gabrielle maintained her silence. When *The Australian* attacked her for inaction, she read what was written and it hurt her. Her reasons for saying nothing were, she thought, quite proper: she did not want to prejudge the work of those lawyers who were reviewing the case. But in the newspaper and on talkback radio and maybe in the conversations she guessed were happening between her colleagues in the corridors and offices of Parliament House, she feared these reasons were being upended. There, her silence was being interpreted as either 'I don't care' or 'I don't know what I'm doing' when really, she told herself, she did care and the work was being done.

The real decision was made during a telephone call with her chief-of-staff, himself a former reporter who once covered the trial in which James Hide was found not guilty of killing Evelyn. Gabrielle wanted to know what advice they had received from the Department of Justice's lawyers.

'Are we there yet? Do you think it's an arguable case?' she asked him.

'I think we could get there, but ultimately, you know, Attorney General, it's your call. You can say no,' he told her.

Gabrielle calls the children's families at about three thirty in the afternoon. Members of each of the three families are on the conference call – Leonie Duroux from Clinton's family, Evelyn's aunt, Michelle Jarrett, and two of Colleen's siblings, Paula and Lucas Craig.

'I have good news,' the attorney general tells them. 'I've just signed off on the document to allow special leave to appeal to the Court of Criminal Appeal, seeking a possible retrial.'

There is a silence, then she can hear the sound of people crying.

Sitting beside Gabrielle listening to this sobbing are several lawyers, including Wendy Abraham QC, who has been asked to take charge of the case from here. Wendy has a reputation for her work with serial murders – having prosecuted those found guilty of the eleven killings in South Australia known as the Snowtown murders – and she is there to answer the questions that now pour out from the families: What does this mean? What happens next? Will James be arrested? Will he get bail? When will it go to court?

Wendy explains that the appeal court will be asked to overturn the not-guilty verdicts of the two previous trials, over the murders of Evelyn and Clinton. If the court allows this to happen, they can seek to charge James with all three of the murders together. What happens next will be more work. It will take the lawyers months to go through the evidence and build a case, and for the court to be ready to hear it. It could be a year. They don't know if James will be arrested, probably not, but this is the first time anyone has tried to do this, to make use of the new double jeopardy legislation and have a not-guilty verdict overturned. These are uncharted waters. Please, she says, be patient while we work our way through.

The attorney general often tells herself, 'Don't cry about work,' but this is an exception. Whatever happens, she thinks, this is about seeing justice happen. Whatever the outcome, the appeal court will now hear the evidence about all three murders together. At least now the families would see justice exhaust itself.

I'm standing in the newsroom when Leonie sends a text message: 'She's sending it to the Court of Criminal Appeal, still on the phone'.

Minutes later, when we speak, her words come in bursts. 'I wanted to scream — Really excited — We just wanted that chance to argue the three cases — Everyone was crying —'

Evelyn's aunt, Michelle Jarrett, is also bubbling: 'I'm ecstatic. It's just fantastic news. I never thought we'd get to this stage.'

Then I call Colleen's mother, Muriel Craig, unaware that she was not on the call to the attorney general. Somehow, neither of her children, who were on the conference call, have yet told her the news.

'That's so good, I can't believe it. I'm so happy,' she says when I tell her the decision. She hesitates, her voice shaking. I remember how she once showed me a memorial to her daughter, on the coast near her home in Sawtell, where Bonville Creek runs out into the Pacific Ocean. The memorial is simple: three wooden posts and a bench inscribed with her date of birth and date of death. They used to come here as a family, Muriel had said, and the kids would run ahead towards the rocky headland and wade out into the water.

Standing there, looking out to where the creek meets the ocean, Muriel had told me how she still clings to the little bit of hope that, one day, they might find her daughter's body. She trembled. The hardest part was not knowing, she'd said.

On the telephone, Muriel is crying.

'Now I might at least be able to find out something about what happened to Colleen,' she says.

Wednesday, 25 May 2016

The wave rushes towards us. My daughter laughs and turns away, running up the beach to avoid the crash. I stand facing the ocean and wait for it to hit me. For the first time in weeks, it seems, I'm not at work. Instead, I've brought her down to the bay close to where we are living. Elsewhere, tomorrow's newspaper is being put together without me. There will not be a story about the murders in it.

What now? The newspaper's campaign is over. We got what we wanted. This morning's final front-page headline, reporting on the the attorney general's decision, reads 'Justice over Bowraville murders'. If this were not a true crime story, it might end with that headline. But real life does not end there. People keep living. The children's families are now bracing for the impact of the court.

*

A woman from Bowraville who calls herself Danielle comments on *The Australian*'s website beneath one of the articles I wrote about the murders, calling it 'a total misrepresentation'.

She seems most angry with my portrayal of the town itself. I'd described the fading main street, where wooden-fronted shops stood empty and seemingly abandoned. I'd quoted one of the white people living in Bowraville, who'd sat on his front porch smoking a cigarette and smiled, exposing a ruin of decayed teeth, as he'd told me: 'Why the blacks hate us is because of the Bowraville murders.' I still clearly remember the sense of a community divided.

But Danielle says, 'I have lived in capital cities, inland towns and remote desert and Top End communities, I would say race relations are better here than any other place I've lived – and I'm certainly not saying they're perfect.'

My article described a shuttered garage on the High Street with the handpainted sign saying 'Welcome to Bowradise' hanging in its cracked glass window. It seemed to represent the town around it, broken and unable to move forward. How the modern world seemed yet to come to Bowraville, as if the town was held in place by the trauma of its past. Danielle says, 'If you'd actually taken the time to look more closely, you'd have seen it houses a workshop for some of the most awe-inspiring giant paper lanterns.' Is she right? Did I not look closely? Had I been looking at Bowraville through a lens coloured by the murders and failed to see clearly? I'd seen only shadows. If I was wrong about the service station, maybe I was wrong about the town and wrong about Gary Jubelin, and wrong about James Hide as well.

*

'How can I help you?'

His voice is still dull and heavy. I want to know why James called me the last time we spoke. I'd made his name public as a suspect in the murder of three children, so why would he pick up the telephone, why answer my questions, and agree for the answers to be recorded and played in a podcast, available to any-one, anywhere in the world?

'Kind of things written that aren't true,' he says when I ask him. He mentions other, older, media reports that claimed he had a job working with Aboriginal children after being found not guilty. That wasn't true. 'There's just so much other stuff that I never even got to talk to you about,' he says. Like another old report that claimed the police investigating Clinton's murder allowed him to take a set of weights out of his caravan before they could be foren-sically examined. It seems a minor detail, but James insists the police actually allowed him to keep living in the caravan for weeks after Clinton disappeared, and also to keep whatever clothes he had. But they took the weights and did not return them. That part was not true, he says.

James also denies other stories I was told during the past few months of reporting on the murders. Like when Alison Walker, James's former girlfriend and the aunt of Colleen, told me James was quiet when he was sober but became the devil as soon as he got alcohol in him. Alison said that James beat her and tried to shoot her. On the telephone, I can hear James's laboured breathing.

'I'd never been charged with anything,' he says. It was Alison, he says, who fired the rifle in the house. Later, 'she was going on about wanting to kill herself. I grabbed the gun off the rack and said, "Here, go ahead and do it"'. Only, he'd removed the firing pin by then, meaning the gun was harmless. Alison still reported him, and a police sergeant turned up at the house and took his guns.

I try to ask James about himself. He says his mum and dad split up when he was seven but, really, he wants to talk about the evidence. It seems obsessive, the way he keeps coming back to what people have said about him, either to deny it or to show that it cannot be proved. Particularly, James wants to talk about Michael Scafidi, the truck driver who told me he'd seen a white man standing over the body of a black teenager lying on the road at Norco Corner, and later to have recognised a photograph of James taken at a local footy carnival as the white man he'd seen standing on the road that morning.

We'd broadcast the interview with Michael in the podcast. James heard it.

'I find it hard to believe, or hard to think of what possible photo of me there could be floating around there. I was just as shy of photographs then as, well, even more so now,' he says.

I ask him, 'Why?'

'I don't know. Just shy guy, I suppose. Grew up that way.'

'What else did you want to clear up with me?' I ask him.

'I've just got to browse through this folder,' he replies and I imagine him sitting surrounded by stacks of paper collected over the decades, from the two trials and the inquest he'd already been through. 'I had a little document there somewhere, with just some points in it.' He pauses, his breath rasping over the telephone. 'It's just a point of evidence —'

'Yeah, go on,' I tell him.

After a moment's silence, he inhales slowly and starts speaking: 'In the original trial they said I took Mum's car out to the Congarinni Road' – the red Galant, the one the prosecution claimed was used to dispose of Clinton's body. 'They forensically searched that car inside and out, they even searched under it for specks of dirt from Congarinni Road, for grass seeds.' Anything that would prove it had been up in the forest above Bowraville, where Clinton's body was discovered. 'They never found anything like that, you know.'

I start to argue with him: 'But they wouldn't have done that for weeks, because they didn't discover the body, let alone start looking until then.'

'I just need to go through some of this stuff,' he says, turning away from that discussion and back to the list of things he wanted to talk about. 'The only thing I've got left there is things about Witness X' – the prison witness who claimed James confessed to the murders of Evelyn and Clinton. James says that when he went into prison, his lawyers told him, 'Do not talk about your case to anyone.' So he didn't.

He and Witness X were in protective custody within the prison, James says. There are only three reasons for someone to be in protective custody: 'You've committed a crime, or accused of committing a crime, against children; you are pretty enough to be a possible rape victim; or you are a known police informant. This guy was none of the first two.' So think about it, he says, why would he go up to a possible informant and confess to murder?

Thinking back to Danielle's reaction to my description of Bowraville, and whether I've been looking at this through a cracked glass from the beginning, I ask him, 'You think the cops were having a go at you?'

'Of course,' he says.

'And do you think the cops are still targeting you?'

He is uncertain. 'The original guys, when I looked at the brief, they had charged me before they had gotten back all the results of the forensic tests . . . I don't know whether it was pressure or they didn't have anywhere else to look, or what, but you pile these things up together and you can make anyone look pretty bad.'

If you went through anybody's life as thoroughly as the police did, you'd find something, James says. Especially someone living the way he was, with the drink and drugs and partying on the Mission. 'They've gone into it with eyes directly on me, as if I'm guilty and anything that doesn't match to that theory needs to be discredited,' he says. 'I think the police probably think it was me but I think they've done things wrong.'

James say he's heard nothing from the police or attorney general about the case going to the appeal court. He doesn't watch the news. He hasn't left the house for weeks, since the podcast and our reporting on the murders started.

What impact has it had on him, being pursued by the police over the past quarter of a century? I ask.

'God, well, uprooted from where I was living. Moved to a place I didn't want to go,' he says. But then again, if it hadn't happened, he would never have met his wife, he never would have had his kids. 'So I suppose everything's got to have a silver lining, if you try to find it.' I'm thrown by his sense of acceptance, of optimism almost. James has built a life beyond the murders.

In June 2016, the lawyers appointed by the attorney general begin working on the case. Their job is to convince the appeal court, which will consist of three senior judges and no jury, to overturn the not-guilty verdicts James received in the past, and order that he face another trial for all three of the murders together. They know this will not be easy. The double jeopardy laws were changed ten years before, in 2006, a decade past, but no one before now has actually attempted to use them to overturn a not-guilty verdict. Like James, the lawyers can also see the fault lines in the evidence.

Some witnesses, both white and black, have moved since the murders happened, or grown sick, or died. The tanning factory where James worked has closed and its employees scattered. Some exhibits, the files reveal, are missing. These include the pillowslip found stuffed down Clinton's shorts when they recovered his body.

The lawyers fire questions at the police on the task force, Gary, Jerry Bowden and Bianca Comina: is this all you have here? Can this be strengthened? Are you certain?

Bianca, the precise, bird-like, civilian intelligence analyst, fields the first of what will be dozens of such requisitions for information sent from the legal team over the next few months. She searches through dusty boxes for old records, some dating back to those kept during the earliest days of the first investigation.

Gary is protective of his task force. He likes working with Jerry because, behind his constant smile, Jerry feels his emotions keenly. As a detective working murders, this means he gets angry. Angry that witnesses won't tell him what they know. Angry at prosecutors who don't work hard enough in court to jail the suspects Jerry brings them. Angry that anyone could murder these three children. Anger's good, thinks Gary. He can use it.

Bianca is more diligent than angry and started working homicides almost by chance. She was working as a teller in the Commonwealth Bank when a friend recommended her for a vacancy with the police force. She started doing clerical work, but picked up bits of intelligence analysis and thought, 'This is amazing.' She started to come in on her days off. She took work home. By the time Gary asked her to join the task force, she'd worked as an analyst on several murders. He thought there was no one better at what she did.

Over the years, Bianca has read almost every piece of paper that exists on the murders and she works on the case full-time, unlike the detectives, who must fit preparing for the appeal court around the other investigations with which they are dealing. Ask her about a half-remembered notion that someone saw a white Holden Commodore on the Mission around the time that the first of the children went missing, and she'll respond saying it is in this witness statement, at that line. Say you want to check where exactly the remains of Evelyn were discovered, and she'll send you a text message:

> *Body located 4 kms from Bowraville township, along Congarinni Rd on a dirt track off western shoulder of the road, 48 ms down the track, a further 10 ms into bushland and a further 24.5 ms in a westerly direction.*

Unlike most other analysts, who satisfy themselves with their files and rarely meet the families of those people whose deaths these documents describe, Bianca likes to visit Bowraville. She knows the families. Such is her knowledge of the case, and her ability to swoop down and pick out one piece of information among the thicket of running sheets, witness statements and court transcripts, that Gary and Jerry joke that she is really the officer in charge of the Bowraville investigation. Without her, the lawyers' job would be much harder, if not impossible. Just like the two detectives, they start to rely on her.

I ask to meet Bianca at the Homicide Squad offices in Parramatta, and we sit down in the same windowless room in which Gary first introduced me to the case. Bianca says that when she started on the task force, she'd just done what Gary asked of her, checking information, organising the material they'd gathered. 'I wasn't really involved in the fight,' she says.

At times, Gary had to also fight to keep her, when his bosses tried to move Bianca onto some other murder investigation. A year or two ago, Bianca started thinking that even his efforts couldn't last forever. She cared about this case. She decided to do everything she could to see it get some resolution. This was their last chance.

After our conversation, Bianca sends me an email: 'I forgot to say that I am married.' I read on, puzzled. 'Our marriage has been shaky for the last couple of years, and this has coincided with working on Bowraville, it is not the cause of our difficulties but my husband often says I put the work before him.'

I know, from speaking to Jerry, that sometimes she has been in tears when Gary has been driving her to keep on working, which means another late night, or losing another weekend. I know that sometimes he has also taken out his own frustrations by criticising her. He needs her, says Jerry. He couldn't do the job without her, but it is almost bullying at times.

'On a lighter note, when I talk about this job my stepdaughter says she wants to be a detective, my younger children will call me in when Gary is on TV. They also think he is amazing,' her email reads. Right now, she wants to solve these murders. 'When my husband rolls his eyes, that's my cue to stop talking about work.' However hard it is that Gary drives her, she also knows he's driving himself harder. And they need to drive themselves right now, whatever the impact of that at home.

'We're hanging in there, just,' her email reads.

So much hangs on this appeal court hearing.

*

In Sydney, waiting for the lawyers to prepare their case and the court to schedule a first hearing, it feels like it has been too long since I was last in Bowraville. Perhaps the decision to send the murders back to court has changed it. Perhaps some of the shadows have disappeared.

I contact Danielle, who wrote the comments criticising my description of the town in the newspaper, and we speak on the telephone. She is defensive at first, then angry. Did I need to mention the rotting teeth of one of the men I spoke to? Did I need to write about the bare-chested men drinking in the street, or the businesses that had closed down? Maybe I was wrong to, I say. Having arrived to report on an unsolved triple murder, maybe that crime became the lens through which I looked at Bowraville itself. Danielle is not impressed with my explanation. A quick fly-by from a Sydney journalist that ridiculed their town has done them no justice, either, she says.

I tell her that I'll try to look more clearly when I return.

'You're coming back?' She sounds surprised. Then cautious. 'Well, have you heard about the fourth victim?'

No, I tell her. Danielle says the victim's name was Craig.

In my mind, the shadows return to Bowraville. It's not a matter of not seeing things clearly, there are parts of this about which I know nothing at all.

Saturday, 4 June 2016

Go looking, and rumours about a fourth murder victim are everywhere in Bowraville. He had a shack down there on the Mission. A blackfella. James Hide knew him. He and James were mates, they used to smoke together. James knew something about what happened to him. No one ever caught the killer. James did it himself.

But nothing is substantial. The strangest part, speaking again to the people I met the last time I was here, is how few seem to question the story that there was another murder. That another person died and nothing happened. Walking past the old garage on the main street with its ' Welcome to Bowradise' sign, sun-bleached, corrugated iron roof and two dead bowsers standing on the footpath, I see that Danielle was right. Inside, in darkness, hang giant, ghost-like paper lanterns. Only, they give no light. That's just how it is in Bowraville, it seems.

I visit Michelle Jarrett, aunt to four-year-old Evelyn. Last time,

she was my guide around the town. She showed me the Mission
and took me up into the forest, where they found the bodies. This
time, I realise that her house stands on Norco Corner, opposite
the service station. It overlooks the place where Michael Scafidi
said he saw a white man standing over the body of a black teen. In
Bowraville you can't escape the murders. You live on the same street
as where they happened, or where James's family lives, or where a
white man was seen standing over the body of a black teen.

A small dog barks in fear and anger until it's silenced by a shout
from inside the house. When I walk in, Michelle is sitting at her
kitchen table with her sister Rebecca Stadhams, Evelyn's mother,
surrounded by sheets of A4 paper covered with designs that Rebecca
has drawn. Rebecca says they're for her daughter's memorial. The
2014 parliamentary inquiry into the murders recommended that
the government provide funding for a memorial to be built for
each of the children. Colleen's stands near where Bonville Creek
meets the Pacific Ocean, near her mother's home in Sawtell, where
she taught her younger brother Lucas how to swim. Evelyn's will
be built here, in Bowraville. Clinton's will be up near his mother's
home in Tenterfield, in parkland overlooking the creek where he
used to do backflips and somersaults into the water.

Another memorial, to all three of the children, already stands
down on the Mission. Then there's the homemade monument to
Clinton that his family built out of a scaffold pole and sheet of
painted metal, standing up there in the forest where they found
his body. The geographies of the children's young lives and deaths
marked out so people don't forget them.

Rebecca shows me one of her designs, which has a flock of
pink and purple butterflies. Because, she says, Evelyn would flut-
ter around her, and had a gentle touch. Another shows a white

dove encircled by an orange snake, with a wide red-and-yellow fish suspended in the space above them. The carpet python is the Ballangary totem, says Rebecca, while the red bass is the totem of the Buchanans. The totems are inherited by each person in these families, and help define their responsibilities and relationships to each other and to the country around them. There are other totems, also, outside a person's family. All Gumbaynggirr people have the gaagal, the ocean, as their totem. All Gumbaynggirr men have girrimarring, the bat. All Gumbaynggirr women have the niyin, the tree-creeper.

I've heard these names, Ballangary and Buchanan, elsewhere on the Mission. Michelle says the Buchanans came from north of the Nambucca River, which runs through Bowraville itself, while the Ballangaries came from the south of the river. The Ballangaries are mountain people. The Buchanans are an ocean people, says Michelle. Later, I ask an elder about this explanation, who smiles and says, that's right, but it is a simple way of understanding something much more complicated.

Michelle pulls a computer across the table and opens a folder on the desktop containing the images of old sepia photographs showing their great-grandparents, two stern couples staring at the camera.

'Their two kids,' says Michelle, pointing at one couple, 'had to marry two of these fellows' kids,' pointing at the other. In each generation, children from one side of the river had to marry children from the other side. Most people here can trace their families back to one or the other.

'Who said they had to marry?' I ask.

'It was just the lore,' she says. 'Traditional. And its lore, not law. L–O–R–E.' This time, having returned to Bowraville, I sense she wants me to understand more about what I am getting into.

I ask about the possible fourth murder victim. Michelle nods and looks at Rebecca for a moment before speaking. They have also heard that story, Michelle says.

I tell them what I've been told. Which isn't much. Just a handful of rumours and that the victim's name was Craig. Michelle leans forward and crosses her arms, resting them on the kitchen table. Craig was her cousin, she says, looking straight at me. He was a Ballangary.

Craig's father raised Michelle and Rebecca up in the house across the road from that in which we are sitting. Their own mother wasn't always around when they were younger, so they lived there with Craig.

He was found hanged in a shack behind the Bowraville Mission in 1989, Michelle says, almost a year before the first of the three murdered children went missing.

Rebecca's youngest daughter walks into the kitchen and opens the fridge. She's five, a year older than Evelyn. Her mother tells her to take some chocolate and the young girl grins. Michelle frowns at this indulgence, waits until the girl has left the room clutching her chocolate in both hands, then continues to talk about her cousin.

Craig and James were mates, she says. They grew yarndi together. Word spread that Craig worked for James, selling yarndi, or that they even shared a girlfriend. Craig had dated Kelly Jarrett, who later went out with Clinton, she says. Perhaps they are referring to her. Another rumour was that someone saw James near the shack on the day that Craig was hanged. Michelle looks at me for a moment, then suggests I speak to their uncle, Craig's father, who looked after her and Rebecca when they were kids. His name is Fred Walker.

Fred lives in a small estate of houses in Nambucca Heads, where the river running through Bowraville empties into the ocean. When I arrive, he welcomes me into a darkened living room, the curtains drawn against the sun, the corners of the walls retreating into blackness. Fred's in his sixties now and says his health is failing, but he smiles still at the memory of Michelle and Rebecca as children, living with him and his family.

When Rebecca became a mother to Evelyn, Fred also often looked after the toddler. Evelyn was staying at his house the week before she disappeared. Rebecca had been out of town for something, Fred says, but she came home. She came to his place and took her daughter with her to the Mission for the party.

Fred was there the next day, when they reported Evelyn missing. After they found the children's bodies, he became a police liaison officer, trying to bridge the gap between black and white, trying to hold the community together. The Mission changed, he says, after they brought the dole in after 1960, and the grog followed and everyone was fighting.

'I'll tell you something now,' he says. Whoever killed the children, 'I think he'd done it before this.'

He's talking about Craig.

Fred says his son and James were always together. James spent a lot of time out there in the shack Craig had in the bushland out the back of the Mission. On the day Craig died, Fred says his son came to him and said Fred owed him money, and could he buy him some oranges?

Craig said that he would be up on the Mission. But when Fred arrived with the oranges, he couldn't find him. 'That was the day he went. The last time I seen him.'

I ask him if he thinks the police did a good job of their investigation.

'No,' he says. The local constable showed up. 'They didn't do any forensics or anything.'

Later, I will read the coronial file into Craig's death, which includes the police record of this investigation. It's only fourteen pages long, including several pages written in the constable's note-book after he cut down the body in the early evening on Sunday, 26 November 1989. On these are a single, rough sketch of inside the shack, showing a mattress, what looks like it could be a stool and a child-like drawing of a man with curly hair hanging from a rope slung over a rafter, stick legs splayed out on the ground in front of him. There are no photographs and, like Fred said, no forensic evidence from the scene.

After he returned to the Bowraville police station, the constable typed up a report saying:

> *It would appear that he tied the rope to the rafter and then sat on a wooden platform that was used as a bed and had a mattress on it, this platform being 1.2 mts off the ground, whereby he then proceeded to slip or jump from the platform with the rope around his neck.*

The report said, 'A thorough search of the hut failed to locate a sui-cide note or any thing of a suspicious nature,' although he had found a few grams of marijuana. Another man – not James – had found the body, and told the constable that 'the deceased had informed him some four months ago that he had tried to hang himself as he got "a buzz" out of it'. There is little evidence in those fourteen pages of any other, real investigation: The file also contains a two-page autopsy report, which is handwritten and in places illegible, but says the cause of death was 'asphyxia due to hanging' and that it may have taken Craig half an hour to die. I will stare at that conclusion. Half an hour, when his legs were resting on the ground?

Perhaps that's right. Ultimately, the thin inquest file says little about Craig's death. It contains no evidence that he was murdered. No evidence he committed suicide. There is little solid evidence, in fact, of much, and little to suggest the police spent much time or effort trying to be certain of the actual cause of death. No interviews were done with his family or friends. No search was made of his room or possessions. As I turn the pages, I will feel ashamed that anybody's death could be treated so briefly. For me, the discovery is not how Craig Ballangary died but how little the police seemed to care.

'After they took his body out of that shack, somebody went and burned it down,' Fred tells me.

'Somebody burned the shack down?' I ask, surprised. There is no mention of this in the police report. 'How long after?'

'The next day.' Fred went out there to look and it was gone. 'Someone went out and tipped some stuff over it. That night they must have burned it down,' he tells me.

'So all the evidence was gone?'

'Yes.'

The official finding of the inquest into Craig's death was that 'he willfully hanged himself' sometime between Saturday, 25 November and Sunday, 26 November 1989.

'I'm sorry. I'm really sorry,' I tell Fred, feeling helpless. His son was twenty at the time. I wasn't wrong when I visited Bowraville before and saw a darkness, I think.

God knows how Fred himself must feel.

*

There's a term for what this community is feeling, says Barry Toohey, exhaling cigarette smoke. 'Chronic collective grief.'

We're sitting outside his house, high on the hillside above Bowraville, watching the sun sink through the forest. Cattle are lowing somewhere in the fields beneath us.

It was the detective, Gary Jubelin, who first suggested I meet up with Barry, the last time I was in Bowraville. Barry knows everyone, Gary had said, and he understands blackfellas better than most white people, the result of working as a grief counsellor with the children's families after James was found not guilty of killing Evelyn.

Back then, Barry had been based in a little clinic on the Mission. When I met him, during that first visit, he was newly retired but had still used his connections in the community to help me find people to interview. A tough, sinewy bloke with a wild smile, like Michelle, Barry acted as a guide and never asked for anything. It seemed enough that I was trying to tell the story of the murders. On this trip, he's invited me to stay with him and his wife, Monica Pullen, an Aboriginal woman and a nurse, who grew up on a mission herself in the nearby town of Kempsey.

To get up to Barry and Monica's, you drive out of Bowraville and follow Congarinni Road deep into the forest, between thick bars of eucalyptus trunks. After a few kilometres the road forks at the quarry, the left turn leading to where Evelyn and Clinton were discovered and the right becoming rutted, where the car wheels bounce and spit out dust and stones. Here, the gum trees seem to crowd in closer. One final turn, up onto the high point of the ridge, takes you into a little clearing. There is the house that Barry built; a long-handled axe is buried in the chopping block outside.

'To understand chronic collective grief, we can go back to colonisation.' Barry stubs out his roll-up. His voice crackles as he talks.

'So the effects of that two hundred years, and then the effects of ongoing racism, poor housing, poor health, those layers impacted. And then add this, these tragic murders.'

The layers weigh down upon each other. Unable to escape, the trauma spreads throughout the community, until everybody feels it. Bowraville is only a small town. There's little work and, apart from the school bus, no public transport to leave it.

I tell Barry about Craig Ballangary, and how his shack burned down and the police did not launch an investigation. It shocked me, I tell him. Perhaps it helps explain how, when Colleen and Evelyn went missing, there was so little reaction. Barry nods, holding a thin paper in the corner of his mouth while shaping a line of tobacco in one palm to roll another cigarette. The rest of the world might be changing, he says, but here in the Nambucca you still get the same racism.

He talks about going into a shop in town, where a blackfella was queueing ahead of him, only the shopkeeper tried to serve Barry first. Or when an Aboriginal woman put out her hand to take her change, only to have the money placed on the counter instead.

'Oh yeah, it's still alive and well,' says Monica, who sits curled up on the sofa. Her daughter wrote a school essay once about how Monica's bags get checked every time she goes shopping.

There're different forms of exploitation. Monica looks at me. Have I thought about what I can do for the murdered children's families?

The question brings me to a halt. I hadn't. The podcast might be finished, but I still expect to cover the appeal court hearing for the newspaper. I'd thought the families would be pleased that I would do so. I'd given no thought to what they might get from me in return.

Don't just be another white reporter who comes out here, stays a couple of days, then leaves and they hear nothing from you, Barry tells me. Monica is nodding.

'You need to ask them, "What can I do for you?"' she says.

The question unnerves me. What if they ask for money? What if they ask for something else entirely? Something which I cannot give them? Monica must be able to see my confusion. 'You need to ask the question,' she repeats.

That night, I lie in my little bedroom, where the heights of Barry and Monica's children at different ages have been marked in pencil on the doorjamb. Monica's instruction is running through my mind. She's right, I think. I owe it to them. I came to Bowraville, asked questions, then went away and took their answers and published them, but never asked what I could do for the families in return.

When I wake up in the morning, the wind carries the smell of bushfire with it and, outside, the sun rises through a pall of smoke. A kookaburra swoops down from the forest, barking. A four-foot-long goanna is marching across the garden. The lizard looks up at the bird and hisses. The kookaburra wheels and launches itself again at the goanna, defying this invasion of its patch of land.

Sunday, 5 June 2016

The first time I met Martin Ballangary, he challenged me, 'Try and find a white man who's been jailed for murdering a black man. Because it hasn't happened.'

We were standing outside Fred Walker's house, where I'd been talking about the death of Fred's son, Craig. Fred and Martin were old mates and, when Martin arrived, wearing a Hawaiian shirt, red shorts and round, John Lennon sunglasses, I got the sense he wanted to check out the interloper who had come to ask his friend these questions.

In that moment, I could not think of a single white man who'd been jailed for killing a black person.

'I'm sure it's happened,' I'd said. Martin shrugged.

This time, a few days later, I have got an answer: five white men who killed a black man who they attacked in a dry riverbed in Alice Springs in 2010. They each got between four and six years in prison. I've arranged to meet him again, in the Bowraville Hotel, where scattered groups of solid, sunburnt people are drinking in fluorescent work gear after a day spent working on the roads.

But Martin is not impressed.

'Maybe that did happen that time, but it never used to,' he says, dismissing the subject. He refuses my offer of a drink. 'This is redneck through and through,' he says, looking around the hotel and scratching at his stubble. We leave, buy pies and a sliced white loaf at the bakery opposite, then sit together on a bench overlooking the empty main street. A sports car hoons across both lanes beside the town's clock tower, wheels howling as the driver guns it down a side road.

'If that was a blackfella, he would have been booked by the police,' says Martin, wrinkling his nose. I feel myself bridle at this prejudice but say nothing. When he learned that I was planning to meet Martin, Barry Toohey, who I'm staying with, nodded his encouragement. Martin's an elder, he said. If I am going to spend time with this community, and keep reporting on the murders, I needed to pay my respects.

Martin leads me across the road towards the town cinema, and points through a metal gate to where Aboriginal people used to enter through a side door to sit on wooden chairs behind a rope. Martin says he was a boy when the bus carrying the Freedom Riders arrived in 1965, and the activists on board it took him in with them to buy a ticket, then went up and sat in the cushy seats reserved for the white folks. He wiggles his hips from side to side, grinning, to show how comfortable they were.

'And then the bloody police come in: "Get out, you little black bastard."' He makes a jabbing motion with his hands, acting out the way the police had shoved him. 'Poked me out. You wonder why I hate the police?'

We get in the car. I drive, he eats his pie between two slices of white bread and directs me to the old hide factory, where James once worked and which now sits silently behind locked gates. Martin points down the hillside to our left across which runs a pair of barbed wire fences.

'Access to river's fenced off,' he says.

'Why?'

'Because the council are dickheads.' He's silent for a moment, staring. 'Used to walk across here to go swimming. Family, all big family, used to come here from the Mission. Used to be big tribe but since, whitefellas put up all the bloody gates.'

He wants to show me the river, so I turn the car around and drive to where the road meets the treeline. We get out and Martin leads me down an old vehicle track that falls away over a few dozen metres to the riverbank. As a child, Martin says that he would walk with his father and uncles all the way from here to the coast at Nambucca. As kids, he says, they came to play here at the river, but never to camp. Not without the elders. A gumburr – a bad spirit – walks up and down the river, stealing children.

'You won't see him. You feel him,' says Martin, nodding at the trees behind us, which bend down so low their green limbs almost touch their own reflections in the water. This gumburr can change himself into a little girl or boy, so that he can get right in among you. Gesturing at my feet with the hand holding the pie sand-wich, Martin says that the only way to know that he is there is when you look down at his feet, you see he's got a cloven hoof. 'He got devil-foot. He a demon-foot,' says Martin. Never leave your clothes, because the gumburr will pick them up and then he'll come and attack you at night. Never leave your footprints. He looks at a tree where a fork in the trunk has left a space just large enough for something child-sized to crouch there. 'He is up there. Sitting there, watching you.'

If the gumburr catches you, you lose your mind, or die.

Martin hands me a camcorder and walks away, towards the water's edge, telling me to film him and that I can get a good shot where a fallen tree leads the eye down towards the river.

I press record and he leans into the frame, grinning: 'I got to go down to get blessing from the water.' He kicks off his Crocs and wades out up to his knees, bending to cup his hands and calling out, 'Legs! Arms! Face! Head!' as he scoops up the river, using the green water to clean each in turn.

Afterwards, he walks back up the bank, water running down his face from the tightly twisted curls of white hair. I stop the camera and he looks at me. I ask what he was doing.

'Why do it? Because my culture. To keep you safe while you do what you got to do here. Gumburr get your smell, he smell you.' Martin says he needed to do this with me so I know where I stand. He's not a Cleverman, he says, but he knows protocol.

None of this is fully explained. Nor do I know how much he knows about me and the reporting I've been doing. Bowraville, and particularly the Mission, are small communities so he must have been told something, but I don't know if he's been asked to bring me to the river today, or if this is something he chose to do himself, or if he's mad, or winding me up, or how exposed I am to the gumburr, or if the lore says all visitors to Bowraville should receive this protection. I realise just how little I understand about this place and its people.

I think of what Barry and Monica Pullen told me, about not being just another white reporter who turns up, then goes.

Squatting down on the riverbank, I tell Martin that I know I have asked a lot of the people in this town, with all my questions about themselves, their lives and the murder of their children. I ask him, 'What can I do for them in return?'

'You know what you can do.' He looks straight at me. 'We've trusted you so far, hey? You keep going.'

Thursday, 11 August 2016

'Police brought racism into all this, people tend to forget that. It was actual police, not the people of this town,' says Michelle Jarrett, standing at the sink in her kitchen. The police commissioner arrives in Bowraville this afternoon to say that he is sorry. Michelle, whose four-year-old niece Evelyn was the second of the murdered children, runs cold water into the kettle and stares out of the window at the empty fields.

Outside, the winter has been a long time going. The brown leaves are dying on the gum trees and a faint frost is lying on the ground. Inside, the metal stove near the table is heavy with last night's ashes, while magazines and books and ornaments loom in untidy piles on the kitchen furniture where Michelle stacked them before the decorators came in the day before I got here. The room still smells of the fresh, white paint that they left on the walls.

Michelle breathes heavily and leans on the sink to support her weight. 'It was the police who told us our kids went walkabout, the police who ignored us,' she says. It's too late now for an apology. She fetches two mugs from the cupboard and bangs them down upon the countertop.

On one of the piles of her possessions sits a framed photograph of Evelyn wearing a neat pink cardigan and smiling, her hair clipped up, her brown eyes looking past the camera. Michelle sees me looking at the portrait, then hands me a mug. Her eyes are brown like her niece's, only with shadows on the skin around them. On her neck I notice the line of scar tissue where she had part of her thyroid gland cut out a couple of years before, leaving her voice with a rasp, particularly when she is angry.

'Our kids weren't even kids, they were just blackfellas who went walkabout,' says Michelle. That was how they got treated. That was what the police told them. She wants the police commissioner to know what her family put up with and how it made them feel.

Thomas Duroux stands outside his house on the Mission, watching a group of men in hi-vis jackets mow the grass ahead of today's visit by the police commissioner. Thomas has lived here since before his son Clinton went missing. Over that time, his home's become surrounded by plastic chairs and garden ornaments, an oar, a pair of boats, a beaten-up Holden ute, four more cars, some tyres, a jack, and a street sign lying in the garden. The layers of possessions settle down upon each other.

'We've been trying for years to get him up here,' he says, meaning the commissioner. Twenty-five years ago, Thomas was part of the big mob who marched from the Mission to Bowraville's police station demanding that they do something about the missing children. 'That was the only way we could get an answer from them,' Thomas says. He'd watched the police inspector walk out in the rain to meet them. Maybe the man was frightened, Thomas thought afterwards, because he was just a skinny bloke.

A naked, blond-haired child runs out of one of his neighbour's gardens, pushing a tricycle along the footpath. A woman walks behind him wearing a blue dressing-gown and a man follows and starts screaming at the woman: 'Shut your cunt! Shut your cunt!' She says nothing. He stands on the grass verge, shouting, a green bottle swinging from one hand.

'Drunk,' says Thomas, frowning. It's nine-thirty in the morning. 'It was his birthday yesterday but it should be over.' The man is Aaron, Evelyn's brother, who was a year younger when she was murdered. I remember their mother telling me how the two of them used to be so close, like two peas in a pod. You couldn't part them, she'd said.

Thomas's own two-year-old granddaughter stands watching the confrontation from his open door. Another child, her brother, is in the front window, crying. The blond child ignores the two adults on the street and plays with his tricycle. I think of what Barry Toohey told me, about how trauma ripples out through the community, and if you could follow ripples back, you'd end up at one summer when three black children went missing and the police did little to investigate.

I ask Thomas what he thinks about the commissioner's plan to apologise for the way the murders were handled.

'What can they say?' he answers. It's now twenty-five years later. 'I don't think it's up to him. He wasn't in the picture at the time.'

*

On the grass opposite Thomas's house, beside the memorial to the murdered children, Martin Ballangary is burning gum leaves on a tripod made of spears, one each for Colleen, Evelyn and Clinton. Dozens of the children's relatives, some of whom have driven for hours to be here today, stand around him. Martin, who took me to get a blessing from the river, says this ceremony is different. The smoke takes with it sins and ghosts, he says. Only the police commissioner, Andrew Scipione, is late arriving.

'Where's that Skippy?' Martin mutters, dousing the flames.

Time passes. Eventually a convoy of cars swings down the road from Bowraville and Martin blows on the flames again to whip them higher. The cars roll to a halt and Andrew gets out in his blue uniform, walking over the grass to meet Michelle, who is wearing a bright pink t-shirt with a photograph of Evelyn. The commissioner also meets Evelyn's mother, Rebecca Stadhams, then shakes hands with Thomas and with Muriel Craig, Colleen's mother, who thanks him for coming.

'Thank you for letting me,' he says.

Standing at a small lectern that's been placed on the grass beside the memorial, the commissioner is encircled by the watching families. Ash from the burning gum leaves settles on our shoulders. Around me are several television news crews, waiting to record the commissioner's apology, and advance copies of his speech have been handed out to the reporters but, almost immediately, he starts to go off-script.

'I want to pay my respects,' Andrew tells the families. 'I want to acknowledge that for twenty-five years you have been fighting for justice. A dignified and committed fight for the truth about what happened to your children.' Among the crowd, there is a shift in the silence. People are listening more intently to his words than a moment before.

'I want to publicly acknowledge that the New South Wales police force could have done more,' Andrew continues. 'We could have done more for your families when these crimes first occurred. We should have done more. I know this has added to your pain.'

He looks up from the words written in front of him. 'And can I say to you that I am sorry,' he says, looking at the families.

Reading the prepared version of the speech that we've been given, I can see that he has now left it behind him completely. 'I'm sorry that you had to endure that. No one should have to endure that and it's important you understand that I'm looking you in the eye and saying that I'm sorry.'

The crowd holds its breath. He repeats those words – 'I'm sorry' – four times over. He thanks Gary for the work he has put in to set right those mistakes and find the children's killer. 'You accepted him,' Andrew tells the families, 'and he's helped you to get to where you are today.'

The police force will not forget the murdered children, he says. 'We will continue to do everything possible to find justice.' Afterwards, Andrew carries a wreath of flowers through the smoke to the children's memorial. Everyone is silent, other than the television crews who stand on the fringes of the crowd to record their reports: 'Today, the police commissioner has renewed hope that the families might finally find justice when these cases go to the Court of Criminal Appeal.'

Martin extinguishes the fire and takes a single red chrysanthemum, which he adds to those at the memorial. Michelle is crying. She says that, whatever she had been expecting, to have someone finally admit that the police had done the families wrong feels like a stone pressing down upon her heart has been removed. For the commissioner to come here and apologise in person means the police are now prepared to treat the Mission as their equal. It will not repair what happened, but it is one less thing for Michelle to be angry about, she says.

Thomas is also quietly impressed. He talks again about that confrontation between the mob and the lone police inspector after his son went missing, and the months that followed. Back then, the two sides were antagonists, he tells me: the police doubting what the families were saying and treating them as suspects, the families convinced the police treated them differently because of their race.

'It took a while coming but we finally got an apology,' says Thomas. 'It gives us a better understanding of the police. We know they've done a hard job,' he says.

The lectern is deserted. The people who came here to watch the police commissioner begin to drift away. Elsewhere in the park, children start playing footy. Andrew himself is standing on his own reading the dedications on the children's memorial.

'He did say all the right things, what we wanted to hear. It felt genuine from him,' says Colleen's mother, Muriel. 'We just want to keep the momentum going, follow it through so we can get it to the court.'

As I drive back through Bowraville that evening, the sun is warming up the pastel colours of the buildings. The corner store has been fitted with fresh hoardings and the War Memorial has new concrete around its base. Passing the Lands Council office, I see bright dot paintings hanging inside and two women sitting, laughing as one plaits the other's hair.

Outside the old, shuttered service station, with its cracked glass windows and dark interior, I see the doors are standing open. Just inside them is a giant paper bird, a brolga, with its head reared back, bill open to the ceiling. Beside this, a painted whale spurts water while a mermaid stands there with tumbling blonde hair, staring at a giant turtle. They're the lanterns, the ones that I was told I'd see if I looked more closely.

Margrit Rickenbach, one of the artists who made them, is standing in the doorway, a red scarf in her hair matching her red, chipped toenails. Her partner, Claude Teyssier, walks past carrying a bamboo pole, ready to bend it into the frame of another giant animal, and stops to shake my hand. Yes, the service station is unsafe, he says, the floorboards are rotted underneath the layered squares of carpet and wires hang like hungry snakes from the roof joists. But they like it. It is a space for them to work.

Why lanterns? I ask the couple.

'Lanterns is good,' says Claude, looking up and smiling at a seahorse hanging from the ceiling. 'It's not sad. It's light.' He smiles at me again.

As night falls, Michelle shifts a bookcase back into her freshly painted bedroom – breathing in laboured rasps and with the straps of her vest barely containing her straining shoulders, but refusing to let me help. She talks about the work she's doing in Bowraville, feeding breakfast to the Mission kids. She's also on the committee setting up a youth group. They want new buses so people can leave the town to work outside it, and there is talk of a new clinic. A skate park is being built.

It feels optimistic. I say how I'd been looking forward to this conversation, where I hoped she could tell me how Bowraville was getting better, now that the decision had been made to send the murders to the appeal court, and the police had apologised.

'Not in an Aboriginal community,' says Michelle, laughing. She leans against the bookcase. Her breathing, I notice, is heavy even when she's not hauling furniture around.

Michelle tells me how her mother, Patricia Stadhams, grew up among the Stolen Generations, when Aboriginal children were taken from their parents by order of the government and fostered out to white families or put in institutions. Patricia was taken by a lady on a train to Brisbane where she met her foster parents. When she grew up, she met a soldier, Michelle's father, but when the family came back to Bowraville to visit, the elders there would not let him on the Mission because he was white.

When they were a little older, Michelle and her sisters moved to Bowraville, where they grew up. In time, when Michelle was old enough to start dating, she began seeing a white boy, a boxer, whose parents did not want him to be with a black woman. His mother used to stand out the front of Michelle's house, calling for him to come back.

In 1988, Michelle split up with this boyfriend and he shot himself. In 1989, her cousin Craig Ballangary was found hanging in a wooden shack behind the Mission. A year later, in 1990, her niece Evelyn went missing. In 1991, Evelyn's body was found.

'You toughen up after a while, you've got to,' she says, turning back to the bookcase and trying to force it through the doorway. 'You can't say you get used to it but you're not shocked as much. I've got to keep going.' Shoving the shelves through and up against a wall with a dull thud, Michelle comes back into the kitchen, clangs a metal bowl down on the counter and pours in flour, water and salt.

The dark is coming in now through the windows. It creeps across the new white walls. Another of Michelle's nieces, Evelyn's younger sister, who was born years after the murders happened, walks in wearing a footy shirt printed with a picture of the murdered four-year-old and turns on the television. The noise of the quiz show mingles with the cooking noises as Michelle warms a frying pan, then sprinkles it with flour before taking the first of several balls of dough she's made in the mixing bowl and dropping it onto the heat.

She tells me how, after the trial in which James Hide was found not guilty of killing Evelyn, she hoped never to go through anything like that again. Three years later, in 2009, her nephew by marriage, Caleb Jarrett, was stabbed to death in Nambucca Heads, where the river meets the ocean. He was only eighteen.

Caleb was out walking with his mates shortly before midnight when his killer, who was white and drunk and had been arguing with his girlfriend, reversed suddenly out of his drive across the footpath. Caleb punched the car and the man came after him, flicking open a spring-loaded knife. They fought, and Caleb was stabbed three times in the chest and once in the stomach. The fatal strike went into his heart. Caleb's mates, who were the same age or younger, said they heard the man say, 'I got you, you black cunts.' The man said he fought Caleb in self-defence.

Afterwards, Michelle watched her nephew's family drowning in the same loss and the lack of understanding that overwhelmed her family after the loss of Evelyn. She watched them struggle to understand the trial, just as her family had. The first time Michelle walked into court for the trial over Caleb's killing, the barrister looked up at her and said, 'Hello, Michelle.' It was the same man who'd prosecuted James Hide over Evelyn's killing, when the jury came back with a not-guilty verdict. Now he was prosecuting this case as well.

The jury found the white man not guilty of murder but guilty of manslaughter. He went down for a few years but is now eligible for parole, says Michelle, and will be released within weeks. She sits, framed against the night sky visible through the window, and we eat the damper hot with melted butter. She worries about a sister, who's recently been told that she has cancer. Michelle has already nursed two cousins who died from cancer. She knows what it will involve.

I sit there, stunned and sickened by this history, and the naivety with which I'd begun the conversation. It was only this morning that Michelle told me that the police brought racism into this story, but with the commissioner's apology, I'd let myself believe that everything could be resolved. Caleb's killing, and the trial of his killer, was a lesson. The gulf between white and black, between my life and Michelle's, remained unchanged. Michelle has seen so much more of death than I have.

'There's hidden treasures in Bowraville,' says Michelle, trying to smile and failing.

Living here in Bowraville, she still has every reason to be suspicious of the police and justice system. A single apology won't change that. Having the house repainted can't clean this all away, I think.

Tomorrow, people will still be living on the Mission.

'How do you endure all this?' I ask.

She's close to tears. There's counselling and sleeping tablets. Michelle picks up our plates and carries them over to the sink beneath the window. 'It gets hard,' she whispers, running the tap and washing our plates clean.

Wednesday, 31 August 2016

While listening to the stories of Caleb Jarrett, who was stabbed to death in Nambucca Heads, and Craig Ballangary, found hanging in a shack behind the Mission, I started to hear about other black people dying.

There was Lynette Daley, left naked and bleeding on a beach a few hours north of Bowraville in 2011. Paula Craig, whose sixteen-year-old sister Colleen was the first of the three children to be murdered in Bowraville, sent me a text message about Lynette, saying, 'It's so unfair how the Australian justice system can let down another family.' The police did charge two men over her killing, but the New South Wales director of public prosecutions decided to drop the charges. This decision was reversed five years later, after reports by the *Daily Telegraph* and the ABC.

Then there was Rebecca Maher, a 36-year-old mother of four children, who was found dead in a police cell in Maitland, south of Bowraville in July 2016. The police said Rebecca was detained because it looked like she'd been drinking. There were also unsolved murders, such as that of Lois Roberts, found dead in 1999, lying in the Whian Whian forest near Lismore in northern New South Wales. Other deaths had been written off by the authorities as accidents, only their families were not convinced, such as that of Mark Haines, whose body was found lying near the railway tracks at Tamworth, in 1988. Or Stephen Smith, struck and killed by a freight train in uncertain circumstances on the same stretch of track in 1995.

All of these deaths were in New South Wales. All unresolved. It wasn't that the stories themselves were new. Nor was it that they were being told any louder. Most, in fact, I read about in newspapers or watched on the television news. The difference was myself. I had not been listening.

A woman writes to me on Facebook, saying she's just finished listening to the podcast and it chilled her because of the similarities to the death of a friend who was killed in western New South Wales in 1999.

Her friend's 'mother reported her missing, and police assumed she had run away,' she writes. Like Colleen and Evelyn. Her 'body lay exposed to the elements and was found by a neighbour'. Like Clinton. 'This destroyed a lot of evidence, and the investigation was handled by country police.' Like all three of the murders in Bowraville. Like the murdered Bowraville children, Her friend was Indigenous, she writes.

I call the woman and she insists that her friend's race played no part in how her life was taken. Maybe not, I find myself saying. Maybe all these different people's blackness played no part in how, or why, their life was ended. But what difference did it make to the way in which the police, the lawyers and the juries responded to their deaths?

A reporter, Danny Teece-Johnson from NITV, contacts me to talk about another murder. He says the body of an Aboriginal woman was found lying in a concrete culvert beneath an empty country road, outside Boggabilla near the northern border of the state. Once again, nobody has been convicted, Danny tells me. What's more, she was a cousin of Clinton.

Her name was Theresa Binge.

I start looking at another journey north, towards the state border.

A crow falls, like a black void, tumbling towards the blue horizon. Beneath it, here on the Moree Plains in far-north New South Wales, the rich, dark earth is laid out in alternating blocks of living crops and harvested, or burned, dry ground. A semitrailer on the road ahead is veering back and forth across the centre line as if exhausted. As I drive closer to the Queensland border the landscape becomes more desolate, with withered pink cactus fruits providing the only bright stabs of colour amid the sun-bleached grasslands and eucalypts in stands of shifting greens and grey.

After several hours, the gum trees give way to grain silos, a row of gleaming harvesting machinery and a burst of red and yellow pansies planted around a picket fence. This is Goondiwindi, Queensland, a small farming town where the buildings seem to loom over the highway after the long journey through the bush. On one corner stands an ornate, brick-and-timber hotel. A few hundred metres further down the main street stands another pub, which is squat and more modern, like a bunker. A shadow divides the road between them sharply. Theresa was last seen here.

On the evening of Thursday, 17 July 2003 she was drinking in the Victoria Hotel with a local man who bought her six or seven beers and himself put away about twelve heavy pots of XXXX. The two of them were seen leaving together at around midnight. Theresa was forty-three and part of a big family – one of seventeen if you include her half brothers and sisters – and due to attend a birthday party the following night on the nearby Toomelah Aboriginal mission where she had grown up. She did not arrive.

Her family began looking for her on Saturday and reported her missing to police a day later, on the Sunday. Her disappearance was treated as a missing persons investigation, led by the Queensland Police.

More than a week later, on Tuesday, 29 July, dozens of Theresa's friends and relatives were out searching along the banks of the Macintyre River, which runs through Goondiwindi and marks the border between Queensland and New South Wales. Three of them drove south-west on the empty Boomi Road, which runs dead-straight between the plains on the south side of the border, to search near a lagoon, without success. Heading back, they stopped their car where the highway passes over a creek known as Black Gully, about eight kilometres south of Goondiwindi. One of them saw a figure lying beneath it in the dirt.

Theresa was on her back inside the culvert, naked except for a pair of silver tracksuit trousers pulled down around her right ankle. A running shoe was still on her right foot. She had a ring on her right wedding finger and bruises around her neck, arms and thigh as well as the right side of her face, suggesting she'd been punched and kicked. On the ground around her body was an old Pepsi Max bottle, a latex glove and an empty packet of Peter Jackson

Virginia cigarettes. As the culvert was across the border from Goondiwindi, in New South Wales, that state's police force sent a forensic team and established a strike force to investigate her death.

I drive out to the culvert with Theresa's niece, Elenore Binge, who first came here herself two days after her aunt's body was discovered. Alone, it would have been easy to miss the place and barrel past, unknowing. The only signs you've reached the creek are two low, metal crash barriers spray-painted with the words 'Justice 4 Theresa B'. Elenore comes out here each year for Theresa's birthday – which is on 9 September, two days from now – to leave flowers and a tallie of VB and to repaint those words.

A straggly cactus crawls along the culvert towards the green-brown water. The creek was dry back then, Elenore says. When she first came here, after Theresa disappeared, the surrounding sand and grit still bore traces of what happened.

'You could see that they drove down. This side was dry, you could see the tyre marks,' she tells me. You could see where Theresa's feet had been dragged backwards through the dirt.

According to the man who was drinking with Theresa on the night she disappeared, she left the hotel with him and they crossed the High Street together, heading towards the council chambers. They then turned right, cutting a corner through the servo and onto Bowen Street, where he lived. That, at least, is the version he gave to the police following the discovery of her body. CCTV also recorded the man walking with one arm around Theresa, the other carrying two longnecks.

When I knock on his front door, there is no answer, nor does he respond to the handwritten messages I leave. Sitting in my motel room, reading through the photocopied witness statements and interview transcripts from the coronial investigation into Theresa's death, I learn a little about him. He told police Theresa stayed over at his home that night, then she left in the morning. He smokes Peter Jackson Virginia cigarettes.

The New South Wales police officer in charge of the investigation was an acting sergeant based around 130 kilometres to the south in Moree. Like the detective who led the first Bowraville investigation, Greg Lamey was not a specialist homicide investigator and feels he was let down by his commanders in the city.

'If you compare her murder with others, and the level of investigation and attention they were given, one has to ask the question, Why?' he writes in an email. 'Sometimes, like in the Bowraville case, it's difficult to get people (and that includes city cops AND media) interested in things that happen a long way from Sydney. Perhaps even harder to get people interested in crime that happens to Aboriginal victims.'

There were other problems, also. Theresa disappeared on one side of the state border, in Queensland, and her body was found on the other, in New South Wales. The coronial files show that the Queensland police poured resources into their missing person investigation, deploying trained homicide investigators to work with the Goondiwindi detectives conducting dozens of interviews, sometimes going back to the same people again and again. But after the New South Wales police took over, when it became a murder investigation, things began to feel uncertain. Their homicide detectives spent a day at the scene, before heading back to Sydney. Without them, Greg was left in charge. He had no murder scene, no witnesses to the murder and little forensic evidence. The Queensland police also scaled back their resources and, while Greg kept talking to his colleagues across the border, cooperation between the two forces was hampered by different methods and distinct legislation.

Over time, without a clear suspect, many of the New South Wales officers working on the murder were redeployed to other urgent cases. Greg felt the police force owed more to Theresa and her family but, eventually, he too was promoted and moved away.

'I still think about Theresa every day,' he tells me. 'Think about the investigation. I feel an enormous amount of guilt that I'm not able to continue trying to bring her and her family justice.' Because of this emotion, he asked to exchange written questions and answers rather than meet face-to-face. I go through the pages of his email with a highlighter. It's a remorseful and complicated piece of writing, which changes the way I think about murder investigation.

'What are your lasting feelings about the case?' I had asked Greg.

'It's easy to just blame the police as the root of all racism (overt or not). But it's wider than that and includes the community at large,' he replied. Yes, the police are tasked with bringing justice, but they don't do this alone. With the investigation into Theresa's murder, 'not one person has come forward with any real evidence – even useful information – to help solve this case.'

The Macintyre River flows through the centre of Goondiwindi, past the house of the man who was last seen with Theresa and on, almost out of town, to the place on the steep-sided riverbank, on the Queensland side of the border, where there is a memorial to another murdered woman.

Like Theresa, she was a mother to three children. Like Theresa, her body was found after a night spent drinking at a hotel in Goondiwindi.

This woman died almost a decade after Theresa, on Sunday, 16 March 2014. CCTV recorded her at 2.16 a.m., walking past the Victoria Hotel wearing a strappy top and it looked as if she was carrying her shoes. The footage shows a man approach her and they stop to talk, then continue walking hand in hand.

Theresa's sister Bonnie watched the Queensland police swarming through Goondiwindi in the days that followed. 'They were all on the case ASAP and within a couple of weeks or a month it was solved,' she remembers. A man was convicted of murder and jailed.

There's no justice, Bonnie tells me. She now thinks the two deaths were treated differently because the second murder victim was white, while her sister was Aboriginal. She says her sister was a very well-loved lady, who drank and smoked and gambled like everybody did but would light up a room with her smile when she walked in.

Over instant coffee, I sit down with one of the officers involved in the more recent of the two murder investigations, who tells me they don't care about the colour of a person. Murder is murder and it's their job to solve it, he says, especially in a small community like Goondiwindi. Who wants a killer free on these few streets?

I'm stuck, then, how to account for the divide between the results of these two investigations. Going back to Greg Lamey's email about no one coming forward, I look at the witnesses. Looking through the police and inquest documents relating to Theresa's murder, I see that, again and again, people say that they know nothing, even when that seems unlikely, or they simply refuse to talk. The police cannot solve a murder in isolation. Whoever in Goondiwindi knows what happened to Theresa, they've decided her life is not worth enough for them to tell the police what they know about it.

This decision to not come forward with information is another kind of violence, forcing Theresa's family to live with their trauma, unresolved, as the years since her murder pass. I remember a conversation with Evelyn's mother, Rebecca Stadhams, after she showed me her drawings for her daughter's memorial, to be built in Bowraville.

Designing the memorial had seemed like a healing process. I'd seen Rebecca smile as she described the drawings. But then Rebecca looked straight at me and said, 'I can't sleep at night.'

She suffers nightmares, four or five times each night, which leave her terrified, walking around, alone in the darkness. She fears that whoever took her daughter is going to come back.

'I think about whether he's going to come up here and take another one of the kids off me.' To stop herself sleeping, she gets up and cleans the house. 'I clean to keep these things out of my head,' Rebecca told me. She does this because whoever killed her daughter has not been put in prison. If anyone in Bowraville knows for certain who killed Rebecca's daughter, and the two other missing children, they have not come forward.

In Goondiwindi, how many of Theresa's family members suffer nightmares because of the silence that met the police investigation into her death?

One of the witnesses named in the records of that police investigation still lives in the same wooden house as he did when she went missing. His phone number is painted on a For Sale sign hanging on a boat in the drive. I call him.

'No, I don't even like to talk about it, to be honest,' he says, barely controlling his temper at my interruption. 'It's just something I'd rather put behind me and not rehash.'

He says that unfair suspicion fell on him during the police investigation.

So why did it?

'Guilt by association. I was just associated with people at the time that was in a chain of events.'

I say that I don't understand what he means by a chain of events.

'Understand this,' he says, hanging up. When I drive past his house a day later, the For Sale sign has been thrown down on the ground.

Elenore Binge, Theresa's niece, was with her aunt on the day she went missing, the two of them among a group of other women who met at a flat in Goondiwindi. When Elenore walked into the room that afternoon, Theresa looked at her, then looked away, then said, 'Come here, my baby, give me a big kiss and cuddle.' Standing at the culvert where Theresa's body was discovered, Elenore says, 'I can hear her voice now. She was cheeky. Cheeky voice, cheeky smile.'

A bird calls from somewhere in the gum trees.

'Her spirit never left here, hey?' says Elenore's partner, Leroy Connors, who's watching as we walk back from the creek bed towards where he is standing with the car. There are sacred sites all the way along this stretch of Boomi Road, he tells me. A few kilometres further to the south is the Boobera Lagoon, home to the Rainbow Serpent. For Theresa to be found so close unsettled everything.

Elenore says her family have heard nothing from the police now for over five years. She shivers. I'm taken aback, as I was in Bowraville, at the sense of duty, or of desperation, that made her revisit this place and these memories to share them with a reporter. She hopes, of course, by talking to me to provoke some action on the investigation into her aunt's murder. I've told her I can't promise anything. She says that she knows this, but still wants to do the interview. She wraps her arms around herself, one hand worrying at the back of her neck.

Leroy Connors keeps on talking. He says that, about two and a half years ago, he was arrested for drink-driving and got chatting to another man inside the prison truck taking them to court. The two men realised they were related; his uncle was married to Leroy's aunt.

'This young man, I didn't know him from a bar of soap but he just blurted it all out while me and him were in a truck together,' says Leroy. 'He said to me that he was assaulted by the same people that assaulted Theresa and that he was there.' He saw what happened to Theresa but was knocked unconscious and, when he woke, he was alone beside the empty road. Leroy doesn't know how much truth there is in the young man's story, but he does know the names of the people who the young man claimed attacked Theresa.

After their journey together in the prison truck, the two of them were sent to different jails.

Leroy catches Elenore's eye and points to where an eagle is circling. The eagle is his totem, he says, and also Elenore's father's. It is trying to tell them something. A few months ago, Leroy called Crime Stoppers and, a few weeks before my visit, a detective called him back. Of all people, that detective was Gary Jubelin. Gary is coming up to meet him, Leroy says.

I ask if the young man he met in the prison truck will talk to Gary but Leroy says he doubts it. He thinks that the young man is frightened. Frightened of the men he says attacked Theresa and frightened of what will happen if he speaks out. The young man doesn't trust the police, says Leroy, because he is himself a prisoner. He's been punished by the justice system. He doesn't want anything to do with that system anymore.

I ask about other witnesses. If this young man claims to know something and has not come forward, could there be others who haven't spoken to the police?

Leroy says he's certain. Someone in his community knows more than they're saying. But he says that I need to understand the relationship between Aboriginal people living around Goondiwindi and the authorities. He says they watched the investigation into Theresa's death not being done the right way from the very beginning. If the police really wanted to learn what people living on the Toomelah Mission were saying, Leroy says, they'd come and give people an ear, sit and talk to them, and show a bit of respect. But that doesn't happen.

'I've seen it with my own eyes,' he says. 'I've seen the way the police come out to our communities and try to stand over people. They treat us like we're nobodies, and we are somebody. And Aunty Theresa was somebody and she is somebody, and she's always going to be somebody.'

The distrust, I think, is understandable. In 2004, a year after Theresa was killed, four Aboriginal teenagers and young men from her mission were chased by two white farmers who suspected them of theft. The men caught one, a sixteen-year-old, and slung a noose around his neck, dragging him like that across the ground before calling the police. A Goondiwindi court fined the two farmers $500 and ordered they walk free. If you're black and that's the kind of justice that gets dealt out in Goondiwindi, you are going to feel fear, anger and resentment towards the justice system.

It feels like this case is where the Bowraville murders were before the police launched the reinvestigation, mired in distrust between the different communities living together in a small country town.

The mission community won't talk because they don't trust the authorities.

The white witnesses in town say they won't talk about the murder.

The young man in the prison truck is too frightened to come forward.

'I don't give a fuck.' Elenore breaks her silence. 'What about Theresa?'

Saturday, 15 October 2016

The lawyers who will argue the case that James Hide should face a retrial over the children's murders have kept their calculations hidden, even from the police. Although there has been a steady stream of requests for more information or to test this or that different statement made in the brief of evidence, which have kept Bianca Comina, the analyst with the police task force, working full-time on the case for months, the lawyers have provided precious little indication of what they are doing in return. For Gary Jubelin and Jerry Bowden, the two detectives on the task force, this is not unusual. Although they like to say that both the police and prosecutors are on the same side – they call it the side of the angels – the reality is that they are two separate organisations and, while the police collect the evidence, the lawyers decide how it will be presented in court. For now, the police have been left to guess what to expect.

For the past decade, Gary has held tight to the account of the truck drivers who claimed to have seen a white man standing over the body of a black teenager at Norco Corner during their journey into Bowraville. This, he convinced himself, was 'fresh and compelling' evidence about the murder of Clinton, and as such the best chance of convincing the judges to do away with the double jeopardy protection that says James could not be tried over this killing again.

But the lawyers have decided to abandon this approach. The Norco Corner evidence is uncertain. The drivers' descriptions of what the black teenager was wearing do not completely match the clothes that Clinton had on that night. If you trace back the separate accounts that they gave of what they saw that morning, the colour of the car they say the white man was driving changes over the years, from mustard when they were interviewed during the first police investigation, to red when interviewed during the reinvestigation, to mucky-coloured when talking to me for the podcast.

Worse, the fact that a detective, Allan Williams, did meet with the truck drivers in the months after Clinton's murder, even if no witness statements were taken and so their evidence was never used in court, means the lawyers have to accept that the police did know about Norco Corner at the time when James was first put on trial for killing Clinton. This means they would struggle to convince the judges that this evidence is 'fresh'.

According to the legislation, evidence is fresh if it 'was not adduced in the proceedings in which the person was acquitted' and 'could not have been adduced in those proceedings with the exercise of reasonable diligence'. The police could have presented the Norco Corner evidence in court during that first trial, in 1994, if they had been reasonably diligent. So, arguably, it cannot be 'fresh' today.

Already, the challenge facing the lawyers is daunting. While the Court of Criminal Appeal has often overturned a guilty verdict in a case of murder, this is the first time it's been asked to do so for a not-guilty verdict. The lawyers, led by Wendy Abraham QC, know there is a great reluctance among many of their colleagues, and among many judges, to set such a precedent. The appeal court's decision will determine not only what happens in this case but in countless future murder cases. The fear is that allowing James to face trial again for these killings could open the floodgates to a wave of other similar appeals, where the police or grieving families want to overturn other not-guilty verdicts. Such a flood could overwhelm the system, washing away the defences that currently prevent innocent people ending up in jail.

So, in asking that the appeal court order James face trial again, Wendy must ask the judges to do something that they are reluctant to attempt and that neither they nor their predecessors have done. She must also ask them to make this decision not once, over the killing of Clinton, but twice, over the murder also of Evelyn. She dare not risk such a decision on the Norco Corner evidence, because if the police could have presented this evidence in court before now, then it clearly does not pass the test that it be both 'fresh' and 'compelling'.

The lawyers have not told him yet, but Gary's best hope for getting a retrial is gone.

Gary sits in the boxing gym beneath the Sydney Police Centre, wrapping protective tape around his left wrist, over the palm, then in between each finger. Satisfied, he tapes the other hand then pulls on his boxing gloves and stands, his black t-shirt and shorts in sharp contrast to the white walls of the old cells around him. He closes his eyes and rolls his neck from right to left, then left to right, loosening the muscles.

A month ago, in September, Gary travelled up to Tenterfield, near the Queensland border, for the unveiling of a memorial to Clinton in the town where his mother still lives. Gary was asked to speak at the ceremony and when he took the microphone he asked the families to trust the lawyers taking the case to appeal court. Gary said he knew that they'd done that before and got kicked in the guts, when the director of public prosecutions or previous attorneys general had refused to take the case to the appeal court. This time was different, Gary told them. This time, he liked the prosecution lawyers. He'd met Wendy several times, when she had fired questions at him about the case. An unyielding, seemingly austere woman, as quiet on the surface as a mill pond, it was obvious that she went deeper. Gary saw something of himself in her. She did not like being beaten. She was a fighter, Gary thought.

'If I didn't think they were the right people for the job, I'd say it,' Gary told the watching families, asking them to overcome their past suspicions of the legal profession. 'I'm not just saying that. I'm vouching for them. They are genuinely trying to make an effort and find you justice, so let's hope that is where it takes us.'

Standing in the boxing gym, Gary says he hopes that the families will trust him. By now, he says, they have spent two decades working with him on this investigation. At the memorial ceremony in Tenterfield, one of Clinton's cousins introduced him as 'part of the family, fighting our fight for us and with us . . . our warrior'.

The buzzer sounds to start his training session and Gary slams his fist into the punch bag, making the chains that hold it rattle.

He knows that the coming months will prove to be his hardest challenge. Everything that he has done over the past twenty years in the reinvestigation of the murders will be pulled apart and criticised inside a public courtroom. James has his own lawyers, funded through Legal Aid by the state government, who will be able to come back at Gary. They'll be looking for weakness in the evidence that he's collected. If he has made a mistake, they'll find it.

If there is one thing Gary fears, it's failing. The buzzer sounds.

I tape my fists, pull on my gloves and start on the heavy bag. Gary watches. Widen your feet, he tells me, gesturing with one gloved fist. It stops you being knocked off balance when your opponent attacks.

'Keep your weight on your back foot,' he tells me. The jab is thrown with your left hand, forcing your opponent to keep their distance. 'Now snap in a hook.' He shakes his head. Do that again but without taking time to wind it up. Don't signal what you're doing. That leaves you vulnerable. He's going to hit you back.

I frown and throw the punch again, with feeling, trying to shake the bad spirit that has settled on me during my own work on these murders. The deaths of Colleen, Evelyn and Clinton as well as those of Craig Ballangary, Caleb Jarrett and Theresa Binge have led me to ask just how common such tragedies are. Aboriginal people, I'd learned, make up around 3 per cent of the country's population but, according to a paper from the Australian Institute of Criminology, represent 13 per cent of its homicide victims, and more than one in ten of its known killers. The reasons given were that Indigenous children are more likely to experience substance

abuse, sexual abuse, being displaced from their homes and to witness violence, gambling addiction or mental illness. All of these
increase their chances of being involved in a violent offence. That
means that the three children in Bowraville grew up roughly five
times more likely to be murdered than a white Australian.

Thinking about Theresa, her body found lying in a culvert and
with no one sent to jail as a result, I'd asked the independent NSW
Bureau of Crime Statistics and Research for figures on the number
of murder investigations that were cleared within a year, meaning a killer was identified. Given what I'd seen in Bowraville and
Goondiwindi, the result was surprising: since 1995, 84 per cent of
murders involving an Indigenous victim were cleared, compared to
74 per cent where the victim was of any other race. In New South
Wales, at least, murders were more likely to be solved when the
victim was black, not white.

Uncertain what to make of this, I asked the National Homicide
Monitoring Program, run by the Australian government, for figures collected from every state and territory police force. Their data
also goes further back, to the time when the murders in Bowraville
took place. It showed the same result. Across the country, 5 per cent
of murders involving an Indigenous victim went unsolved, while
the proportion of unsolved murders where the victim was white
is twice as high.

Seeking some explanation, I spoke to several homicide detectives, including Gary, all of whom said that they weren't sure, but
maybe there could be an explanation. They see a lot of domestic
violence in Indigenous communities. It's often caught up with the
same factors laid out in the Australian Institute of Criminology
paper on homicide statistics: substance abuse, booze, gambling
addiction, past exposure to violence, insecurity and mental illness.

Domestics are often easier for the police to solve than other murders, which might explain why a higher rate of homicides involving an Indigenous victim are quickly cleared. Sometimes, when the police arrive, the drunken husband is still standing over the bloodied body of his wife.

These things did not get spoken of in the Sydney in which I live, where I rarely see a black face on the journey from my home to the offices of *The Australian*. Or if they did, I'd not been listening. As a reporter, I'd failed to notice what was happening around me, where people of one skin colour died younger and were more likely to be murdered than people who had the same skin colour as me. How had I not known this? The only answer was that I ignored it. I'd been part of a national pact of silence. But now that I'd met the families of these murdered people, the world around me seemed a darker place than I'd pretended all those years.

At *The Australian*, I'd written about Theresa's murder. There is nothing to report on the Bowraville murders until the case gets to court. Instead, I spend weeks covering the hearings of a royal commission into child sexual abuse and, again, feel that work leading me into a world I did not know existed, where children are raped, beaten and murdered by adults.

One day in October, after a two-week royal commission hearing, my chief-of-staff asked me to go to western Sydney to report on the gang rape of a teenage girl. Without warning, I felt hot and weak, as if I had a fever. The buildings around me in the street were shaking. Another sexual crime against a child, I thought. I could not do it. I couldn't face what I might find. I was frightened of what I would find. Instead, I told my chief-of-staff I would not do the story. To my relief, he understood. For the first time, I wondered if I should stop reporting on crime.

The buzzer sounds and Gary sends one last fist into the punching bag. His breathing is heavy and his black t-shirt is stuck to his torso with sweat. The reason he likes boxing, he says, is that it's just you and your opponent. You have to face your fear of failure in the shape of your opponent when you step into the ring.

Sometimes, he says, you have to do the thing that scares you. Bringing up the Bowraville case unprompted, Gary says the lawyers are interested in the interview I did with James for the podcast. Can they have a copy? I agree to send over the recording.

He points one gloved fist at the boxing ring. 'Now step in there and let's see how tough you are.'

Inside the ring, Gary jabs with his left fist, advancing. He circles quickly, forcing me to follow him, then slips my attempted cross and snakes a hook into my side. I try again. He blocks my fist. Behind his guard, Gary is staring at me. I realise that he's dropped his fists, leaving himself open. He's inviting me to hit him. I throw a punch. There's a feeling of relief when it connects.

On Monday, 12 December 2016, the attorney general calls the three murdered children's families and, choosing her words carefully, tells them that proceedings will begin before the year is over.

They do not understand exactly what she means. Such is the uncertainty around this first test of the new double jeopardy legislation that even Gary is unsure of what will happen. To start the court process, the police have been told that James must be charged again with the murders of Evelyn and Clinton. They don't know whether he will also be charged with Colleen's murder, or whether this will somehow happen later, or if it will only happen if the appeal court orders that James face a retrial.

Gary wants to arrest James in person, but he doesn't know if he will get to do this. He may instead be told to simply issue James with a written order to appear in court.

Allan Williams, the detective who led the first investigation into the murders, gets little sleep on the overnight train from Coffs Harbour to Sydney, and looks pale and drawn when I meet him at a cafe near the New South Wales parliament building. As the case gets closer to the appeal court, it seems to have provoked a reaction in Allan. In front of him on the table is a notebook, open to a page that reads:

> *I was extremely disappointed*
> *I was ruthlessly sacrificed*
> *I was embarrassed on national TV on many occasions*
> *Death sentence for my career*
> *Wife / family suffered as well*
> *I call on Gary to justify his public statements.*

'That's how I felt about the whole thing, how I come out of it,' says Allan, showing me the notebook. He didn't like the way Gary had taken over and become the hero. He didn't like the way Gary had stood up at the parliamentary inquiry and in the media, talking about how Allan's investigation made mistakes, implying his would put them right.

There are no heroes in this story, I tell him. Gary has his failings. He's not seen anyone convicted for these murders either.

Allan says that the murders in Bowraville have hurt him. They're part of the reason he has not worked now for over a decade.

He had a bit of a nervous breakdown, retired early and has been diagnosed with post-traumatic stress disorder, he says. The reason he's in Sydney, where he asked to meet me, is to meet with his psychiatrist.

'You know you're important?' he says.

I say I'm not, but he insists: 'You don't realise how important you are.'

I realise he wants me, as a reporter, to give an account of what happened as he saw it. To salvage his reputation. That's not my job, I tell him. Yes, I think that he was unprepared and ill-equipped and, at worst, not equal to the task that he was given of leading the murder investigation, but there were also more senior officers within the police who allowed him to be all those things. It was his bosses who allowed Allan to lead a triple murder investigation when he had no experience of running a homicide inquiry, who left him with only three detectives and using a manual typewriter which he brought from home to take his witness statements.

'Why not request more detectives?' I ask him.

'I did it time and time again, of course I did.'

'What was the answer?'

'No one available, you're doing a good job. Keep doing it.'

I can't imagine Gary accepting the same answer. More than once, Gary had walked into his bosses office and squared off, swearing or threatening until he got what he wanted. Allan was allowed to fail by his bosses. Allan allowed himself to fail.

On Wednesday, 14 December, the attorney general telephones the three children's families again. She says the legal process is now about to begin.

Thursday, 15 December 2016

Gary leaves Sydney at four in the morning, driving through the smacking rain. He is to serve James Hide with a Court Attendance Notice to face charges over the murders of Evelyn and Clinton rather than arrest him, but Gary still wants to hand over the documents in person. Just as he did thirteen years ago, with Jason Evers, when Gary drove up here to deliver the order to appear at the inquest into the children's deaths.

Do it now, the lawyers had decided, before the courts shut down for the long Christmas holiday. Gary's been waiting a decade for this moment, ever since the court in Port Macquarie found James not guilty over the murder of Evelyn. But as he stares through the thudding windscreen wipers, the journey feels like an anticlimax. There are no other police cars fanning out behind him on the Pacific Highway, no lights, no uniforms, no show of force; just Gary, driving north alone in a grey Holden Commodore to meet the other detective on the task force, Jerry Bowden, outside a small police station, where they will sit together in the car park, reading through the paperwork.

The two of them agree this should not be a confrontation. But still, inside their car, Gary turns to Jerry and tells him, 'Let's be switched on because I'm going to ask him whether he wants to say anything.' Maybe, he thinks, if they can rattle James a little, he might give something away. Before they drive out of the car park for the final journey to the house where James is living, Gary says, 'Let's just be prepared in case it takes a twist.'

The detectives arrive around seven in the morning, step out of the car and put on their suit jackets, let themselves through the wooden gate and take the few steps between the wheelie bins and scrap of garden that lead to James's front door. The door itself is open, although the black screen door in front of it is closed. Behind it, James's wife walks past the doorway and sees the two detectives. A dog starts barking. James fills the doorway, his wide shoulders and heavy frame shutting out the electric light shining inside the house.

The men stare at each other through the black mesh screen. The police hold up their badges.

Gary speaks first: 'James, it's Detective Chief Inspector —'

'I know who you are.' The shadow in the doorway interrupts him.

'Fine, then.' Gary puts his badge back inside his pocket. 'Do you want to open the door?'

'No.'

Now they have a problem. Gary says he needs to serve the order requiring James to attend Newcastle Local Court on 9 February 2017. He stands there, holding out the paper. James looks at it and opens the screen door a crack but Gary moves the paper backwards, out of reach.

James stares at Gary but says nothing and reaches his hand further through the narrow gap to take the sheet of paper. Gary gives it up this time and James retreats into the building.

'Did you enjoy that?' asks Jerry, as the two detectives walk out of the front garden and back towards their car.

Gary says that he deserved to enjoy the moment. It's twenty-five years, eight months and seven days since James was first charged with Clinton's murder. This month, December 2016, Gary has been working on the case for twenty of those years.

In Bowraville that evening, the giant paper lanterns are carried out from the old service station and tied in place between the palm trees running down High Street. As night falls, they cast their light on crowds of children, white and black, running past with popcorn and fairy floss bought from the market stalls. More children are playing on a bouncy castle, their whoops and cheers competing with the Salvation Army brass band, which is playing Christmas carols.

Plenty of the adults from the Mission have also walked up to town for the Christmas Festival, and a small group of men join in the music, playing didgeridoos and clapping sticks. Santa Claus arrives and hands out presents. By 10 p.m., when the last of the partygoers start to head home, the lanterns are still shining, visible from the surrounding hills.

The next day, Friday, 16 December, the attorney general's lawyers file their written submissions with the Court of Criminal Appeal, asking the judges to order that James face a retrial. James himself is named only once, on the first of the 108 closely argued pages of the document. Afterwards, he is called only 'the respondent'.

The case to which James must respond is this: that evidence about the disappearance of Colleen, the first of the children to go missing, was not used in either of the two previous, separate trials, over the murders of Clinton and Evelyn. In fact, the lawyers argue, the trial judges' decision to hear each of these cases in isolation – so neither jury was told that other children went missing from Bowraville – meant it became impossible for evidence about Colleen's murder to be heard. As such, in the language of section 100 of the *Crimes (Appeal and Review) Act 2001*, not only was this evidence 'not adduced in the proceedings', but also it 'could not have been adduced in those proceedings with the exercise of reasonable diligence'. This evidence therefore remains 'fresh and compelling' – not because it is new, but because it has never previously been heard in court.

And when you do consider this evidence, the lawyers argue that it allows you to establish similarities or coincidences between all three of the children's killings. Together, 'the coincidence evidence establishes each of the children were murdered; they were murdered by the same person; and that person was the respondent'.

It is a brilliant strategy. In effect, the oldest of the murders is being used as the 'fresh' reason that the court should send all three of the killings to retrial today. The dry language of the lawyers' submissions makes no appeal to goodness or morality, or to the torment of the children's families. Instead its argument is built upon what it calls the Legislative Landscape, explaining how their case satisfies the exact wording of the double jeopardy legislation. Upon this foundation, the lawyers place their other blocks of new evidence: the prison informants and Hilton Walker, who said James told him he had bodies out on the Congarinni near his crops. Neither of those, alone, are enough to convince the judges to overturn the previous not-guilty verdicts. But together with the fresh evidence about Colleen's disappearance, the lawyers say the case is made.

Almost thirty pages of the written submission are dedicated to a framework of legal principles supporting their construction: discussing the meaning of 'adduced'; the 'application of the Law to Facts'; and whether the case is 'reliable', 'substantial and highly probative' and in the 'interests of justice'. The capstone is fashioned from an appeal to legal precedent, and to the seriousness of the undertaking which now faces the appeal judges. The lawyers quote a past court judgement: 'For the conviction of the guilty is a public interest as is the acquittal of the innocent.' A retrial is the right decision, they argue. 'This is a case where, to use the language in *R v H*, "Not to have one would damage the credibility of the criminal justice system."'

Now we have to wait until the court will hear it.

The road to Bowraville crosses the train tracks and turns sharply right before meeting a wooden bridge over the Nambucca River, where a line of children in bright bathers stand balanced on the railings, high above the water. The eldest, a boy, looks down, grins and dives, his impact scattering the sunlight reflecting on the surface.

On the Mission, the house at number 13 has been gutted by fire. The roof lies flat and shattered on the ground, the windows stare out blindly from the wreckage. The walls are scorched but the flames seem not to have touched the child's trampoline standing in the front garden. Around it all is yellow tape, which reads: 'Danger – No Entry / NSW Fire Brigade'.

Next door is the house where Evelyn's mother says her daughter went missing from their bedroom. Beyond that is Thomas Duroux's house, where his son Clinton was staying before he disappeared, and where Colleen was last seen.

'Oh, gee, I don't know,' sighs Thomas when I ask what happened to his neighbour. He invites me in and we sit together amid framed photographs of children and grandchildren, baskets of laundry, and boxes of food shopping stacked up the walls ready for unpacking. There'd been a stabbing, Thomas says, or rather two. One man was stabbed twice. Then a shooting. Then a brawl started on the day of another person's funeral held at the Bowraville cemetery, just as the mourners were heading back through the Mission from the service. People were throwing bricks at each other, says Thomas. Someone sang out that one of the people living in number 13 had a hand in the shooting.

'Go and get petrol, set the house on fire!' someone called out. The building burned during the wake.

'The way things are going we're just getting further and further and further apart,' Thomas tells me, looking down at the floor. 'Whatever happens now with the appeal court, we'll still have problems to deal with.' The people living in number 13 had just had new furniture and beds for the kids delivered. He's not seen the family since.

A young boy walks into the kitchen wearing his school uniform, grinning. Thomas introduces his grandson, Clinton, who steps forward to shake my hand. Named after his uncle who was murdered, Thomas tells me. Clinton changes into footy gear, grabs a bag of chips and heads back out. I follow him into the sunshine and see Evelyn's father, Billy Greenup, sitting next door in the shade of the carport, drinking.

Clinton heads up the footpath, past the yellow tape hanging outside number 13.

In her kitchen, Evelyn's aunt, Michelle Jarrett, types 'house fire Bowraville' into her computer, then does the same with 'stabbing Bowraville' and 'shooting in Nambucca', pulling up a series of brief, local newspaper articles.

'What actually happened?' I ask.

'So, about twelve, half past twelve, one o'clock,' she starts to answer.

'In the morning?'

'Yes, in the morning. There were two, they're saying it was blackfellas.' One of the men got mistaken for the other, she says, and the story Michelle heard is he was in sitting in his car when a group of people walked right up and shot him. He survived it but got arrested in hospital because the police had a warrant out for him over something else. The second man, the real target of the shooting, also got arrested on the same night, on another warrant. Word is the police wanted this second man over a home invasion in Bowraville where someone almost had their arm cut off with a machete.

'Jesus, Michelle.'

'Now this leads up to the fire thing,' she says, clicking between the newspaper stories. The man who got shot had been blamed for the stabbing on the Mission that Thomas told me about earlier this afternoon. There'd also been another shooting, two weeks earlier, in Nambucca, only no one was hurt that time.

'Everyone's connected,' she says. 'All this mob, all these are my family, on both sides.' The funeral brought both sides together in Bowraville, and the fire was started.

'Michelle, what's happening?' I ask her.

'It's not normally this bad.' She pushes her chair back and rolls her shoulders to work out her frustration. Most of the people causing problems are outsiders, she says. They've got family connections to the Mission but weren't reared up in Bowraville themselves.

'I love this town, I love it. I've grown up here since I was a kid, it's the best place I think and it's just outsiders coming in and making it bad for us,' says Michelle, her voice rising in volume. She stands up, letting her anger fill the room with its presence. Because she's been trying, she says. All the work they're doing to set up a youth group, the breakfasts for the young ones, the new sports equipment. Trying to make things right, to help the town get over the murders, and these bastards – she waves one hand out the window, over the paddocks towards the wreck of number 13 – they knew nothing about what happened here.

She says she knows what the white people in Bowraville will say about the shootings and the burnt-out building: 'Oh, it's the black folks on the Mission. Just going off the edge again.' She can picture them over their beers in the Bowra Hotel, turning to look and check that no one else is listening, then saying, 'Why don't they let them all go and kill themselves? Hopefully, they'll wipe each other out.'

Michelle reckons they thought the same thing after the children's murders. Back then, she says, the white people's response was, 'It's none of our business. That's blackfella business see.'

The storm subsides. Watching Michelle take her seat again, I think that she has changed over the time I've known her. She's older and more determined, more intent to drag her community along with her to where she wants to take them. More willing to work with people like Gary – and like me – to get some answers to her niece's murder. I realise she is more like Aunty Elaine, the elder who first came to view Gary as an ally in her own attempt to have the children's killers brought to justice.

'I need to ask you something,' I say. I try to explain how I have been reporting on these murders for however long it's been, and in that time leaned heavily on her and her community. That I keep coming up, or phoning up and asking questions. That I should have asked them before now: 'What can I do for you?'

She answers straight: 'Do what you're doing.'

'But is there anything —'

She cuts me off. 'Do what you're doing. 'Cause we didn't have any of this, support of newspapers and that. Keep doing what you're doing, get the message out that there's problems in this town, in this community and how we were treated.'

That night, driving along the darkened Congarinni Road, I stop the car and kill the engine, turning off the headlights. Outside the trees stand in silhouette against the starlight. There is the constant stabbing noise of insects. I get out and stand there, silent, breathing, looking at the forest. I think about Evelyn and Clinton, left lying here alone.

From Bowraville, I drive about an hour north, to the end of a lonely road where there is a small village, a campsite and a beach that stinks of dying seaweed. The bodies of the limp, brown plants lie tumbled by the surf. From here, a footpath worn into the sand dunes leads up onto the narrow headland. Walk along it and the wind batters at you while the waves beat themselves against the land.

This ragged path passes a metal plaque set into a boulder. 'In memory of the victims and survivors of the Blood Rock Massacres'. A few troubled footsteps further forward, bent into the wind, and the path disappears among the rocks and grass. Beyond this lies the jagged cliff edge where, years ago, after white colonisation of the area, Gumbaynggirr men, women and children were chased to this headland by mounted police, and driven over into the spitting ocean. Looking down, you can see the violent white surf hurling itself against a giant, blood-red rock.

I stand on the cliff top, where those people would have turned in terror to see the advancing line of police on their snorting horses. Looking down, I catch myself thinking that it is not high enough to ensure that those who fell would be killed by the impact. Was the tide higher at the time of the massacre, or the waves more powerful? Or did their pursuers wade into the water, using their guns and knives to finish the survivors off?

The wind sends a few loose pebbles scattering down the sharp rock of the cliff face. Turning to walk back to safety, I notice a concrete pillar standing behind me on the highest point of the headland. The letters JAMES are carved into it and painted black on white.

Everything begins to shake, and I feel feverish. Sick at the world and sick at myself also. Is it normal, at the scene of an atrocity, to question the mechanics of how it was conducted? Is it normal that my first thought is to connect these letters carved into the concrete to the Bowraville murders when, surely, no connection exists?

I hurry back along the footpath through the sand dunes, while the wind rages all around me. Past the metal plaque that reads, 'Gumbaynggirr descendants, especially women, still avoid this headland' and turn the car around, heading south. It is time for a court to hear about all three of the Bowraville children's deaths.

Wednesday, 8 February 2017

The night before James Hide appears in court, Jerry Bowden, the detective working on the Bowraville task force alongside Gary Jubelin, is standing in the setting sunlight outside Newcastle's Customs House Hotel, surrounded by his family and grinning in disbelief.

Jerry has spent a decade working on the murder reinvestigation. Outside of work, he has spent the past year and a half working on a play about the police. It's something of a confession. After a career spent wearing the 'two-blues' New South Wales police uniform and the dark suit of a detective, Jerry wants to tell other people what that's like.

It's not common for cops to turn playwrights, and Jerry has had to battle with his bosses to get their permission to do so. At first, he had an idea for a different story, based on another real investigation, but then he got talking to the woman who became the play's co-director about a police shooting that took place near Newcastle itself. In video footage of the confrontation, Jerry reckoned you could hear the officers armed with pistols shouting, 'We don't want to do this' at the man wielding the knife before they shot him. For months now, Jerry has been writing and rewriting the script and finally, tonight, the play will open. He grins again, sunnies pushed up on top of his salt-and-pepper hair, as if he can't believe what is about to happen.

Jerry says he was a Homicide detective before Gary asked him to join the Bowraville reinvestigation. It's only in hindsight, looking back at those sixteen-, eighteen- or twenty-hour days at the beginning of each new murder investigation, that you realise what it takes. He'd spend months, or years, taking a case from the first moment when he saw the victim's body to the jury's verdict, and then there would always be another case, and then another. Each meant another grieving mother, father, sister, brother. Another post-mortem.

'Not only did it not bother me, I really enjoyed it,' Jerry says. He used to stare at his mobile, wanting it to ring. 'Give me a job, I want to go and do it. Tell me where the next murder is.'

Eventually, the work takes something out of you, however. Jerry's marriage broke down and he moved away from Sydney. Now, when he travels back and walks into the Homicide Squad offices again to work on the Bowraville murders, he no longer feels like an old colleague welcomed back into the workplace. Instead, he feels the other detectives' eyes burning into him.

'Why?' I ask him.

'Because I'm working with Gary.'

I look at him, surprised. They resent him, Jerry says. Gary pushes his investigations hard, burning people or the road behind him;

always demanding resources that have to be taken from elsewhere. Some people also dislike the way Gary gets his face on television and don't believe him when he says he's only using the media to advance his investigations. He's ruthless and demanding, and maybe he is lonely. Some of those who've worked with him on big investigations now don't talk to him. And those were great jobs, says Jerry, shaking his head. The sort of thing you build a friendship out of.

'You know they call him Crazy Fuck?' he asks me. I had heard that, I tell him.

Jerry says other detectives ask him why he works with Gary. His answer is that the things that enrage him, like Gary's relentless determination, his willingness to drive an investigation forward at a cost, are the same things he respects. The two of them, says Jerry, have sat with the Bowraville families and talked about their children. They've felt the grief rising up in the room and threatening to overwhelm them. Working with Gary is the best way to get these murders solved.

'There's not too many jobs that I take away from work, that stick with you, but this is one,' says Jerry.

'You took this one home?' I ask.

He looks away. His lips tremble. He gulps at the water in a tall glass on the table beside him. Takes a breath and recovers. Another deep breath shakes him.

Jerry looks at me, then looks away and swallows more water. He says that he is sorry. He is no longer smiling.

As it gets dark, Jerry's family and friends join the queue outside Newcastle's old police station, where the play will open. We walk in through a single, clanging iron door to find a room, perhaps

10 metres wide by 40 long, with sandstone walls and metal bars in place of a ceiling. Prisoners were once kept in here awaiting court.

The audience sits at the two ends of the room, facing each other across the empty lock-up floor. Jerry is sitting opposite, two rows back, and looking nervous. Against one wall is a pin board, the type you imagine the police using to track the progress of an investigation. As each actor enters, they pin a photograph of themselves on the board, connecting the different images together with red string.

The play begins with a young officer buttoning his shirt and buckling his gun-belt. His uniform is a light-blue shirt and dark-blue trousers, just like that of the New South Wales police. He's young, the child of immigrants, like Jerry. He says he's happy to be working.

'Good cops enjoy chasing good crooks,' another police officer replies.

A teenager gets into trouble. It's something minor. The policeman could charge him, but speaks to the boy's mother and lets him off with a caution. Jerry's eyes are fixed on the actors' faces. At home, the policeman's wife tells him she is pregnant. On stage, she jumps, wrapping her arms and legs around him.

We do not see the shooting, though we hear it. A crowded shopping mall. The teenager, armed with a knife, stands over a female police officer. The policeman is also there.

'I don't want to do this,' the policeman says, over and over. She's screaming. We hear the shot. When we see him, the policeman is sitting in his t-shirt, shivering. It's warm in the lock-up and the audience start to fan themselves, stirring up the hot and heavy air.

A year passes. The baby is born and the policeman is drinking. He won't engage with his psychiatrist. His wife calls him a coward. By now the pin board is a tangle of red lines.

The policeman finally admits what he is feeling: 'You start to look for confrontation, someone to fight, something to hit. You're a missile seeking a target.'

The stage lights draw our attention to a young man slouching against the side of the heavy door through which we entered. The policeman reads a file and sees that the young man was arrested for assaulting children.

'Stand up,' he says.

'Get fucked.'

'Stand up.'

'Or what?' The policeman starts taking down his details. Height, race, eye colour. Asked if he has any tattoos, the young man pulls down his shirt collar to reveal the words 'Such is Life' written on the skin around his neck. The last words of the bushranger Ned Kelly.

'You know it's just a myth?' the policeman asks him. 'He never said that.'

'You're right,' the young man replies. 'I should have just got one that said "I. Fucked. Your. Wife."'

The policeman hits him in the mouth.

A single spotlight shines as the policeman unbuttons his uniform and beats the suspect to the floor. He stands over him, punching the prone figure who is now lying in the doorway. It's brutal and unpleasant and it makes you start to question what it feels like to be a missile searching for a target. How you must sometimes wish that you could take off the uniform, if only once, to overcome the evil in this world.

The house lights go up. We applaud the actors, then stand to applaud Jerry, who is still sitting in the second row, still smiling, but exhausted.

I later ask if he will write another play, but he replies, 'There's nothing there.'

I wake up hot. The morning news shows a rough, purple circle of extreme heat lying bloated across eastern Australia. At 8.30 a.m. a barrister in thick black robes and I are sitting together in the shadow cast by Newcastle's courthouse, trying to avoid the sun. I'm waiting to see who will arrive for James's first court appearance. The barrister is here for a different case, where his role will be to defend the accused.

'It's intricate,' he says, his face lined with distaste. 'Decades ago. There's no evidence. Witnesses die, witnesses become infirm. They lose their ability to recollect.' It is almost as if he is talking about the Bowraville murders, I think to myself. The problem is when the case became political, he tells me. 'It's red hot. The politicians make you go ahead when there's no evidence.' He says it eats at him, that it's an affront to his professional capacity. I think he means that it's an affront him having to defend it. That, in his mind, it is offensive that the prosecutors have pursued the case at all.

Thomas Duroux, whose son Clinton was the third child to be murdered, parks his car in front of the courthouse, pulls down his baseball cap against the sun and starts to climb the steps towards us. He says that this will be the first time he's seen the man accused of killing his son in more than a decade, since James was found not guilty of killing Evelyn. Back then, after the verdict, Thomas was walking up the courthouse steps as James was walking out. He thought James looked the same as when he'd lived in Bowraville.

A little fatter maybe. Today, Thomas is uncertain what he should expect.

'You have to do it,' he says. You have to see what happens. Today's hearing may last only a few minutes – the law dictates that James first appear in a local court before the case can be formally referred to the Court of Criminal Appeal – but you have to be there.

The task force – Gary, Jerry and Bianca Comina – walk up together, past the metal plaque fixed to the wall that marks the date, a year ago, when Gabrielle Upton opened this new courthouse. Today, she is no longer the state's attorney general, having been moved in a cabinet reshuffle. Only this physical reminder and the effect of her decisions, including that we are here to watch James return to court over the murders, remain.

Three television news crews arrive. The *Newcastle Herald* newspaper has a reporter here, as does the local ABC radio station. There is a reporter for the *Daily Telegraph*, and me for *The Australian*. We stand in a line at the bottom of the courthouse steps, just inside the shadow of the building. Stand any further back and it feels like the sun is cutting through your skin.

At 10 a.m., Magistrate Robert Stone takes his seat on the raised platform at the front of courtroom 2.1. He holds his head in a splayed hand while reading the paperwork before him. Gary prowls in and out of the courtroom, leaning forward to listen to the whispered conversations between the lawyers, or speaking briefly to the local police prosecutor, a big man with his pen falling out of his shirt pocket. The prosecutor picks up a file from the stack of papers on the bar table and follows Gary out, where they huddle together with two members of the attorney general's legal team who've driven up from Sydney to be here.

Thomas stands just outside their circle and cracks a smile, lips parting to reveal his tongue. He's feeling hopeful, he says. It's the first time I have seen him admit to optimism. Evelyn's aunt, Michelle Jarrett, bustles up behind us, her breathing hard and rasping with the effort of rushing to make it here, and her fear of being late. She flinches and bends forward, pushing one fist into the palm of the other hand.

Wincing, Michelle says that years ago, she picked up one of her nephews and pulled some discs out of place in her spine. Now, when she gets stressed, her back goes into spasm. She's gone and left her painkillers in her pink bag in Bowraville, she says.

Gary is trying to look confident. Yes, he says, this hearing is procedural and should only take a moment. But there's still time for something to go wrong. He stares ahead, jaw set. It's like when you step into the boxing ring. You have to look ready even if you don't feel it, or your opponent will sense that you are weak.

There's a delay. James's lawyers arrive but somehow, no one has told James that he needs to be here also. Gary paces up and down outside the courtroom. James gets a call telling him to get to court right now, and everybody waits.

'We should be used to waiting, hey?' says Michelle, smiling. 'It's been twenty-six years.'

After half an hour, Paula and Lucas Craig arrive, whose sister Colleen was the first of the three children to be murdered. For five hours they've been driving.

'It started to really hit when we walked in here,' says Paula, joining the constellation of anxious faces orbiting the entrance to the courtroom. 'We've come so far.' Through trials and inquests. Through changes to the law and a parliamentary inquiry. Over a quarter of a century, during which time she and her brother have grown into adults, while James himself has had more children, who've grown old and had children of their own.

After an hour, with no sign of James's arrival, the court takes its morning break and the families crowd back into the lift with a flock of lawyers dressed in suits, designer glasses and black gowns. Michelle and her husband are forced up against one side and fall silent while the lawyers chatter. After a cup of coffee outside at a cafe behind the courthouse, we head back in, where one of the newspaper photographers says that James is now inside the building. Michelle clutches at her chest and staggers, grasping for the handrail. Her breath echoes in the lift up to the second floor.

James sits alone against the far wall of the court building, arms crossed, his face betraying no emotion. Colleen's sister, Paula, is standing staring straight at him. She was fifteen the last time she saw him, in the spring of 1990, shortly before her sister went missing. He's older now, of course, and he looks tired, but still big with muscle. His arms are pale like fish bellies beneath a short-sleeved, purple shirt, suggesting that he doesn't see much of the sun these days.

James is staring back at Paula.

The hearing is delayed again, until after lunch. By now, the pain in Michelle's back has got so bad she is forced to lie down on the floor outside the courtroom, feet up on a bench to try to stop it from gnawing at her. A young couple sitting next to Michelle's feet are blueing about something, telling each other to fuck off, the volume rising. A sheriff's officer tries to quiet them down, but they overwhelm her. Gary and Jerry detach themselves from the knot of lawyers standing outside the courtroom and walk over to the

couple, looking as if they would invite trouble at the moment.
It would be a relief from waiting.

Finally, the families are called into the court for the hearing.
Michelle sits upright in the seats at the back of the courtroom.
Paula and Lucas lean in towards each other. Thomas waits for
his partner, Marjorie Jarrett, to take a seat, then joins her, sigh-
ing as he pulls off his baseball cap and runs a hand through his
grey hair.

James holds his head high as he walks across in front of the
watching families. Looking up, you realise just how tall he is.
How solid. He takes a seat in front of Michelle and her breathing
becomes harsh and laboured. It is the only sound in the courtroom.
Nobody speaks.

The magistrate enters and we stand. He nods towards us and we
bow. He sits and opens the file on the desk in front of him.

'This is James Hide, is it?' he asks.

'Yes, Your Honour,' replies the police prosecutor, pulling the
pen from his shirt pocket. There's little to discuss. The case will go
to the appeal court, until which time James will remain on bail,
rather than spending the time until the next hearing in prison. The
police do not oppose this. The magistrate wants James to surrender
his passport, but it turns out he doesn't have one. He is not a flight
risk. The magistrate nods again and closes the file. James leaves the
courtroom alone, staring straight ahead.

'Short and sweet, but at least it's started now. We're on our way,'
says Thomas as we walk out of the courtroom following the
hearing. The families have been told not to speak to the media but,
once outside the building, Thomas is cornered by the waiting

television cameras and is too polite to ignore the microphones thrust towards his face.

'It's something,' he tells them. 'We've waited for a long time so it's good. It's really good to be here. I've travelled a long way and I have to go back a long way. We've all travelled down here, all our families have. Travelled down and we still have a long way to go yet. We've just got to keep fighting, keep going. There's a long way to go. It's been a long travel but hopefully we'll get there.'

Asked how he finds the strength to keep on going, Thomas looks up at where Michelle is walking out of sight around the corner of the building. Paula and Marjorie are not far behind her.

'It's not me,' he says. 'It's the girls. They've done all the work and kept us going. They're the ones who should get the accolades for everything that's happened, I reckon.'

The cameras let him go and line up again, waiting for James. He's still inside, standing at the counter of the court registry, staring out the window, waiting to sign his bail papers.

He smiles when I approach him.

'James? I'm Dan Box.'

'I know.'

I say it did not feel right to both be here and yet ignore each other. I put out a hand. He shakes it.

'I'm not allowed to talk,' he tells me. 'Maybe we can have a talk one day.'

I turn and find a seat near the registry where I start to write up the day's hearing for *The Australian*. After a few minutes of silence, James walks up to me, yellow bail paper in hand and says he wants to say something. We agree it will be off the record, meaning I don't reveal what's said, but we start talking. He's taller than me and physically imposing. He smiles. His teeth look sharp and are stained brown, perhaps from smoking. Seeing him in the flesh, I find myself thinking again about his family, his children and grandchildren. He had a son with Colleen's aunt, Alison Walker, with whom he used to live on the Mission in Bowraville. I'd asked Colleen's family if I could talk to James's son, but they were protective. They said it wouldn't do him any good. He already had a hard enough life, trying to reconcile the two worlds of his parents.

I think again about James's pillowcase found stuffed down Clinton's shorts.

Once again, as in our previous phone calls, James does not express any sympathy for the murdered children's families. There is no desperate appeal about his innocence, no attempt to grab my shirt collar and plead, 'You have to believe me.'

But then, is that so surprising? It's been so many years that, innocent or guilty, perhaps his emotional response has long been blunted. Perhaps he is simply too exhausted to be desperate.

Our conversation ends. After James leaves, pursued by television cameras, a court registry staffer slides a thin bundle of papers towards me across the countertop. There is James's name, his date of birth and the exact wording of the charges against him.

The charge sheet alleges James murdered Clinton at some time between Friday, 1 February 1991, the day he disappeared following the party on the Mission, and Monday, 18 February, the day his remains were discovered.

The charge sheet alleges he murdered Evelyn sometime between 11 a.m. on Friday, 5 October 1990 – when her mother woke up on the morning after another party on the Mission and noticed her daughter was missing – and six months later, Saturday, 27 April 1991, the day the search party found Evelyn's skeleton lying half-covered by leaf litter in the forest beside Congarinni Road.

There are, then, weeks and months of uncertainty between these dates where the police cannot say when these murders happened. Does this mean they are admitting it is possible the children were alive after the parties James attended on the Mission? Without that link between the children's disappearance and James's presence at those parties, the case against him collapses.

The lawyers will have to do better than that when this gets to the appeal court.

Wednesday, 29 November 2017

Colleen Walker-Craig was sixteen when she disappeared on 13 September 1990.

Evelyn Greenup was four when she went missing three weeks later, on 4 October.

Clinton Speedy-Duroux was sixteen when he was last seen in the morning of 1 February 1991.

That's four and a half months between them, Wendy Abraham QC tells the three red-robed appeal court judges.

Three children. Three murders. They were so close together.

This morning Wendy is standing at a lectern on the bar table, the only figure on their feet in the state's Banco Court, the biggest in Sydney's Law Courts building, where rows of plush red chairs are raised in tiers, like in a colosseum, surrounding the arena where the lawyers are lined up. Dressed in a barrister's black gown and white wig, with pale skin and bright red lipstick, she looks ready for

the coming combat. Her opponent, who barrelled into the courtroom moments before the hearing began, black robes trailing out
behind him, is Mark Ierace SC, the state's senior public defender.
He sits, yellowing wig askance, watching Wendy and smiling.

This is a strange fight, I think. Wendy represents the New South
Wales attorney general, attempting to have the previous not-guilty
verdicts overturned and James Hide sent back to trial for the murders. Mark's wages are being met by the state's Legal Aid system as
he tries to stop her. So the New South Wales government is paying
for both prosecution and defence. It's state against state, arguing
over one man, three dead children and the law.

Wendy describes the Bowraville Mission, how it was so small
at the time the murders happened, only eight houses, and how the
children went missing from two of the homes in this small row.
A metre-tall aerial photograph of Bowraville stands propped
behind the judges, showing the physical closeness of the places
where Wendy says Colleen, Evelyn and Clinton went missing. It
must have been taken in the summer, the season when the children
were murdered; the image shows a dry, exhausted land with a thin
lines of trees creating narrow shadows, and the sun-bleached roofs
of the Mission houses blurring into the tired grass.

The children's families have made the journey down to Sydney
for the court hearing in their dozens, travelling in crowded
cars from towns across the state's north and over the border in
Queensland. From Macksville, Warwick, Lismore, Ballina and
Bowraville. From Sawtell and Nambucca and other towns all
fed by the rivers that run down from the mountains of the Great
Dividing Range.

The families have taken seats directly opposite the heavy
wooden court bench, so they are facing the judges. Colleen's

mother, Muriel Craig, is there, along with her remaining children, including Paula and Lucas. Clinton's parents, Thomas Duroux and June Speedy, are there also. Evelyn's mum, Rebecca Stadhams, is twisting her greying hair around the fingers of one hand. Rebecca's sister, Michelle Jarrett, sits hunched forward in pain from the muscles in her back that again have tightened. One of Rebecca's grandchildren sits behind them, on the highest tier of chairs, looking around him at the polished wood and the oil paintings of old judges, his feet dangling down but not reaching the floor.

Others of the children's families are watching in a different courthouse, in Coffs Harbour, the city an hour north of Bowraville where the coast meets the South Pacific, and where a dedicated screen has been set up to show the proceedings live using an audio-visual link.

James, the man accused of these murders, is also sitting, watching. But he does not have to be in court for this hearing in person, and has chosen against it. He will instead follow what happens on a separate screen, set up in another court building nearer his home.

Inside the Banco Court the families sit in silence, their black faces like so many mourners, watching. The other faces in this courtroom – the three judges, who wear red robes with silver sashes on their shoulders; the ranks of lawyers drawn up with their laptops and documents at the bar tables; the police sitting behind them in their dark suits; the journalists gathered together to one side, looking down from our own place in the colosseum seating; and all the portraits of dead judges hung in gilt frames on the walls above us – each and every one of us is white.

Colleen's body was not recovered after her disappearance, says Wendy, so James was not charged over her killing. The evidence about her murder was also not adduced in either previous trial over the deaths of Evelyn and Clinton.

She argues that 'adduced', the meaning of which is not made clear in the new double jeopardy legislation, means 'admitted', the process by which a judge allows evidence to be allowed to be heard by a jury. More than a year has passed now since my first visit to Bowraville in February 2016, meaning it is now more than a quarter-century since James was first charged over the murders of Evelyn and Clinton, and twenty-four years since the first judge to hear the case ruled they must be heard by separate juries, neither of which would be told about the other children who went missing in the town. Because of this history, Wendy argues, the evidence about Colleen could not be adduced as it was inadmissible during the first two trials.

She asks the three judges to look at the photograph of Bowraville. Congarinni Road, beside which Evelyn and Clinton's bodies were discovered, is marked in yellow near the bottom of the photo, heading away from town into the forest, she says.

'Your Honours can see Colleen Walker-Craig's clothes were found on the bottom of the plan. They were found in the Nambucca River, 11.6 kilometres from Bowraville,' Wendy tells the judges.

'Does Congarinni Road cross the Nambucca?' one of the judges, Lucy McCallum, asks her.

'Yes, it does.' Exactly. Wendy wants to show the murders must all be connected, although she hasn't said so, yet.

The key to this is Colleen's murder, Wendy argues. The fact the evidence about her death could not be admitted during the first two trials means that it is 'fresh', satisfying the first demand of the double jeopardy laws that govern the possibility of a retrial. To satisfy the second, that this evidence also be 'compelling', Wendy points to the similarities between Colleen's disappearance and those of the other children. This is why she's worked so hard to emphasise how close together the murders were, both in space and time.

Muriel, Colleen's mother, sits with her arms folded, flanked by her children. This is special, she told me before the hearing. It's the first time her family have all been in court together. But the chief justice, Tom Bathurst, interrupts Wendy. He's troubled, he says. Can all three of the matters – he calls the deaths of each of the murdered children 'matters' – really be joined together? Wendy has appealed to the imagination, encouraging a creeping sense of how similar the three murders seem, but the judge is interested only in a legal understanding. Does the law allow for each of the three murders to be listed on the same indictment – the formal process by which a suspected killer is charged? Wendy argues that they can.

It is the similarities between all three killings that make the case compelling, Wendy argues. All three must be considered together. She does not ask the judges to overturn either of the not-guilty verdicts for the murders of Evelyn and Clinton separately, because then James could face a retrial only on that murder. Were that to happen, the evidence would be less sure.

This similarity 'is the cornerstone of the application,' Wendy tells the judges. Janet Fife-Yeomans, the *Daily Telegraph* chief reporter, who is sitting beside me, whispers, 'She's good, isn't she?'

She is, but the chief justice fires another cannon: 'This legislation takes away a fairly established right.'

His words hang in the courtroom. He's talking about double jeopardy, the principle that no one should face trial for the same

crime twice. Among the watching children's families, Rebecca is
still twisting her hair around her fingers. Michelle is still hunched
forward in pain. The law prevents a suspect being tried twice,
rather than being punished twice, as if being put on trial is punish-
ment itself. By doing so, the law protects the accused man against
the state, which has the power to pursue him, but in this case, if it
prevents a retrial being held, it will mean no jury ever gets to hear
the evidence about what happened to Colleen.

My eyes stray up to the oil paintings hanging around the courtroom, showing the former chief justices of New South Wales right
back to the first in the history of the state, Sir Francis Forbes.

All of them observed the rule of double jeopardy, I think. How
willing is their successor, this chief justice, to surrender this long-
established right?

Wendy doesn't falter. She says that parliament had voted to change
the law, after the campaign by the children's families.

'The whole purpose of the legislation was to remove the principle of double jeopardy,' she says. This is just the first time the appeal
court has been asked to recognise that this change has taken place.
But the shot from the chief justice has forced her onto the defensive.
Following her argument in shorthand in my notebook, I realise she
is now attempting to advance on another front. The judges ought
also to consider the evidence of the prison informants, she says.

This evidence, in contrast with the complexity of the law itself,
is simple. At different times, in different jails, says Wendy, James
shared a cell with other prisoners. One told police that James
claimed, 'Clinton came at him with a knife, he took it off him, give
it to him in the head.'

A second said James told him, 'If I had done a proper job bury-ing the cunt I would never have got pinched.'

A third prison informant claimed James admitted, 'I stabbed the bastard. I took Speedy out in the bush, he had been drinking. I'm going to do the girlfriend too.'

The fourth informant said James once 'specified about the boy being knocked in the caravan and the girl's body just outside of town'.

All prison informants, says Wendy, have issues with their cred-ibility and reliability as witnesses – at this, her opponent, Mark Ierace, smiles in anticipation. Wendy says the strength of this evi-dence is that there are four separate prison witnesses, all giving different versions of the story that James did it. There is no sugges-tion that the four got together to concoct the evidence they gave.

Without warning, Judge McCallum asks about 'the Box transcript'.

I stop writing. She must mean the transcript of my interview with James. The interview which we used in the podcast. The inter-view that Gary Jubelin asked me to give a copy of to Wendy's legal team several months ago.

The walls of the Banco Court grow taller and close in above me. As a reporter, every instinct, every lesson learned in training, says don't become the subject of your own reporting. Because that's not your job. And it's hard to be honest. The interview, I learn with a twist of feeling as Wendy answers the judge's question, will be used to argue what she calls James's 'consciousness of guilt'.

She says James lied in his answers to my questions and, by lying, revealed that he is hiding what he really knows about the murders. I can't remember catching James out in a lie during the conver-sation. Head down, writing in my notepad, I try to hide from all the eyes in the courtroom, which I fear have turned to look at me.

The evidence on which Wendy is relying is contained in white folders, dozens of which are stacked on the bar tables or on trolleys standing on the floor of the courtroom, or are laid out on the bench before the judges themselves. Inside these, I learn, are long stretches of transcript from the interview with James, including the moment when I asked about the night Colleen went missing following a party on the Mission; when James was seen walking towards the rear of the house at number 3 Cemetery Road, while Colleen walked down the other side of the same building.

'On that night of the party did you walk down the side of that house to the back?' I'd asked him.

'No.'

'Were you there at all around midnight, around the time Colleen disappeared?'

'I was there at one point that night, but I left early.'

'You left early?'

'Yeah,' said James.

Except, Wendy's legal team have gone through the other witness statements and say that three separate witnesses saw James at the party between 11.30 pm and midnight; that another saw him at around midnight and a fifth saw him leaving after midnight had passed.

'It is open to the jury to find that what the respondent told Dan Box is a lie,' says their written submission to the judges, which also sits inside those white folders in the courtroom. 'This lie . . . is capable of constituting an admission against interest – that is, it gives rise to an inference that it is told out of a consciousness of guilt.'

Still making my hurried shorthand notes, I listen as this evidence is laid out by Wendy for inspection. I hear how, in another passage from the interview, I asked James about the second party on the Mission, after which Evelyn's mother Rebecca woke up and found her daughter was missing.

No one disputed James was in the house on the night of that party.

'Did you go into that room where Rebecca was sleeping with Evelyn after they went to sleep?' I asked him.

'No,' he answered.

'You're saying you had nothing to do with Evelyn's disappearance?'

'That's right.'

Except another witness saw James coming out of the bedroom in the early hours of the morning, after the party had ended and most people had either left or crashed out. If a jury accepts her evidence, says Wendy's written submission, then 'it is open to them to find that what the respondent told Dan Box in relation to this matter is also false'.

At this point, I realise I am no longer simply a reporter. I'm not sure what I have become. If they are using my interview as evidence, does that make me complicit? When the judges rise to take their morning tea-break, I call my chief-of-staff at *The Australian*, explain what's happened and suggest they send someone else to cover the court hearing in my place. He pauses for a moment's silence, then tells me to stay where I am unless my credibility is questioned during the hearing. If that happens, he says, I cannot report fairly and they will replace me. I hang up and go back into the courtroom, feeling vulnerable.

There is a third exchange between James and myself included in the evidence the lawyers are relying on to make their case that he should face a retrial. I'd asked him about the claim that he got into an argument with two people living on the Mission and tried to smash in their door with a golf club, saying, 'I'll get youse, you two fuck heads, I'll take youse out to Congarinni Road and use youse for fertiliser, under the ground'.

'I never mentioned Congarinni Road in that argument,' James told me.

'But you did threaten to use people for fertiliser?' I asked.

He said he did, but that was just a form of words. 'It's a saying that was getting around there at the time.' Wendy does not accept this. She says James is admitting the conversation, which is, in effect, a threat to kill.

Wendy tells the judges that my conversation with James is 'fresh and compelling'. So, too, are the accounts of the prison informants. When you consider them along with the evidence about Colleen's disappearance, which has never been put to a jury, the argument is overwhelming, she says. The court should order that James face a retrial.

Thursday, 30 November 2017

The three judges walk into the courtroom. We stand and bow. They, too, seem to bow slightly, as if in mirror-image. They sit. We do the same.

The chief justice, Tom Bathurst, sits between the other judges, a wig the colour of an egg yolk flopped on top of his head. He's older and grumpier than he used to be, whispers Janet from the *Daily Telegraph*. During an exchange with one lawyer representing the police force about a delay in providing documents that the court ordered to be handed over, the chief justice snarls that the court orders and it shall be obeyed.

On his right sits the chief judge at common law, Clifton Hoeben, who seems more jovial. Age has hunched his shoulders forward and there is something owl-like in the way he studies the documents before him, and something owl-like, also, in the way he swoops down on any small mistake or point of law left out in the open. In the coming days I will come to appreciate how tight he holds to what is before him in the legislation; to what is allowed, and what is not allowed.

The third of the judges, Lucy McCallum, is younger and sits more upright, peering through heavy spectacles at the children's families opposite her. Years ago, as an undergraduate, she volunteered at the non-profit Legal Centre in Redfern, the hub of Sydney's Aboriginal population, and where they would come for free legal advice. Perhaps she will have more empathy than the two other judges. How hard is it to face Colleen, Evelyn and Clinton's mothers – who sit in court with chins resting on palms, fingers dug into the soft flesh of their cheeks, wearing footy shirts printed with photographs of their murdered children – and not want to help them?

Wendy Abraham, the lawyer leading the argument that James should face a retrial, starts laying out the details of Clinton's murder. Clinton's mother, June Speedy, bites her hands. When Wendy talks about how Evelyn was murdered, it is Rebecca Stadham's turn to be heartbroken. Among the watching families, a child starts to bawl and is carried out of court.

From where I'm sitting, in the court's tiered seating, I can see the lawyers' tables spread with heavy folders spilling out their contents: maps of where the children's bodies were recovered; photographs of the inside of James's caravan; a close-up of Evelyn's bare skull lying in the bush where it was found. I hope Rebecca hasn't seen this. The child outside is wailing, 'Mummy, Mummy,' in the corridor, her voice echoing from the uncaring walls.

Wendy says that when Clinton's girlfriend woke up in James's caravan, he was gone and her trousers had been removed. When Rebecca woke up the next morning, her pants had also been pulled down.

'So the motive is sexual interest in women?' Judge McCallum asks her.

'Yes.'

'So in one case, the victim herself and in the other two cases, the people they were with. That's the evidence in your submission?' It is a bare, necessary way to describe the horror of what's being suggested. Colleen would be the victim. The other two people would be Kelly Jarrett, Clinton's girlfriend, and Rebecca herself.

On this interpretation, whoever killed the children is a potential rapist. The killing was a way to achieve it, or cover up what he was doing. We know that Colleen had been stripped naked because her clothes were found in the Taylors Arm River. Perhaps she was killed after trying to fight him off, or afterwards, to keep her quiet. The other two, Evelyn and Clinton, were not the killer's targets. Instead they were potential witnesses. Perhaps they tried to stop him, and were killed as a result.

Judge McCallum nods and rubs her nose with the back of one hand.

Next to her, the chief justice is concerned with definition, not with motive. He wants Wendy to return to section 102(2) of the *Crimes (Appeal and Review) Act 2006*, which deals with double jeopardy. This says that evidence is 'fresh' if it was not and could not have been adduced in a trial. Wendy has argued 'adduced' means 'admitted'. Judge Hoeben holds up a judgement from another case, which says adduced means something different. It might mean evidence was tendered or presented to a court, rather than accepted by a judge and admitted into evidence.

'In my submission, it does not,' Wendy flashes back.

Their contest over meaning descends into the detail of parliamentary readings of the legislation, the findings in *Alcan (NT) Alumina Pty Ltd v Commissioner of Territory Revenue* [2009] and what was once said in *R v B* [1997] in the United Kingdom appeal court.

Janet, sitting next to me, Googles 'adduced' on her phone and shows me the screen: 'In legal context it refers to bring forward in argument or use in evidence.' I look at the families, sitting patiently. Does this make any sense to them? Are they tired, resigned or frightened – or following every word?

After the day in court is over, I ask Evelyn's aunt, Michelle Jarrett, how she is feeling. Spinning a finger round beside her head, she replies, 'Confused.'

Outside, Clinton's father Thomas Duroux sits alone on a low wall on the edge of Hyde Park, looking at the Law Courts building. He walked out of the hearing at lunchtime and did not go back.

Thomas waves one hand at the city and says that he was hungry.

'I went all up around there and there.' He points at the office blocks in frustration that in all these buildings, he could not find anything to eat.

We sit in silence while the people walking past ignore us.

'The big arguments, the big words they use. You don't understand what they mean for half of it, legal mumbo,' says Thomas. It's as if the lawyers and the judges speak a different language.

I say nothing.

'You going to the boxing tonight?' he asks.

I am.

Gary Jubelin has spent months training for this moment, a charity fundraiser for Legacy, which supports the families of those killed while serving in the police force.

He has also bought tickets for many of the Bowraville families to be here. There, in the tiered seating surrounding the ring at the Norths leagues club are Evelyn's mother, Rebecca Stadhams, pressing her fingers to her lips in excitement, Evelyn's aunt, Michelle Jarrett, and Leonie Duroux, who got together with Clinton's brother Marbuck and who is sitting with their two sons.

Sitting beside them, Jerry Bowden and Bianca Comina from the police task force are roaring in appreciation as they watch one of the earlier bouts scheduled for the evening. Gary's own children, now adults, are here to watch him also. Barry Toohey, the former grief counsellor who worked with the children's families and at whose house I stayed in Bowraville, raises his schooner to me in welcome, then turns his attention back to the boxing. One of the fighters is swaying, unsteady on his feet. The referee looks into his eyes, shakes his head and signals to stop the fight. The boxers leave and two more climb through the ropes to replace them, circling each other until a buzzer sounds and they close in confrontation. A child in the front row shouts, 'Go, Dad!'

That fight ends and Gary appears, framed in the doorway from the changing rooms.

'I'm ready! I'm happy!' booms the ring announcer, his words rolling out of the speakers hanging from the ceiling like a drawn-out thunder. 'This is going to be one hell of a fight!'

The Bowraville families are on their feet, as are Gary's adult son and daughter, cheering.

'Knock him out, Bowra!' shouts Rebecca. It's the first time I've heard them call him that. They've known each other for so long now, Rebecca tells me, her eyes fixed on Gary, and he has fought for them all that time, that he is one of their mob now.

Gary climbs into the ring, throwing punches, fists snaking out dead straight and hard. His opponent is another detective, hollow-eyed and taller but less muscled. One of Leonie's sons looks at him and leans over, telling me, 'He's scared.'

The ring announcer calls Gary 'the Gatekeeper' and his opponent 'the Doctor'. The buzzer sounds.

'Knock him out,' Rebecca shouts. The ring announcer booms: 'Will the Doctor give him his medicine or will the Gatekeeper close the gate on him and call it goodnight?'

The Doctor lands the first two punches, one of which catches Gary out of nowhere. Rebecca is bouncing with excitement. Gary jabs, the Doctor stumbles and looks frightened for a moment.

'Fucking chase him, Dad!' shouts Gary's son. As if in answer, the Doctor hits Gary in the face with a right cross. Gary returns it, with vengeance.

The round ends. Gary has won it, I reckon, but it's close. Both fighters go back into their corners, suck in a few breaths of air then come out for the second round.

Gary jabs, the Doctor's head snaps back and we can see his sweat spray up under the lights. He lifts his fists up higher, to protect his face, and steps backwards.

'He doesn't want to fight,' Bianca says.

'He's done,' Jerry agrees. When the round ends, Gary returns to the stool in his corner, breathing hard and scowling as his trainer sends him out for the last round.

The Doctor throws a straight punch and Gary retaliates with seeming fury, forcing his opponent off balance, then back over the ropes.

'Oh my God, Gary! Oh my God!' Michelle is shouting. The two fighters meet again in the centre of the ring, trading blows that smack home with a dull sound on impact and which must surely hurt.

'Both men want to end it,' roars the ring announcer. 'Who wants it more?'

'Knock 'em down, Bowra! Knock 'em down!' Michelle screams. Gary charges, shoulders hunched, throwing everything he can. There is a violence inside him, I realise, which I have not seen before.

The final buzzer sounds.

'Two warriors. Intensity, tenacity and courage,' growls the ring announcer over the sound system. The two fighters stand together inside the ring, isolated in the stage light.

'He's got it,' says Jerry. It's a unanimous decision. Gary won. Everyone around me roars. Gary ducks under the rope, pausing to look up and stick his hand out to the families, thumb raised, while he grins like a schoolboy. His kids, Rebecca, Michelle and Leonie all leave their seats and surround him, as does Bianca.

'It needed to happen,' says Barry Toohey, watching as Gary heads back into the changing room. It keeps the fairytale alive for one more night before heading back to court.

'I hope they check his knuckles,' says Rebecca, patting my shoulder as she walks back to her seat, and smiling.

*

The following morning, Gary carries a busted lip into the courtroom. Wendy Abraham is there already, waiting and wearing fresh
red lipstick. Her opponent, Mark Ierace, hurries to the lectern,
his yellow wig and long black robes emphasising both his age
and height.

'The history of this case is unique,' Mark says, placing an
emphasis on 'history'. As if he's suggesting that the judges should
be careful. Be reluctant. I look up at the unsmiling portraits of
those other long-dead judges, hung on the courtroom walls. The
living judges sit beneath them, following Mark's argument. There
are fewer of the children's families here this morning, having found
yesterday's legal argument either too upsetting or difficult to
follow. Mark's voice is dry, deliberate and quiet.

Mark says that the judges shouldn't consider all three of the
murders together, as Wendy argued, but rather look at each of
them separately when deciding whether the evidence was 'fresh and
compelling' enough to order a retrial.

Judge McCallum interrupts to ask Wendy a question: 'But
you're saying its compellability is linked to the fact that there
are three?'

'Yes,' Wendy replies.

'So you wouldn't seek an outcome to this that you would have
one of two acquittals?' the judge asks. This is an outcome I had
not considered; that the appeal court could overturn the not-guilty
verdict in, say, Clinton's case but not in Evelyn's.

Wendy does not blink. 'No, going for all three,' she says.

As Mark begins to make the case for James, I realise that he
plans to challenge the evidence that the police have collected. This
is unexpected. Rather than carefully unpicking the complex legal
argument that Wendy spent yesterday constructing, he's taking a

hammer to the building blocks instead. More than once, the chief justice asks if Mark is going to talk about the principle of double jeopardy and its interpretation in the law, about 'adduced' and 'fresh and compelling'. Yes, the barrister replies. He'll get there. Then he continues to smash at the evidence that the police built up.

In our podcast about the murders we tried something similar. The fifth and final episode was called 'The Case for James'.

As part of it, the producer Eric George and I recreated the car journey James claimed he'd made on the morning after Clinton disappeared from his caravan. On James's account, he thought he'd missed his lift to work, so started to drive himself, then saw the car belonging to his mate arrive to collect him so he returned to the caravan, only he then sent his mate to work alone and decided instead to stop and drink a cup of tea.

It seemed to make no sense, as Wendy had also told the appeal judges yesterday. It was irrational, she argued. Did it not make more sense to believe that James had been out disposing of Clinton's body and returned late, finding his mate waiting outside the caravan, so sent him away while he took a moment to regather his thoughts?

Except, when Eric and I drove the same route James claimed to have taken, we'd been surprised at our own reaction. On paper, in the transcript of James's evidence at the trial over Clinton's murder, the route seemed odd – driving around the corner, pulling over when he saw his mate in the rear-view mirror, then heading back. But in person, on the road, it felt plausible.

In court, Mark gathers his black gown around him as he considers this moment. 'My learned friend yesterday made much of what they said was irrational behaviour of the respondent doing these things,' he tells the judges. 'Perhaps the appropriate approach to take is whether it is irrational behaviour, given he was drunk?'

Then there are James's neighbours, Mark continues, who say they heard the red Galant belonging to his mother driving away from the caravan earlier that morning, and saw James behind the wheel when the car returned.

Their account would seem, at first, to undermine James's own. But 'an important issue in the trial and in any retrial would be the credibility of their evidence,' Mark says. One of the couple has died. And, as for the other, so much time has passed since then that no one knows what damage age, health and cognitive ability might wreak.

In fact, he says, so much time has passed since the murders happened that any witness evidence cannot be relied on. Memories play tricks, or warp. A retrial might find some witnesses say something different to what they have said previously. There are great holes in this case that cannot be overlooked, the barrister is saying, swinging his hammer against the stones.

At lunch, Jerry says he thinks they're down, one judge for them, two against. Afterwards, Mark continues his demolition work.

Three witnesses have given evidence saying they saw someone matching Clinton's appearance hitchhiking out of Bowraville after the night police say he disappeared from James's caravan. One of them, a nurse, came close enough to the young Aboriginal hitchhiker to call out, 'Sorry, I can't pick you up,' and later described the t-shirt and shorts that he was wearing, and the fact he was not wearing shoes. Her evidence, 'in every respect', was compelling, Mark tells the judges. When shown a photograph of Clinton, she told the police that he was who she saw.

In contrast, he says, look at the prison informants, who say James told them things about the murders while they shared a jail cell. Here, Mark's voice seems to sharpen, as if with glee or scorn. One of these informants, he says, watched a television appeal for information about the Bowraville murders on *Australia's Most Wanted* and knew a $100,000 reward was being offered in return. This man also had convictions for dishonesty. He heard voices. He'd given evidence at an inquest into the death of two young women, claiming to have heard someone confess to their murder – only the person he accused was himself in prison when the murders were carried out.

Gary, who gathered this evidence, sits unmoving in the courtroom, staring forward, the swollen lip an angry red. I had heard none of this, about the faults with the evidence, from him before this moment. Not when we first met, nor when I started reporting on the case for *The Australian*, nor when the podcast became a success.

Mark says that Gary also made no mention of these flaws in an affidavit detailing his reinvestigation of the murders, which had been submitted to the appeal court to argue that James should face a retrial. Nor did Gary mention that another of the prison informants has a perjury conviction. Or that records show the third such prison witness was known to inform in return for money, while the fourth had been found to have given police false information in relation to other, unrelated killings.

Sitting in court, I don't blame Gary for not telling me this information. Nor will I blame him later, when I read through the folders of written argument put together by Mark's legal team which detail, point by point, the police case against James and attempt to contradict it. Gary told me the murders stopped after James was arrested. 'There have been murders and violent deaths' in Bowraville since this arrest, James's lawyers state.

When Gary and I first met, he was trying to convince me to report on the murders, hoping the exposure would somehow help his case. Since then, he has left me alone to report it. He didn't have to tell me everything. Gary was trying to prosecute an argument. The fault is mine for not finding out these facts before now.

The next morning, Evelyn's aunt, Michelle Jarrett, wakes up with an ear ache, like someone has stuck her with a knife. A doctor says her blood pressure is high, higher than she can remember it before. She's late to the court hearing as a result, walking in just as the lawyers are talking about her niece's murder and the singing pain down the side of her face increases.

At lunch, the children's families gather around four small couches that have been placed outside the courtroom. Children sit on laps and one of them, still wearing his nappy, runs up to me waving his little hands like tiger's paws and roars. The adults have brought neat sandwiches and a bag of Anzac biscuits, which they share out while discussing the barristers' performances. I sit against the wall to file for the newspaper, then get up and walk into the deserted courtroom, climbing the steps between the tiered rows of seating to look more closely at the portraits of the judges hanging on the wall.

Most of the names and faces provoke little recognition, though one stands out. It hangs behind where the children's families were sitting and shows a proud and decent-looking man in black robes with two slashes of red, one across the waist and another falling from the right shoulder. I write the name in my notepad, Sir James Dowling, and Google him. He was the judge who oversaw a trial of the white men accused of massacring twenty-eight Aboriginal men, women and children at Myall Creek in northern New South Wales in 1838, almost two centuries before.

That trial was held in the old stone courthouse across the square from where I am standing in the Law Courts building. It involved men who had been found not guilty but were then charged again by the attorney general. The case against them, too, was largely circumstantial with no eyewitness or direct evidence of who committed the crime. Eventually, the white men who committed the Myall Creek massacre were tried again and found guilty. But the case provoked fierce argument among the white population. The *Sydney Herald* newspaper carried a piece saying, 'The whole gang of black animals are not worth the money the colonists will have to pay for printing the silly court documents on which we have already wasted too much time.'

Earlier this morning, Michelle showed me a Facebook comment beneath an article from the *Nambucca Guardian* headlined 'Bowraville murders: Court of Appeal hearing tomorrow'. In it, a woman from Nambucca Heads, just outside Bowraville, had written, 'Waste of tax payers money stupid stupid.'

I doubt that woman has met the children's families. I walk back out of the courtroom where the toddler, who is still pretending to be a tiger, tries to climb over my foot and stumbles, before his mother picks him up.

Tuesday, 5 December 2017

'It's just frustrating, listening to them fellas,' says Michelle Jarrett outside the appeal court. She's tired, much more tired than she expected, and this afternoon her face is lined with sadness after having sat and watched James Hide's lawyers turn their guns onto her mother, Patricia Stadhams. Patricia was grandmother to four-year-old Evelyn, the second child to be murdered.

Patricia is also the closest thing the police have to a star witness. It was she who claimed to have heard Evelyn cry out on the night when James was in the house at a party, followed by a thud, then silence. It was also Patricia who said she saw Colleen walking down the side of the house at number 3 Cemetery Road on the night the teenager went missing, while James walked down the far side of the same building. But Patricia 'is essentially just patching things together,' the junior barrister on the team representing James, Julia Roy, has told the judges. Patricia lacks a coherent memory, she said.

Take Colleen. In Patricia's first recorded account of what happened, given to the police six months later in March 1991, she described seeing Colleen walk down the side of number 3 towards the back while James was walking out the front of the house. A week later, interviewed again, Patricia said she saw some white boys in a Holden Commodore out on the road, Colleen was walking down the side of the building and 'that's the way [James] was walking'. Six years later, interviewed during the police reinvestigation, Patricia said she saw James's mother's car parked behind the house at number 3, towards which Colleen was walking. This time, Patricia said she saw James walking through the front gate to number 3 and down the far side of the house, towards where Colleen was heading, and the car was parked. She saw all this, Patricia said, because she got 'suspicious' and 'just wanted to know what they were up to'.

Later again, questioned at the inquest into Colleen's death in 2004, Patricia repeated that she had seen James go through the front gate into the garden at number 3. 'He was looking towards the land there . . . where Colleen was,' she said. James and Colleen then walked down either side of number 3, both of them heading towards the back of the building.

Patricia's evidence had changed over time, the different versions contradicting one another, Julia had told the judges. Over time, they become weighted with a sense of suspicion and foreboding. 'The unavoidable and overwhelming inference that arises from all of her accounts and the progression of her accounts is that she has conflated things that she observed with things that she's been informed . . . with a common consensus in the community.' Patricia herself was also now much older, and experiencing short-term memory problems. Her long-term memory is still okay, according to a doctor, but the suggestion that her recollection might be fading had hung heavy in the still air of the courtroom.

What about the evidence of another witness that Colleen was seen in that white Commodore, driving away from the Mission on the night of the party? Julia asked the judges. That she had called out, 'Uncle George, where are you going?' or maybe, 'See ya later, Uncle Martin'? James's lawyers did not accept the police version of events, that Patricia last saw Colleen and that the teenager went missing from the party on Thursday, 13 September 1990. What about the witnesses who say they saw her in James's caravan the following night, or on the morning of the fifteenth, two days later, before the footy tournament in Macksville?

It was the same argument that had been used in James's defence during his trials over the murder of Evelyn and Clinton. The first police investigation had found witnesses who claimed they saw the children alive after the dates on which their families said that they'd gone missing. The police reinvestigation found many of these witnesses were wrong, or had their dates confused, or had the dates suggested to them during the first investigation, but by then it was too late. Their evidence had already been recorded.

'It's totally two different ways of talking and thinking,' says Michelle with a grimace, when we speak outside the courtroom. Aboriginal people don't think in terms of times and dates, she tells me, but in terms of relationships. She doesn't live at number 38, she lives next to this person and that person. Nobody on the Mission would say something happened on 15 September, especially six months later. They'd tell you this happened then that happened. No one on the Mission talks like they do in those old witness statements drawn up by the police in the months after Colleen went missing. 'Didn't then. Don't now,' says Michelle. They sounded too white, she frowns.

Her eyes close and her breathing becomes shallow. The muscles down the backs of her legs have tightened, and the pain meant it took an effort for her to stand and walk away from the courtroom after today's hearing. Each day, as the lawyers attacked the evidence against James, fewer of the children's relatives came back to watch them, their ranks on the seats facing the three judges getting slowly thinner. Colleen's mother, Muriel Craig, has stopped coming. So too has Clinton's father, Thomas Duroux.

'These lawyers don't understand how blackfellas talk,' says Michelle, walking stiffly down the corridor.

Julia plans to take a final swing at the evidence against James, aiming this time at the interview with him I recorded for the podcast. Hitching her black robe up around her shoulders, she stands to face the judges.

'It would be accepted that the Box interview is fresh,' she begins, but it fails to do what the prosecution claims – that is, to catch James out in lies about the murders James is not lying, she says.

She also tells the judges that the media reporting of the three murders itself makes it impossible for them to order a retrial. Her team have prepared an affidavit dozens of pages thick, listing hundreds of the newspaper, television and radio reports about the Bowraville murders over the years.

Some of this reporting, Julia continues, is highly prejudicial. 'Some assume the respondent's guilt, purport to report on evidence that is inaccurate or are otherwise sensationalised.' She hasn't

mentioned my reporting, yet, but watching her across the courtroom, I wait for the moment.

I know that I have changed from being a reporter about this
case to being a campaigner, joining with the police and children's
families in calling for the murders to go back to court. Now that
it's here, with evidence about all three of the killings being heard
together, I realise with a shifting horror I am no longer even a
campaigner. My interview with James is being used in evidence.
What am I then? The affidavit prepared by James's lawyers claims
that many different media reports over the years, by different
reporters, contain 'items that assume the respondent's guilt, and
items that report on "evidence" that is inaccurate and/or inadmissible'. Sitting in court, all I know is the worst thing that could
happen now would be for the judges to decide a retrial cannot pro-
ceed because of my reporting. In a moment, while the courtroom
is silent, I think back over everything I've written or included in
the podcast. I did not doubt them at the time, I think. But so
much is now at stake for those three children's families. What
if the judges uncover some sloppiness, some bias or some poor
choice of words?

Julia shifts her head. She must know I'm watching her. She
begins to describe a feature article I wrote for *The Australian* that
was published on the morning the appeal court hearing started.

The article began, 'The man chased the girl across the golf
course . . .', and described the evidence of a woman on the Mission
who said James chased after a friend of hers in the months before
the children disappeared.

'She just kept running and he didn't catch her,' this witness
had told the 2004 inquest. She also claimed to have seen James
putting an unidentified tablet in a bottle of bourbon during a party.

I'd found her evidence among hundreds of pages stored in the coronial files.

The article I'd written had not mentioned James by name and *The Australian*'s lawyers had gone through it before publication. At the time, there was no criminal trial relating to the murders. Yet Julia argues my reporting could trip up a jury should a trial be established. The woman's claims, repeated in my article, were prejudicial and would be inadmissible in court, Julia says, inviting the three judges to read the feature through to its completion.

She then invites the judges to look at us reporters in the public gallery. Already we've applied to see those documents tendered in evidence to this hearing, as if doing so proves our hunger for sensation. I hate this but cannot say anything, so I stare back at Julia. If a retrial were ordered, she says, any juror could have read our reports and so have formed some view about James's guilt or innocence. As a result, the application to overturn James's previous not-guilty verdicts should fail, she tells the judges. Julia sits. I breathe out, slowly.

That afternoon, once the judges have left the court and the lawyers are packing up their laptops and folders, one of the barristers in the legal team arguing that James should face a retrial waves me over. She's not concerned with what Julia was saying. That's courtroom argument. Instead, she asks, 'You realise that if this goes to trial you could be called as a witness?'

I hadn't. I should have done. I spoke to James. They would want to tender the interview in evidence and put me on the stand to confirm it.

That's what I am now. Not a reporter, nor a campaigner. A witness.

But perhaps I had always known that, really. Perhaps I just
told myself that I could be the objective reporter, who stood back
and kept myself separate from the story of the murders. The truth
is I couldn't. Looking back over the three years since I first met
with Gary, I have to admit that the act of reporting affects both
the reporter and the people he reports on. Perhaps I should have
known that the moment I sat down with Gary at that cafe table
outside the New South Wales Police headquarters in Sydney.

I think Gary knew that. He once told me that he was not supposed to make his investigations personal, but he couldn't help it.
'You can't do it and not get personal. If you're going to do something, get involved.'

During the final minutes of the last day of the appeal court hearing there is a reversal. The chief justice, Tom Bathurst, returns
to what he calls 'the first question', of whether there is evidence
against James Hide that is 'fresh and compelling'. Wendy Abraham
stands at the lectern, listening in silence. Evelyn's aunt, Michelle
Jarrett, stands just outside the courtroom. The pain that has built
through the hearing now runs up and down her legs, meaning she
can no longer sit, so she watches what happens next through the
open courtroom door.

For evidence to be 'fresh', the judge says, it must not have
been adduced in either of the previous murder trials, over the deaths
of Evelyn and Clinton. But, since the first day of the appeal court
hearing, Wendy has argued that the judges should overturn the not-
guilty verdicts over the murders of both Evelyn and Clinton together.

'I just want to make sure I know the hypotheses,' the chief
justice pauses. 'If we came to the view that the evidence was fresh

in the [Clinton] Speedy case, but not in the [Evelyn] Greenup case, such that we justified order in your favour in Speedy but not the other case, would you agitate for that or not?'

He's asking whether Wendy would accept an order that James face retrial on only one, not all of the children's deaths.

'Yes,' Wendy replies.

'So you'd take the fall-back position as it were?'

'Yes.' It is a huge decision, but she seems calm now and confident. Perhaps it is not what they were seeking at the start, but they'd take it. It's still justice of a sort.

Wendy is still hopeful she has done enough to convince the judges to overturn both murders and allow James to be charged again with both, as well as with the murder of Colleen. She wants them to see the case the way she's argued it is, as a serial killing.

'If we are right and we have satisfied the tests,' says Wendy, 'then you're dealing with the murder of three children. In my submission the interests of justice dictate . . . that the application be granted to enable a jury to hear the matter according to law.'

The hearing ends. The judges do not say when they will deliver their decision. As the lawyers, journalists and remaining members of the children's families head outside, Gary stands alone, staring at the bar tables where the case was argued.

'It's difficult, isn't it?' he says, frowning. 'There's a strange hollow. Twenty-one years we've been fighting and now it's in the hands of the judges.'

I walk out of the courtroom and step aside as the two teams of barristers wheel their trolleys full of documents back along the corridor. Michelle, who by the end was lying on the floor to ease her back, gets to her feet and follows them towards the lift. This court hearing has been what they wanted, she says, but it has also been the most exhausting experience since the children were murdered. Worse even than the trial over the murder of Evelyn. Because it was evidence about all three of the children being heard together this time.

Michelle looks at Gary, still standing, hand on hip, alone in the empty courtroom.

'He's fought for this like it was his own children,' she says. 'I can't believe any other policeman would have fought it for so long. Maybe it has had an effect on him, his marriages. You don't get many cops like that.' She walks on towards the exit of the Law Courts building.

Outside, the afternoon heat is rising and the air is heavy and thick, promising a storm. Michelle is happy to be leaving the city, which is too big, too busy, smells too much and has too many people in it. She just wants to be home in Bowraville.

Michelle heads across the courtyard and disappears around a corner of the old courthouse, where the men who committed the Myall Creek massacre were found guilty. Soon after, the sky darkens and begins to weep. Rain falls.

Saturday, 8 September 2018

For almost nine months the appeal judges have been silent. Gary pads barefooted along the corridor of his apartment building, wearing loose black sweatpants and a t-shirt that reveals the muscles in his shoulders and neck. He opens his front door onto a small unit, with a combined kitchen, dining and living room. Through the windows you can see the cranes working along the harbour shore and, above them, the clouds sweeping past, carried on the wind.

'I think it's defined who I am, this investigation,' he says, wiping the kitchen counter. It's left him beaten up and scarred and angry but his time on the Mission also taught him about respect and trust, and how these are earned. The children's families taught Gary about acceptance, he says. His own children are roughly the same age as the Bowraville investigation and he jokes with them that he may have been a fuck-up as a father but the one thing he has taught them is principles. Those principles are what he found in Bowraville.

Stalking over to the sofa, he sits down with one leg curled beneath him. Look at what the children's families have achieved already, he says. The parliamentary inquiry. Changing the laws around double jeopardy. The police force has also changed in the years since the murders happened: today in New South Wales the specialist Homicide Squad will take charge for at least the first seventy-two hours of any suspicious death investigation, rather than leaving it to local officers. Homicide will also take charge of any missing person cases where foul play is suspected. New recruits are now given training about the long, troubled history between police and Aboriginal people. They're taught about the differences, particularly, in communicating with potential witnesses. The Bowraville reinvestigation has been used as a case study for police officers, to train them in working with an Aboriginal community to pursue a crime.

Gary himself has resolved to take a more hardline approach in the future. If he has been tough on himself and others in the past, then from now on he'd be tougher still. He gets up and walks to the kitchen. From the fridge, he offers a carton of coconut water. On the fridge door is the funeral notice for Aunty Elaine Walker, the Bowraville elder who once told him, 'Why should I trust you? You're a cop.' Besides it, the only other pictures visible inside the apartment are a framed flyer for a television series based on another of Gary's investigations, into a gangland murder, and a portrait of Buddha that he painted on a meditation retreat in Nepal.

At the moment, Gary is working through the long drawn-out legal process of his second divorce. 'She wanted me to leave the cops, to move to Perth.' That didn't happen. So he ended up here, in this small apartment.

I say goodbye and Gary walks me to the front door of the building where he pauses, looking down the empty road that runs between a wall of quarried sandstone and another wall of residential units. He didn't want to leave the force. He doesn't want to leave the Bowraville investigation. He made a commitment to the children's families.

'This is what I do,' he says, turning to walk back inside the apartment, where the photographs of family are still stored in boxes, waiting to be unpacked. 'This is what I live.'

I do not sleep the night before the appeal court decision. It's now more than two years since the case was first referred to the court. It is four years since I first met Gary, in the cafe outside the police force headquarters, and he told me about the Bowraville murders. It is eleven years since the police sent the first of four separate applications to the director of public prosecutions and to successive attorneys general asking that the appeal court be asked to reconsider what happened. It's twelve years since the families' campaign helped bring about a change in the laws surrounding double jeopardy, meaning that James Hide could face a retrial if 'fresh and compelling' evidence was uncovered. It is also twelve years since James was found not guilty of Evelyn's murder. It's fourteen years since a coroner found that Colleen and Evelyn were murdered and asked the DPP to look again at prosecuting James over the second of those murders. It's twenty-two years since Gary Jubelin was asked to join the reinvestigation of the children's killings. It is twenty-four years since James was found not guilty of murdering Clinton. When morning comes, it is Thursday, 13 September 2018. Twenty-eight years to the day since Colleen Walker-Craig, the first of the murdered children, disappeared.

'We know that the grief and loss remains fresh in your minds, particularly on a day such as today,' says the chief justice,

Tom Bathurst, as he looks across the courtroom at the assembled children's families, who have again made the long journeys from their homes to be here. They sit, watching him, and listening. Colleen's parents are both there in the courtroom, the first time her father, Michael, has been in any of the court hearings related to the murders. So, too, are Clinton's parents, Thomas Duroux and June Speedy. Evelyn's mother, Rebecca Stadhams, bites her hand to quiet the emotion she is feeling. Leonie Duroux, who was one of the leaders of the families' campaign to change the laws on double jeopardy, is there with her two sons beside her.

The years have taken their toll on everybody. Nineteen witnesses have died over the time since the murders happened, including several of the Mission's residents, the SES volunteer who discovered Evelyn's remains and the forensic pathologist who examined both her and Clinton's bodies. Two more witnesses died during the months we have waited for the judges to come back with their decision. Gary fears that others may soon follow. Particularly, he worries about Patricia Stadhams, Evelyn's grandmother, who says she heard her granddaughter cry out in the night and then heard a thud, and also said that she saw James walking down one side of the house on the Mission on the night that Colleen went missing, and that she saw James walking down the other side. Patricia's getting older, her memory is failing. She may not last another winter, Gary says.

The chief justice repeats the admonition he gave at the beginning of the appeal hearing. This was not a retrial of James over the murders. 'The court was not required to form, and has not formed, any view as to the guilt of the respondent in respect of any of the deaths,' he says. Watching the judge speak, Colleen's parents are optimistic. Today is the anniversary of her disappearance. Surely, the judges would only choose today to deliver their verdict if it were good news.

Of the three judges who heard the appeal, only two are on the bench facing the families. The third, Clifton Hoeben, who contributed to their joint decision, is on leave. Without him, beside the chief justice sits Judge Lucy McCallum, in silence, her head bowed. She seems close to tears.

The chief justice starts to read their verdict. He says the appeal court was asked to overturn both of the previous not-guilty verdicts, for the murders of Evelyn and Clinton, and order a retrial be held for all three of the children's murders together. To do so, there needed to be 'fresh and compelling' evidence available in relation to both these previous acquittals. But the evidence about Colleen's disappearance – the foundation of the case to have these verdicts overturned – was known about at the time of the trial over Evelyn's murder, in 2006. Some of it had come out during Gary's reinvestigation, while other evidence, including the witness accounts that Colleen was seen walking down the side of the house at number 3 Cemetery Road, or that James was heard making advances to Colleen at the party on the night she disappeared, or that Colleen said James mauled her when she stayed over in his caravan a couple of months before the party, had come out during the inquest into Colleen's death in 2004.

As such, says the chief justice, this evidence cannot be called 'fresh'. According to the law, evidence is fresh only if it was not adduced during a previous trial and could not have been adduced with the exercise of reasonable diligence. The appeal court, he says, disagrees with the meaning of the word 'adduced' adopted by the lawyers arguing that James should face retrial. They argued that it meant 'admitted' – the process by which a judge allows evidence to be heard by a jury. The appeal court has ruled that adduced means 'tendered' or 'brought forward' – the process by which evidence is presented to a judge, who may allow it to be admitted.

The evidence about Colleen's disappearance could not have been admitted in the trial over Evelyn's murder, the chief justice continues, because the trials had been separated, meaning a judge had ruled that each jury would hear about only one of the murders in isolation. But the evidence about Colleen's murder could still have been presented to the court, even if the judge would not have admitted it into evidence.

The effect of their decision about the meaning of 'adduced' is that the evidence about Colleen's death cannot be said to be 'fresh' in relation to the murder of Evelyn, the chief justice continues. At the last moment during the appeal court hearing, the lawyers arguing that James should face retrial had tried to reverse their position and ask for the judges to overturn either the not-guilty verdict in relation to Evelyn's killing, or in relation to Clinton. But this came too late, he says. It contradicted their original application to the court, that both verdicts be overturned together.

I close my eyes.

If the appeal court cannot overturn the not-guilty verdict relating to the killing of Evelyn because the evidence about Colleen's murder is not 'fresh', then the chief justice says they cannot overturn the two not-guilty verdicts together.

There will not be a retrial. The evidence about Colleen's murder will not be put to a new jury because it could have been 'adduced' during the previous trial over the murder of Evelyn, even though the judge at the time would have refused to allow it to be heard.

It is bewildering and baffling and means no jury will ever hear evidence about all three deaths together.

'The court recognises that this conclusion does deprive the families of the three children and the Bowraville community of the closure which they justifiably seek,' says the chief justice. 'Nonetheless, the court, in fulfilment of its duty is obliged to give effect to the terms of the statue as it has construed them.' The law is hard. The judges stand, turn and walk out of the courtroom. The families of the three murdered children watch them go.

Rebecca, whose four-year-old daughter Evelyn was the second murder victim, cannot understand what the chief justice said and keeps asking, 'Is that it? Is that it?' as she sits staring at the emptying court.

'I knew it. I knew it,' says Thomas, the father of sixteen-year-old Clinton, as he storms out of the Law Courts building, crosses the road and heads in a straight line, away, through the sunlight and into the shade beneath the fig trees opposite. 'The government has let us down again.' I follow for a moment, mutely, but he keeps on walking.

Colleen's mother, Muriel, has to be physically supported on her way out of the Law Courts building. She is too upset to say anything, she says.

Behind them, life continues in the quiet of the court building. On the ground floor, men and women dressed in suits file in and form two queues, in silence, waiting to pass through the security checks and off towards the lifts that whisk them to different floors. Uniformed guards wave them forward through the scanners. I'm watching their progression, feeling empty, when someone shouts, 'What do we want? Justice! What have we got? Fuck all!'

It's Marbuck Duroux. Clinton's nephew. Leonie's son, named after his late father. Twenty-three years old, part of a generation born after the murders happened, Marbuck is stripped to the waist and painted with white ochre on his chest and back. His palms are also white, and he is walking up and down through the court building, leaving fresh, white handprints on the glass walls and doors.

He wants to show that the families will not stop with this decision. That their fight will continue. Later that day, the families meet with the new state attorney general, Mark Speakman, who announces he will ask the High Court to overturn the judgement of the appeal court.

Eventually, Marbuck walks away from the court building and the TV crews also pack up and leave. Once they are gone, security staff start cleaning off his white ochre handprints. For now at least, and possibly forever, the court's decision means there will be no further trial over the murder of Evelyn and Clinton. James will remain not guilty and will never be asked to give an official account, in court or to the police, of what happened to Colleen.

Walking back to *The Australian*, I do not want to write this story for the paper, although I know I have to. In the office, reading through the court judgement, it says only one piece of the evidence relied upon in the appeal met the judge's definition of 'fresh': the podcast interview with James, where I asked him about the claim that he was seen walking out of the bedroom where Evelyn was sleeping with her mother, on the night the four-year-old had disappeared. The judges single out one section of the transcript:

'Did you go into that room?' I asked him.

'No.'

'You're saying you had nothing to do with Evelyn's disappearance?'

'That's right,' James said.

The judges say this evidence is 'fresh' but it is not 'compelling'. As such, it does not pass the second test to justify a retrial. For it to be compelling, 'would inevitably involve independently proving the respondent's guilt.'

If only, I think, I'd asked James more. If only I had kept him talking because they might lie and if they do, you can catch them. Gary told me once he always liked to keep a suspect talking. I remember James trying to claim his pillowcase was found tucked down the shorts of Clinton's corpse because the teenager might have taken it to get some yarndi. I should have asked James what did happen to Colleen and Evelyn. If he had tried, and lied, to come up with an answer, maybe that would have been enough.

You can tell if a crime story is true because it has no ending. The people left alive after the murder happens keep on living. They don't have any choice.

Nor does a true crime story have a moral. In the *Gumbaynggirr Yuludarla Jandaygam*, the book of dreaming stories from the area of the mid-north coast of New South Wales of which Bowraville is part, it says, 'Many people look for a non-existent "moral" to each story. [But] these stories say how things are, what life is all about.'

According to the *Yuludarla*, 'in these stories nothing happens without a reason and all actions have consequences.' That is Maangun: 'the law'. On Friday, 22 March 2019, the High Court of Australia upheld the decision of the New South Wales appeal court. 'Adduced' meant 'tendered' or 'brought forward'. Justice was delivered.

So no true crime story has a moral. And any that pretends it
does is lying.

In Bowraville, Colleen's family still go out searching for her body.

In the forest, the detective who led the first investigation of the
murders, Allan Williams, pulls his van over on the southern, dirt-
track section of Congarinni Road, a few kilometres from where
Evelyn and Clinton's remains were found. A dog barks on the hillside behind us. In front of us, the ground slopes down for around
50 metres, before a line of gum trunks marks the point where it
suddenly and steeply falls away.

Allan gets out and walks ahead, an old man now in a neat,
short-sleeved shirt tucked into his trousers. He has regrown the
moustache he wore on the day he arrested James Hide in 1991,
although the hair in it is grey.

He's pointing down into the forest. People come here now to
dump their rubbish. There's a grey doona lying bundled at the base
of a eucalypt. A red milk crate. Beyond them both, a plastic bucket
lies half-buried in the leaves.

'Bearing in mind that where the killer took Clinton, and where
he took Evelyn was further in than that,' says Allan, staring at the
place between the gum trunks where the ground gets steeper. 'Can
you see where I'm coming from?' he asks. 'It's Congarinni Road, it's
still on Congarinni Road.'

'Yes.'

'It's a bigger effort than with the other two.' He stares into the
forest. To carry a body down to there would still be easy for a big
man. This stretch of road is also further from Bowraville, closer to
the river where Colleen's clothes were found.

A faint track, like the ones leading to both Evelyn and Clinton's bodies, heads down among the eucalypts. I follow it, swiping at mosquitoes, and can see how the ground drops into a narrow slot carved out by water. It's damp down here. The track becomes more obvious as it runs down towards the creek bed.

'It was his first one so he was probably more careful,' says Allan, who has stayed up on the road. Twenty-eight years ago, he says, he organised the search for Colleen's body, working off aerial photographs laid out on a table in the Bowraville police station.

'This was the area that wasn't searched. I know it wasn't.' There's something nervous in his voice. 'I'll tell you why I missed it.' Everything down there is farmland, says Allan, pointing down the road from where he parked the van. Above us, between here and Bowraville, is forest. When they were looking for the children's bodies, they started the search at the T-junction a couple of hundred metres up from where we're standing, and headed north, away from here, into the forest, towards Bowraville.

Someone had to make the decision where the search would start and that T-junction provided a natural point to do so. 'I remember saying, "South of here is farm country,"' Allan says. No point searching farmland. Too open to hide a body. But between the T-junction and the open farmland, the road runs through these few hundred metres of thick forest on either side, where we are standing. Where nobody looked for Colleen's body.

Allan says his wife brought him here last Father's Day. They'd been to a pub together and, afterwards, he'd said that he wanted to drive home along this stretch of road. For the first time in more than a quarter of a century, he looked out at this forest, and realised they never searched it.

If they had done, maybe they'd have found something, he tells me.

If the police had done more, I think, we wouldn't have so many different versions of what happened on the night that Colleen went missing, all of them culled from witness statements taken only months after she disappeared. If the police had moved much quicker, if they had charged somebody over Colleen's murder, maybe Evelyn and Clinton would not also have gone missing. If the police had done more at the beginning, there might not be so many confused witness sightings claiming each of the three children was alive after the time their families say that they went missing. You only get one chance at the appeal court. Even if they found Colleen's body now, there will be no retrial.

'I didn't see it,' Allan says, looking down into the forest. 'I've fucked up. I've really fucked up here,' he says.

Acknowledgements

This is a true story, but there is one lie in it. Following the High Court decision on Monday, 25 March 2019, Magistrate Robert Stone imposed a suppression order preventing the publication of the name of the man suspected by police of murdering the children in Bowraville. As a result, his name has been changed. All direct speech is quoted either from my interviews, police statements or records of interview, court transcripts or other primary material. Any mistakes in the telling are entirely my fault, however.

Throughout this book the spelling of the word Gumbaynggirr and of words in that language is that used by the Muurrbay Aboriginal Language and Culture Co-Operative. On occasion, where different spellings were used in the source material, I have changed this to the Muurrbay version for consistency.

This book could not, and would not, have been written without the consent and cooperation of many of those involved. In particular, I want to thank the families of Colleen, Evelyn and Clinton, for their trust and kindness. Others on the Mission or with ties to Bowraville also helped me to try to make sense of what took place, and I am grateful. My best efforts were limited; I have attempted to put down the known facts in some order, but do not pretend to understand the pain felt by those involved.

I would also like to thank all of those people who agreed to be interviewed, often more than once and in some cases many times over several years. The following particularly deserve recognition, and my gratitude:

Gary Jubelin, whose support was unfailing; Mick Willing and the NSW Police Force who were generous in the cooperation they extended throughout; Jerry Bowden and Ann Croger, who allowed me to quote from their unpublished manuscript 'Post'; Bianca Comina, who helped me understand the work involved and the cost; Georgie Loudon and Angus Huntsdale at the NSW Department of Justice; Sonya Zedel, Lisa Miller and the staff of the NSW Supreme Court; Ann Lombardino and the staff of the NSW Coroner's Court; Gary Williams and those at Muurrbay, who allowed me to use the story of the stranger shining like the sun, as well as the quote at the start of this book, and whose *Gumbaynggirr Yuludarla Jandaygam* has sat on my desk over the past couple of years now; Isabella Voce at the Australian Institute of Criminology, who provided me with data taken from the National Homicide Monitoring Program. (Please note that the NHMP project is funded by the Australian government. The data used in this publication were made available through the Australian Institute of Criminology. The AIC does not bear any responsibility for the analyses or interpretations presented herein); the staff of the NSW Bureau of Crime Statistics and Research; those at *The Australian*, including Stefanie Balogh, John-Paul Cashen, Stephen Fitzpatrick,

Eric George, Michelle Gunn, Sid Maher, James Tindale, Helen Trinca, Alex Walker and Paul Whittaker. Helen also allowed me to quote from various of the newspaper's articles, while some of the reporting on the death of Theresa Binge in this book previously appeared in *The Weekend Australian Magazine*, edited by Christine Middap; my colleagues outside the newspaper, including Danny Teece-Johnson, Janet Fife-Yeomans and Dan Proudman; Donald Grant, who provided both his time and his insight; Barry Toohey and Monica Pullen, who put me up more than once and in whose house this book started to get written; Stephen Fitzpatrick and Cassie McCullagh, who also put up with a wandering Pom during the appeal hearing and decision, and in whose house that section got drafted; Keith Kirby and Greg Bearup, who read the first draft and told me where it needed to be better; at Penguin Random House, Cate Blake who gave me the opportunity to write this story then made it better, while Clementine Edwards and Elena Gomez also played a big role in making this the book it is; my parents and especially my mum, who transcribed hundreds of pages of interviews and in doing so really wrote the story before I did. I also want to thank my children, who gave up a corner of their playroom for me to work in without complaining. Finally, I want to thank my wife, Nell, who said this book was worth making sacrifices for, and who made them.